AF469636

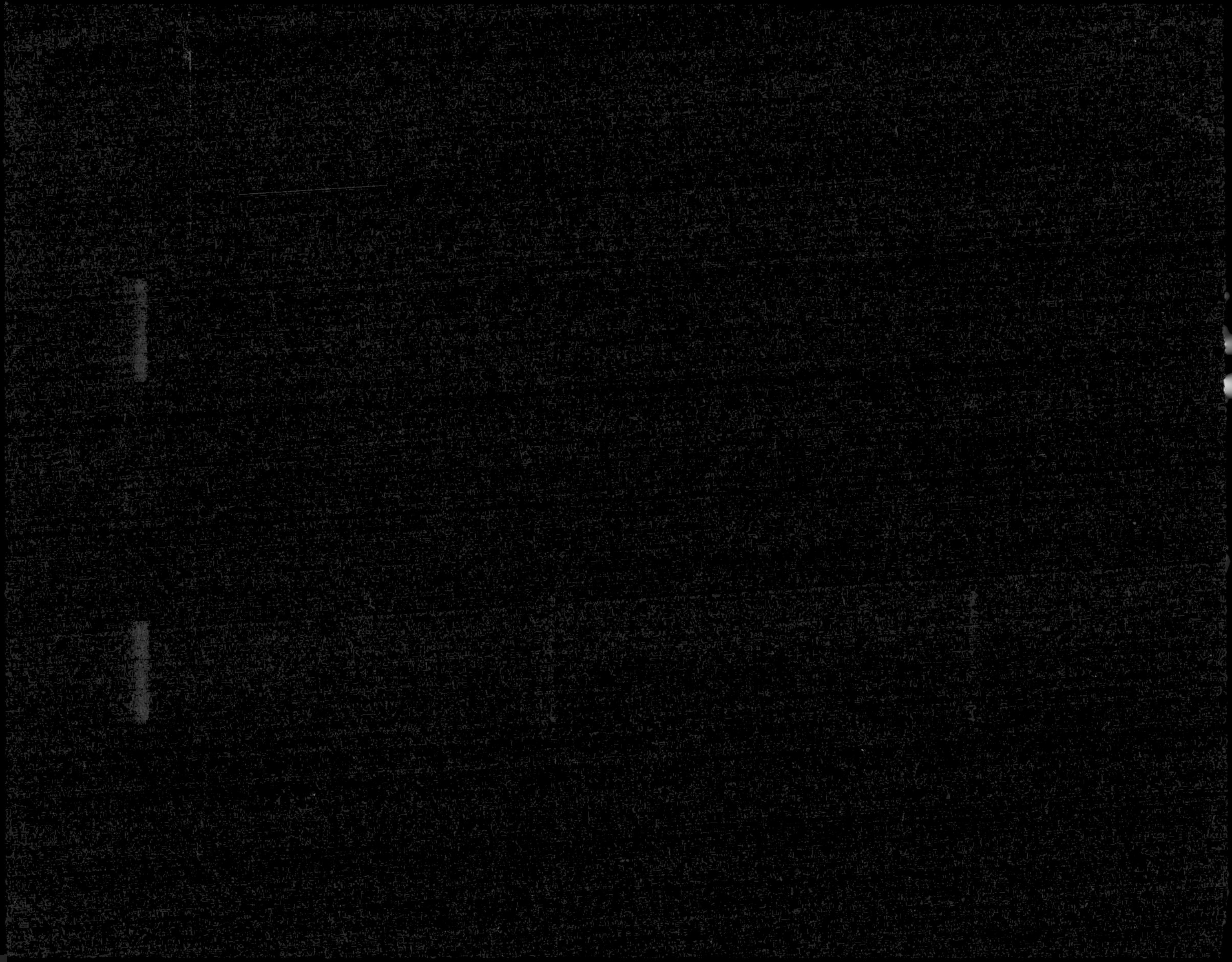

screen time

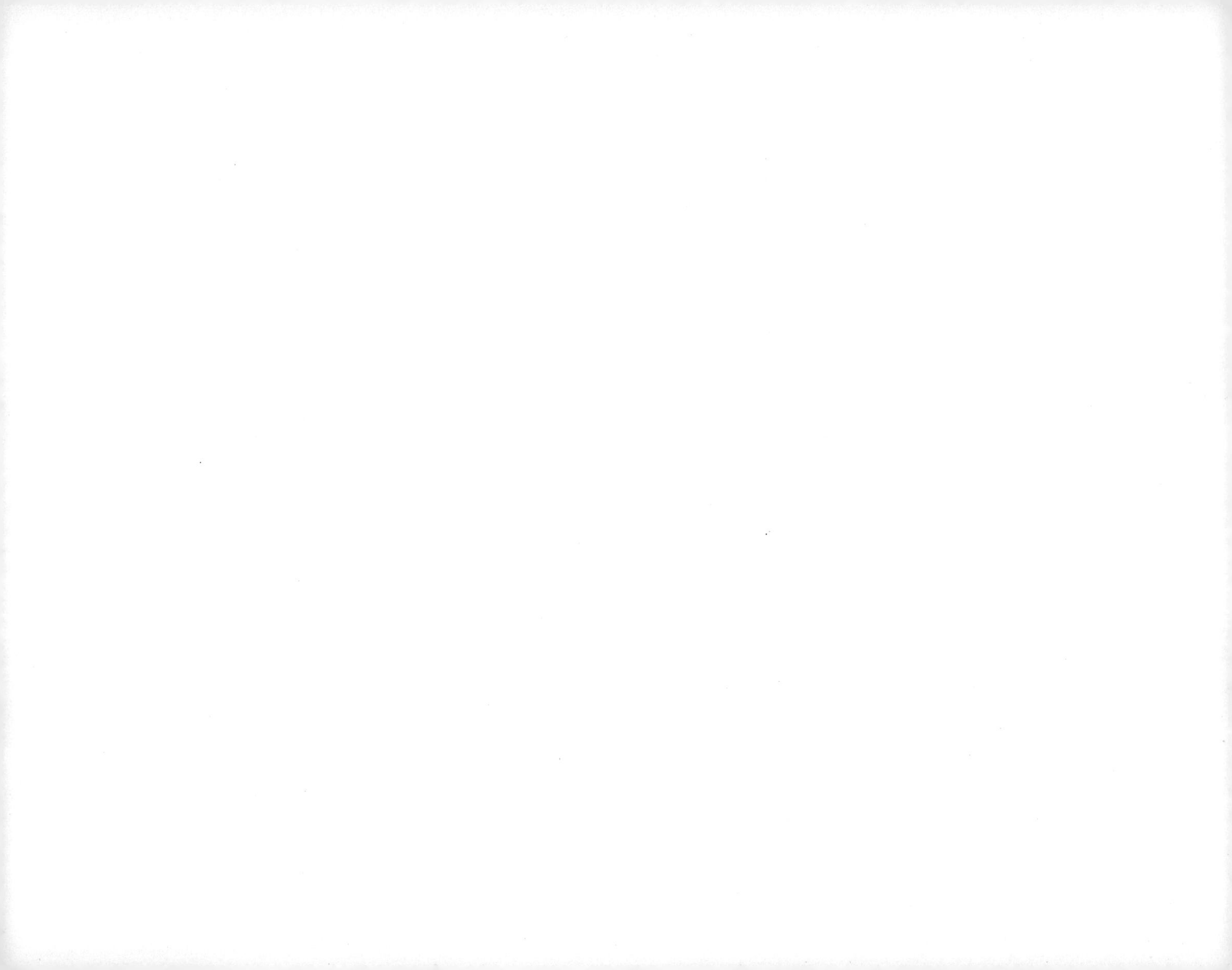

screen time DAFYDD JONES

C I R C A

57th St, Manhattan 2019

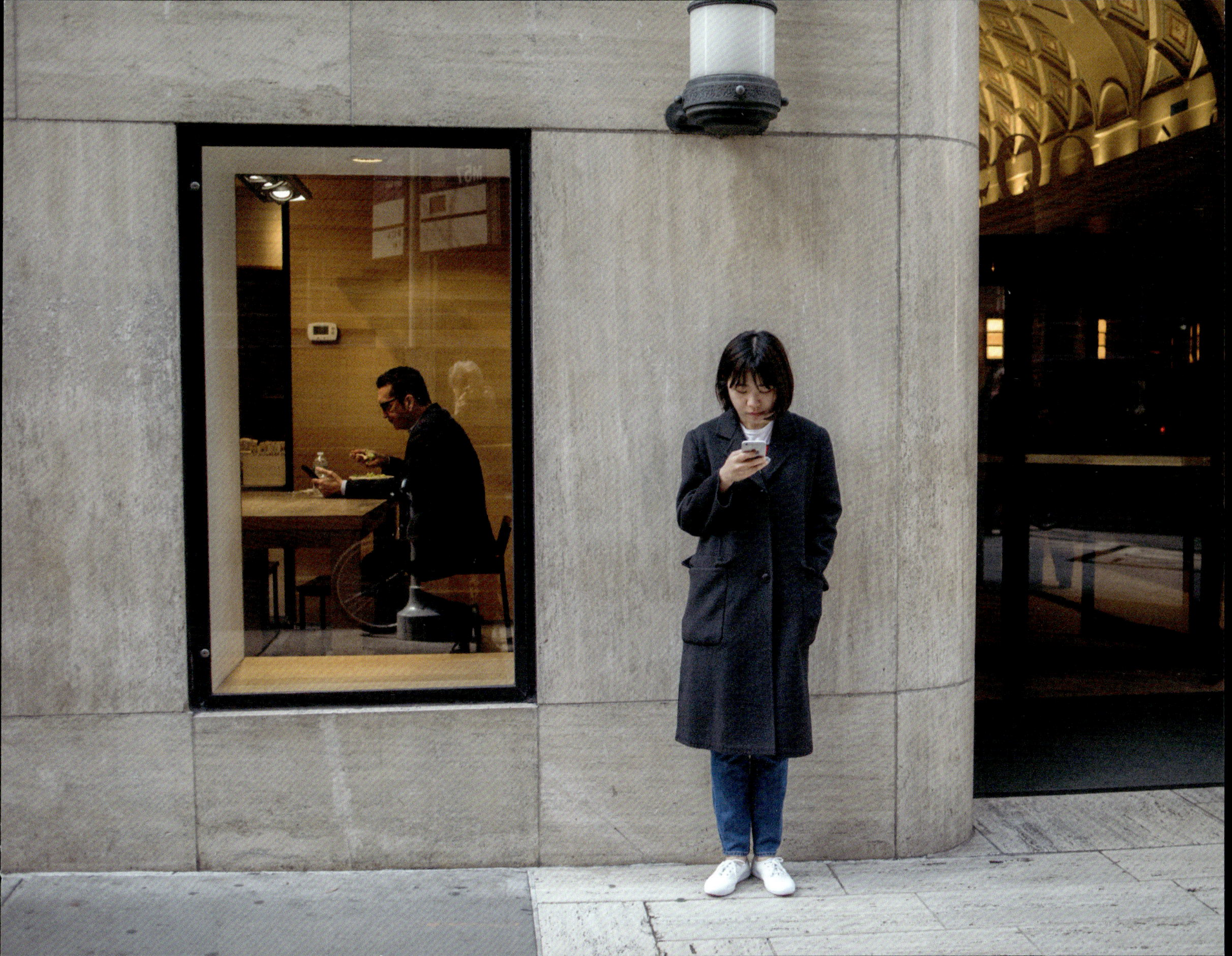

Today almost everyone uses a smartphone, and most of us are addicted. In every social situation the smartphone is not only killing conversation, it's changing the way we look at the world.

Years ago, when I started photographing balls and parties in England for the *Tatler* magazine, I'd find young people chatting, observing one another and generally taking an interest in their fellow guests. Now I see them silently mesmerized by their iPhones, checking their Instagram feeds, their WhatsApps, or whatever it is they're hooked on. They hardly seem to talk or make eye contact.

In the eighties, social photography was the easiest way for an aspiring photographer to get work into print – parties and the upper classes had hitherto been rather overlooked as potential subject matter. Most photographers didn't like the anti-social hours, or bridled at the snobbery they perceived – or sometimes imagined. Moreover, getting a decent picture of a party is actually very difficult.

How do you photograph a room packed full of people holding drinks? My way of working has always been to try to capture the revealing moments. I sought out events that excited me, and although the resulting images were not always complimentary, they caused a stir. As the magazines I worked for prospered, I covered events all over the world, and for a while lived in New York.

In 2008, I was sent to Miami to cover a party hosted by *Vogue Italia* during the Art Basel fair. Although it was one of the week's most glamorous parties, I noticed a single man apparently oblivious to the fabulous group of women he was with, so engrossed was he in his phone. Maybe he was texting his friends to tell them how lucky he was. Possibly he was a pioneer tweeter. Whatever his fixation, he was definitely missing the action.

That was the first time. Then gradually I began to see the same thing happening more and more. The light emitted by the phone can be very flattering, and there is something quite beautiful about someone transfixed in that way, almost in another world, isolated in a crowded scene. Instinctively, at first, I began to seek out these instances.

When the then editor of the *Oldie* magazine, Alexander Chancellor, suggested I contribute a regular feature called 'The Way We Live Now', he noticed how many of my pictures featured people glued to their phones. Old people, young people, mothers with children, workmen, cops, cyclists, everyone – in shops, in the street, on the train, in galleries, in bars and restaurants, everywhere. I've even seen a man standing at a urinal, a phone cradled in his free hand.

Screen time is all-consuming. Who knows what impact it's having in the bedroom. It's probably a race to see what will wipe out humanity first – global climate change or screen-induced sexual indifference. I fear we may have reached the point of no return.

Dafydd Jones

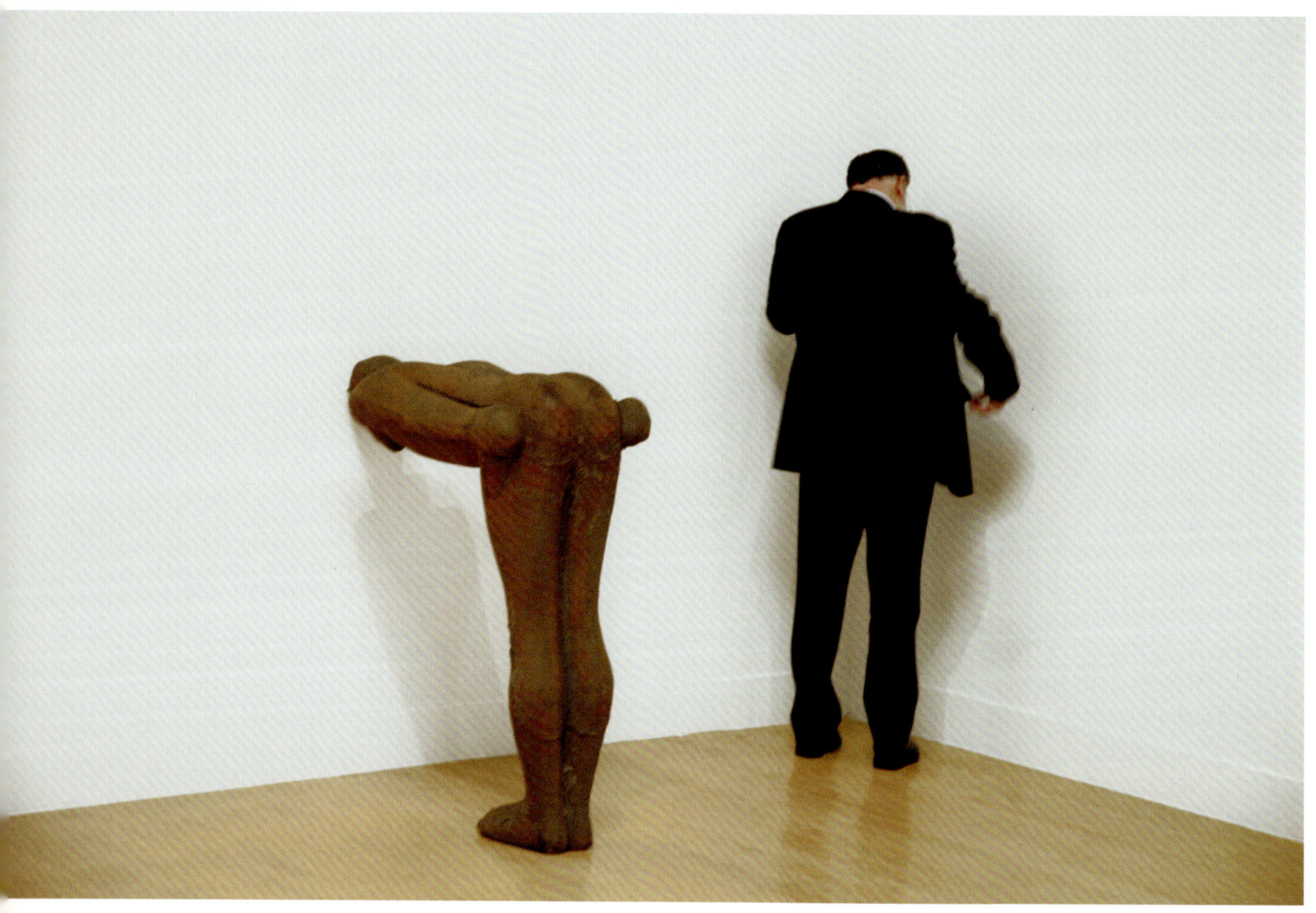

Tate Britain, London 2007

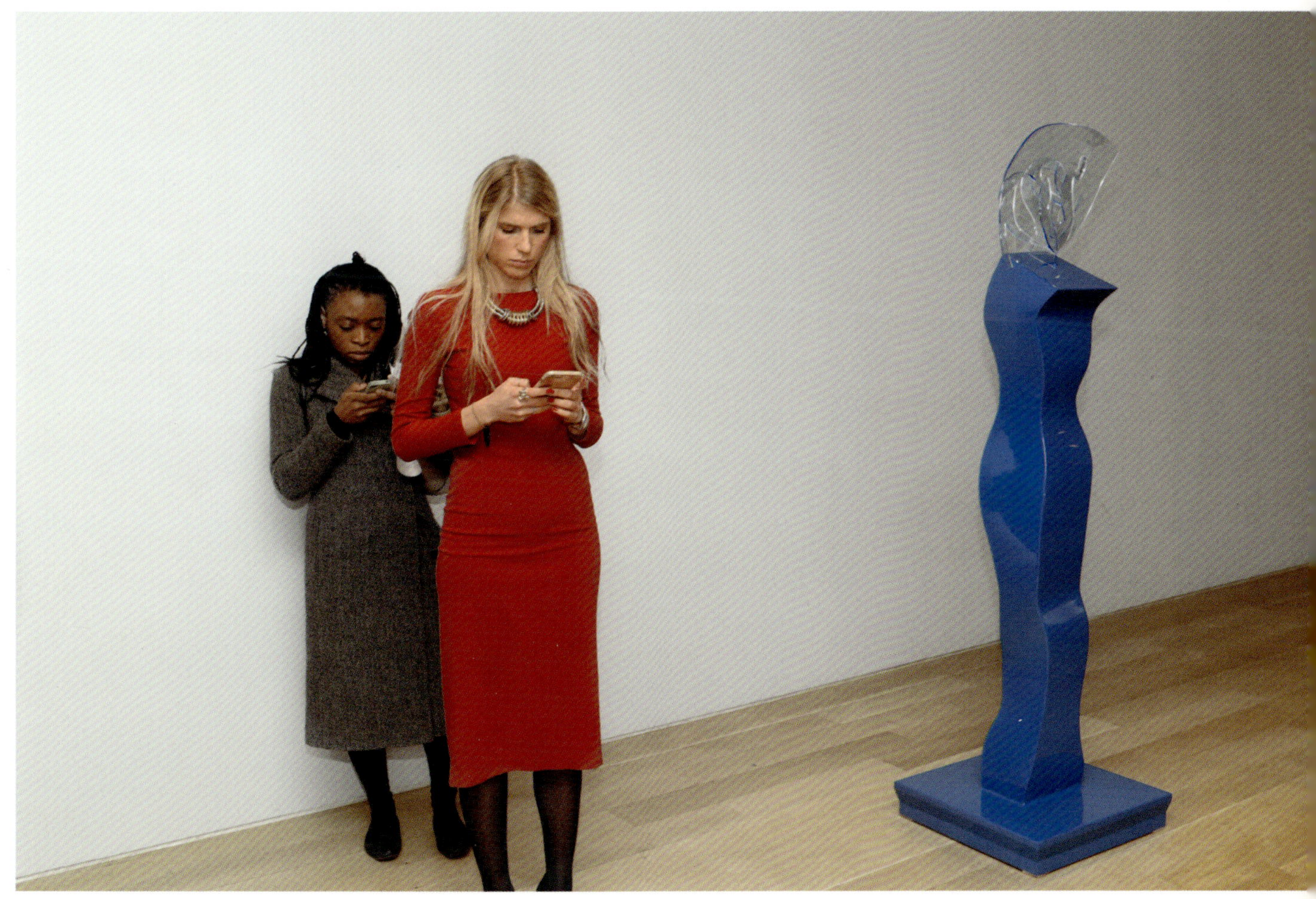

Mayfair, London 2015

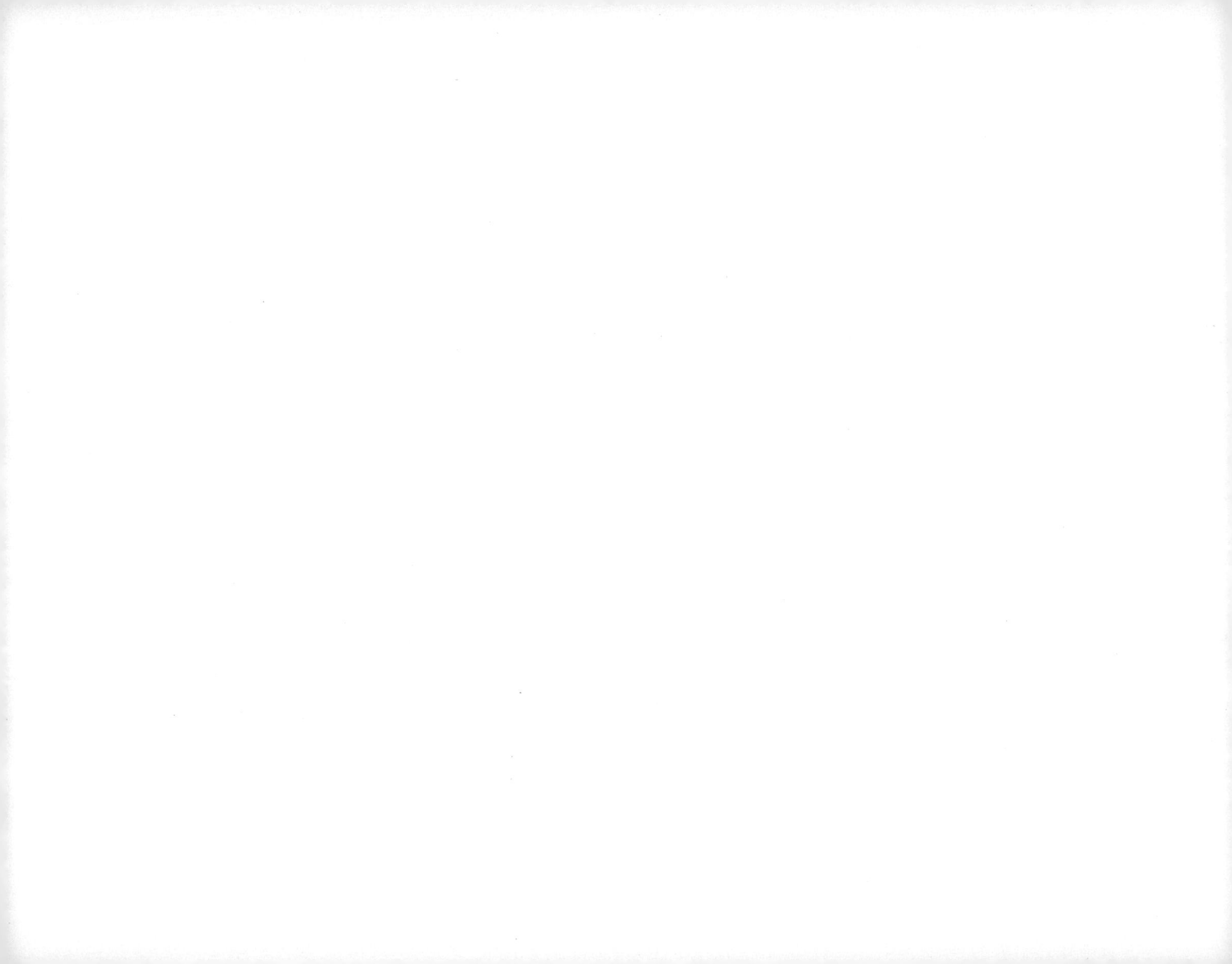

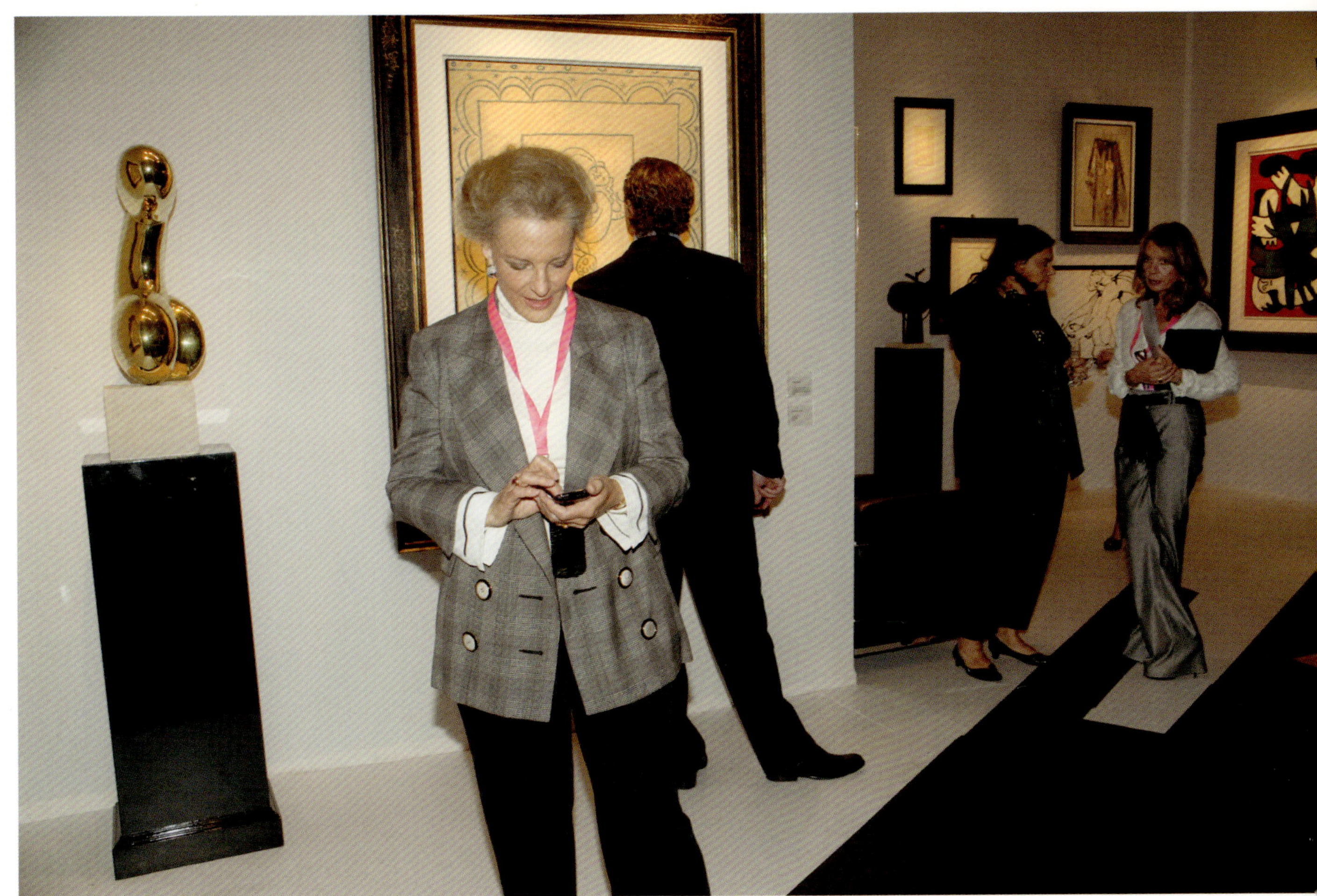

Mayfair, London 2010

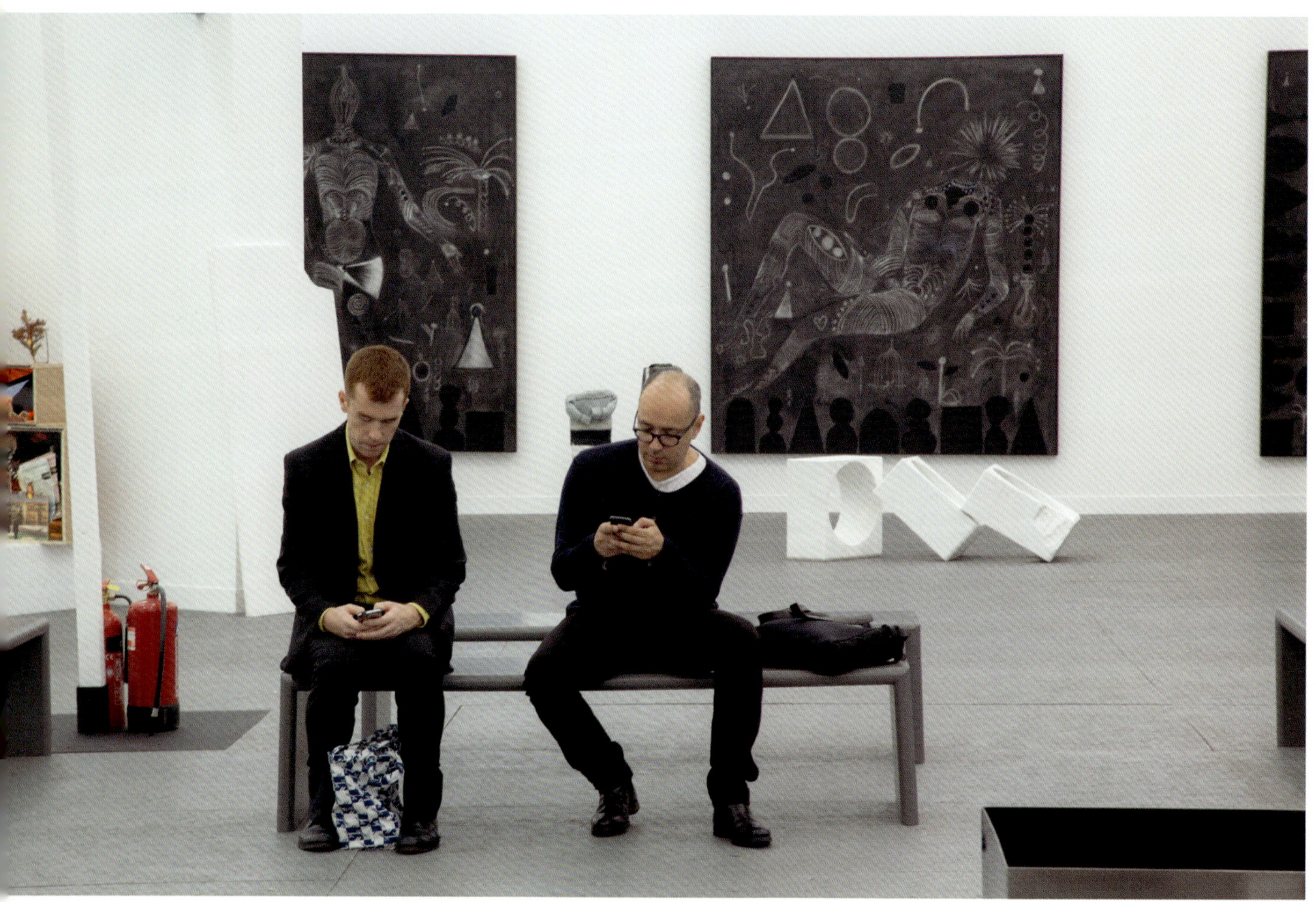

Frieze London 2013

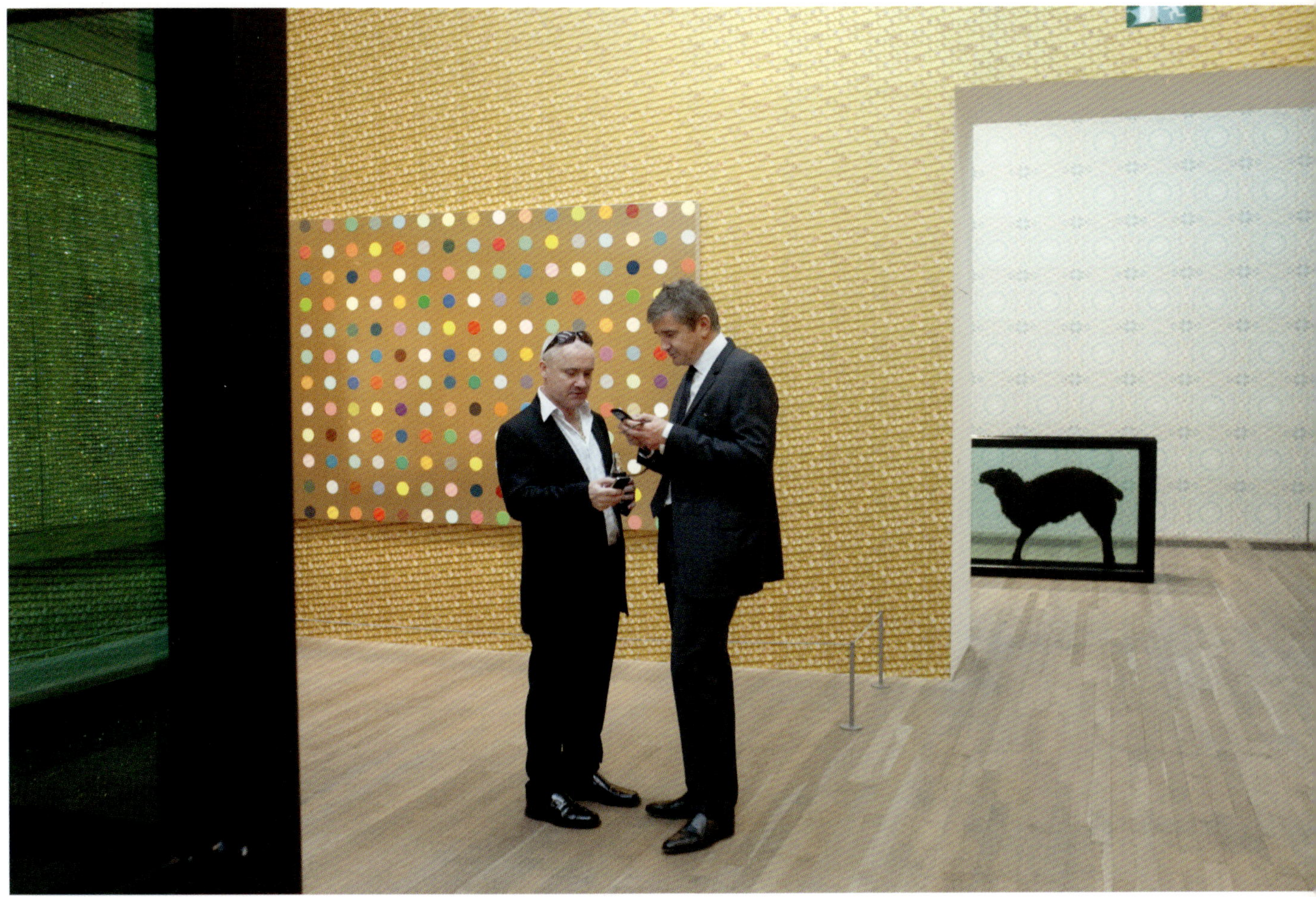

Tate Modern, London 2012

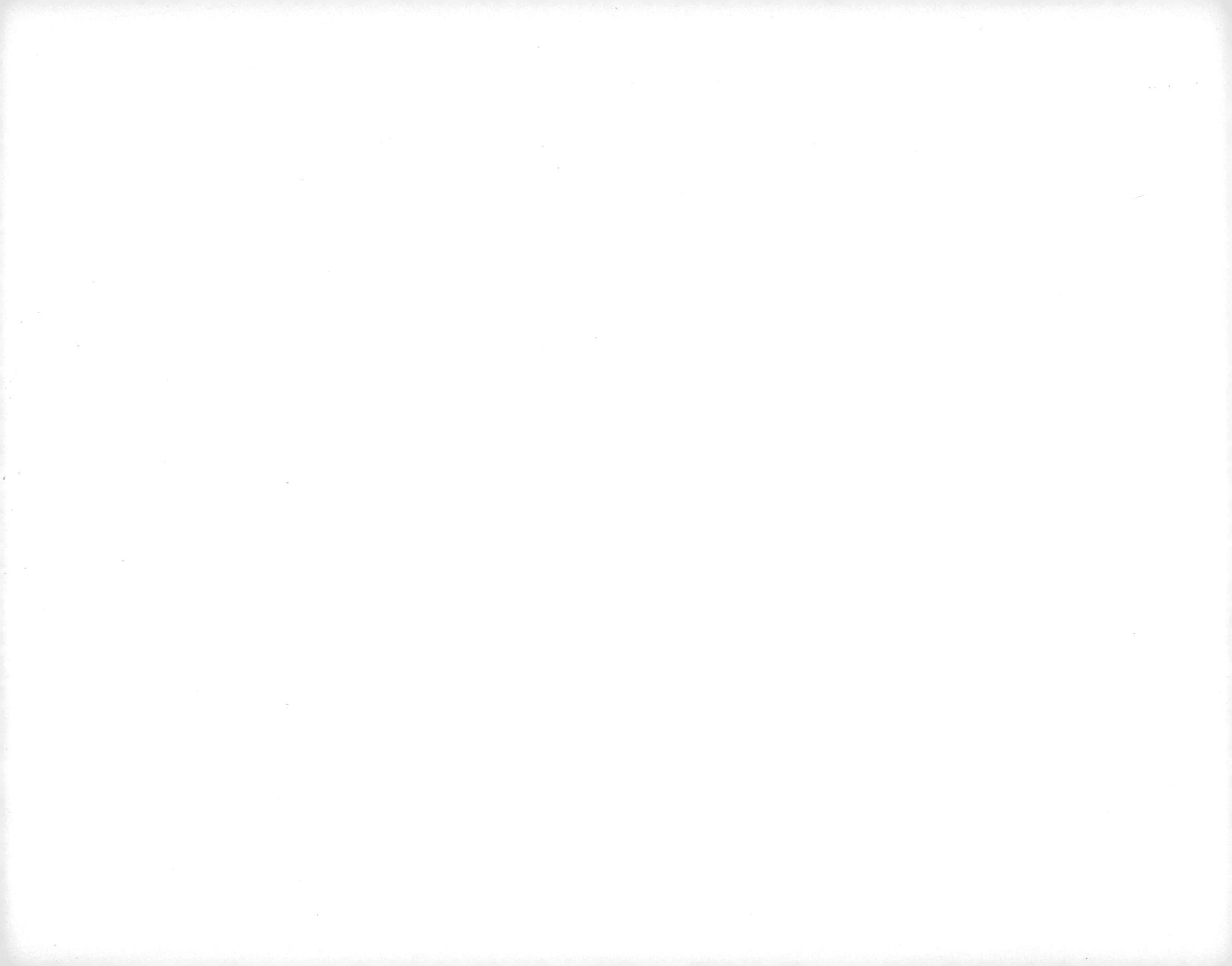

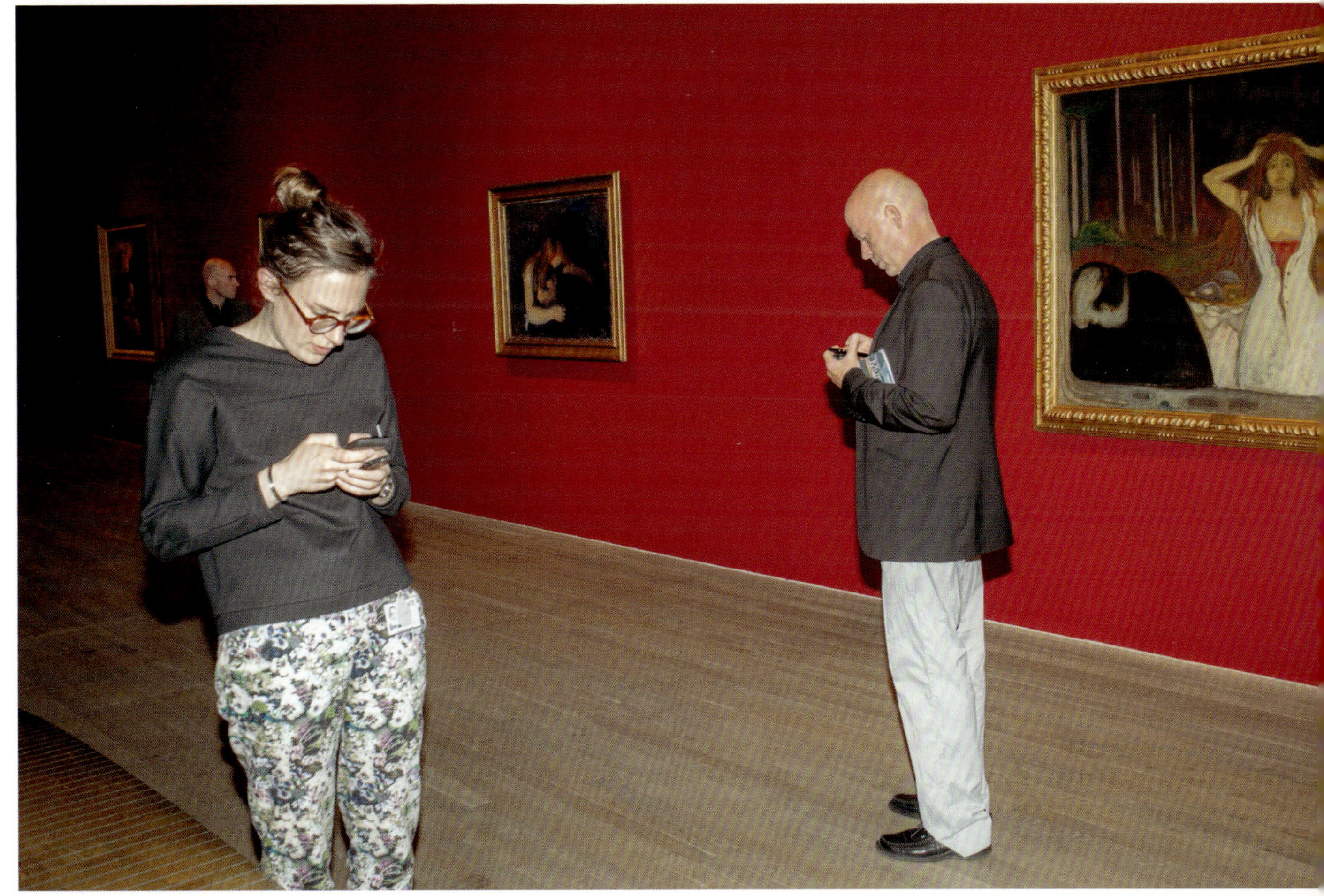

Tate Modern, London 2012

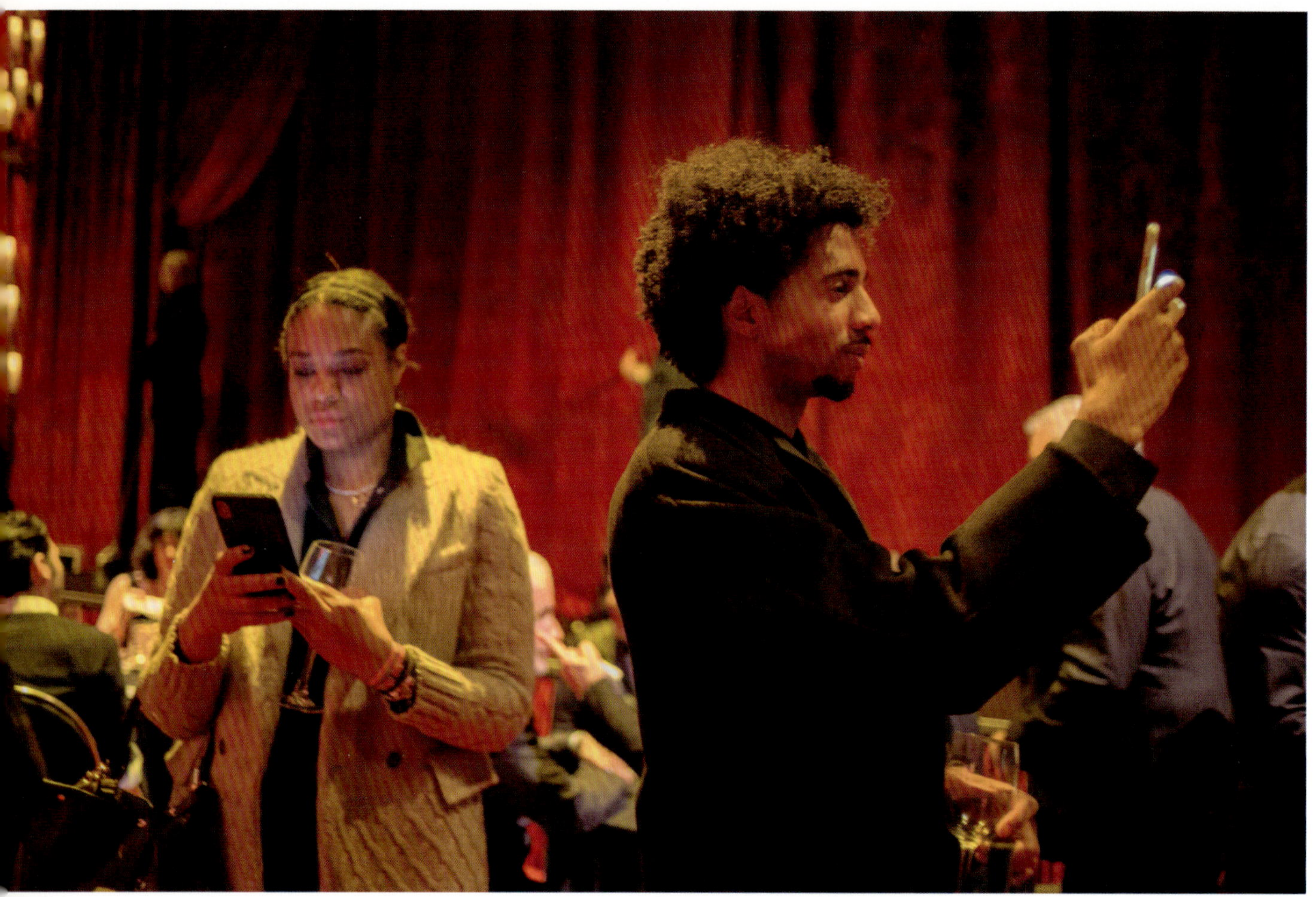

Vesey St, Manhattan 2019

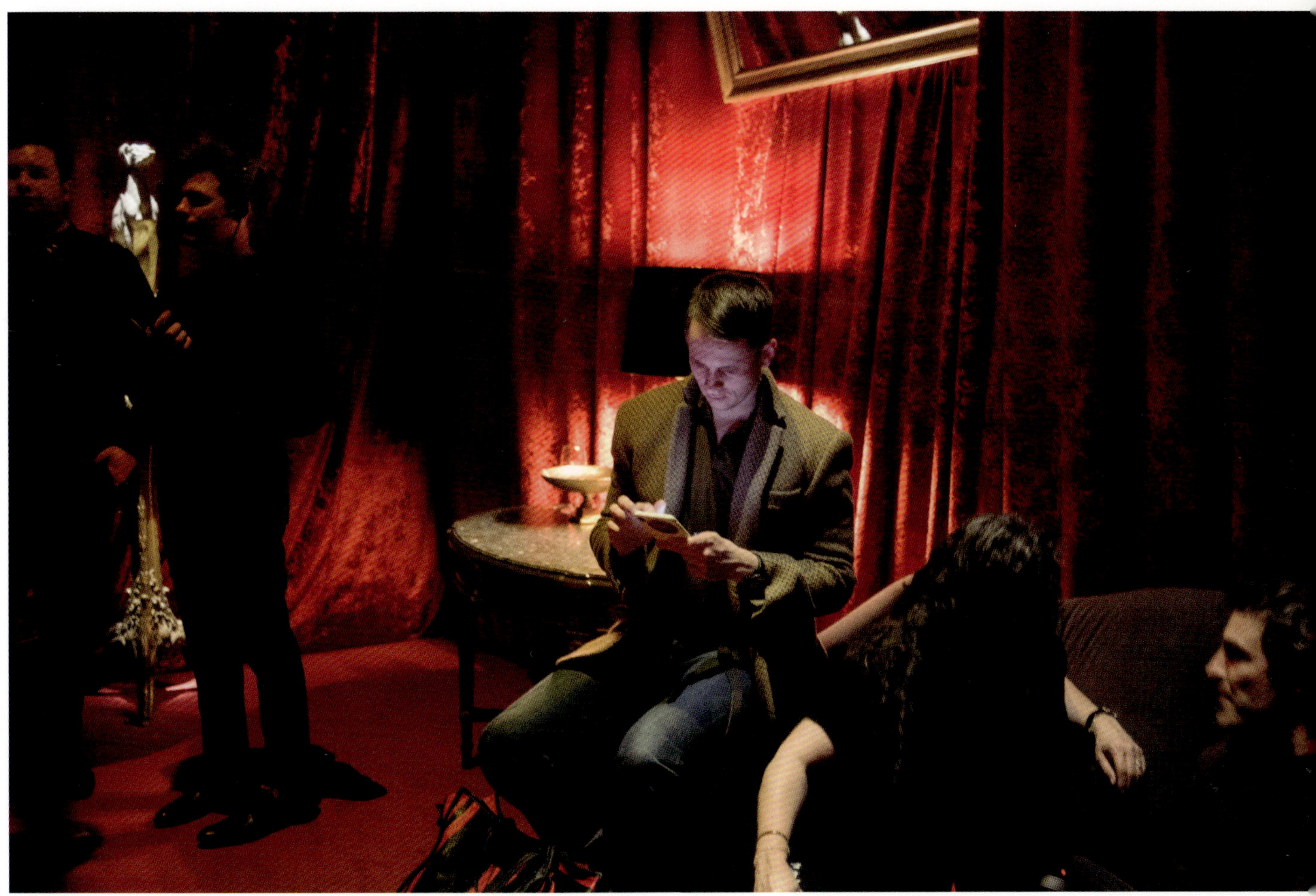

Vesey St, Manhattan 2019

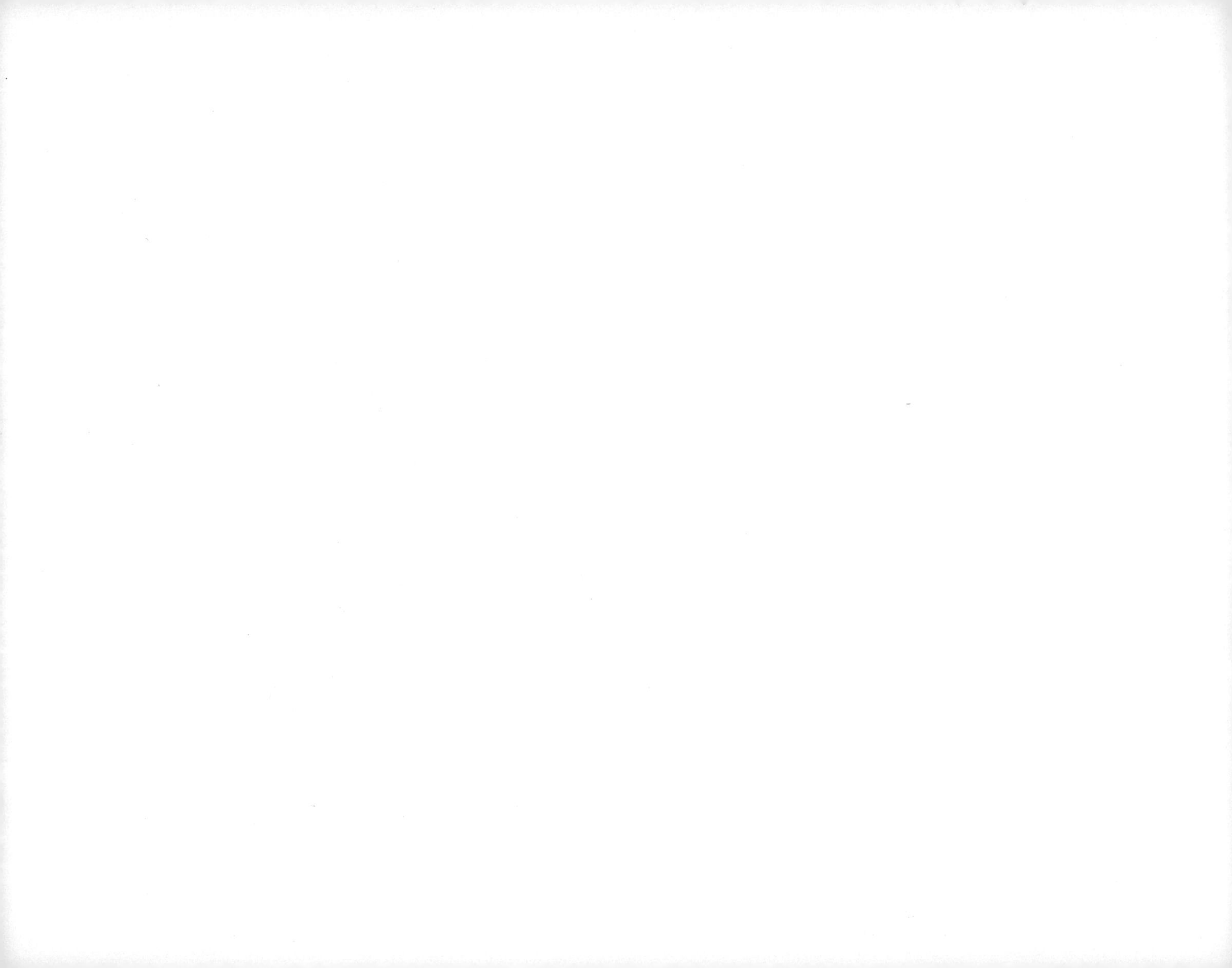

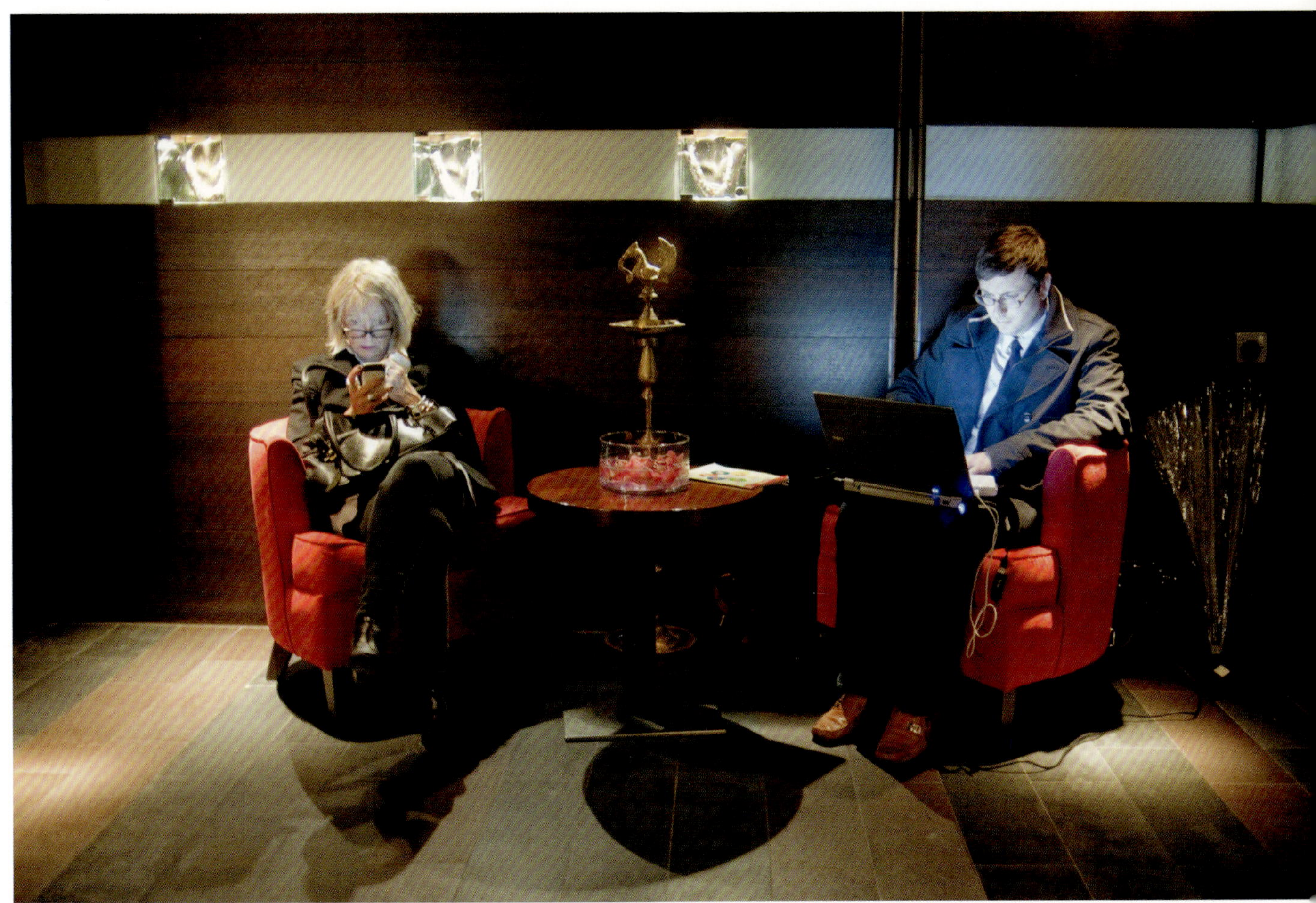

Haymarket, London 2012

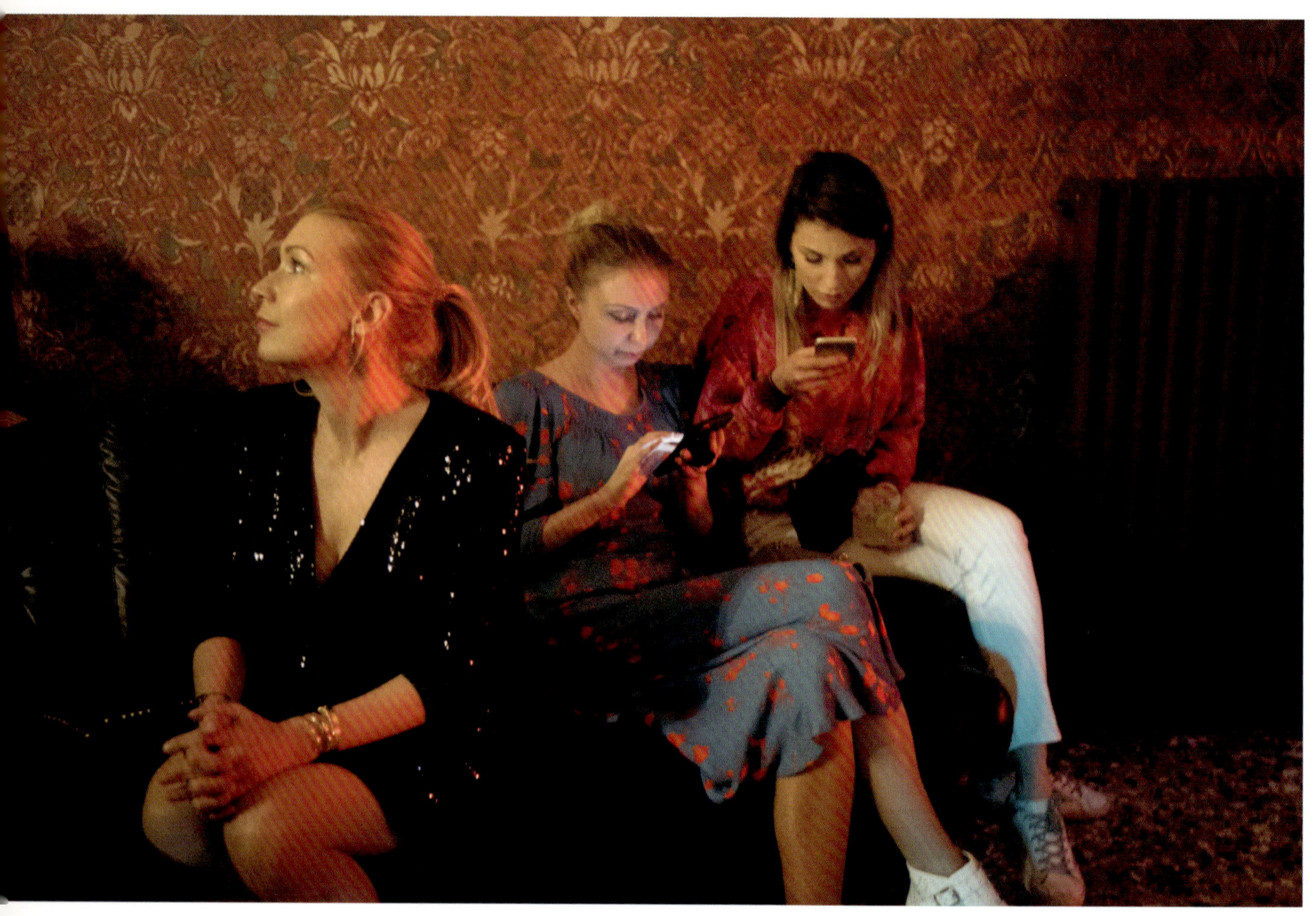

Palazzo Benzon, Venice 2019

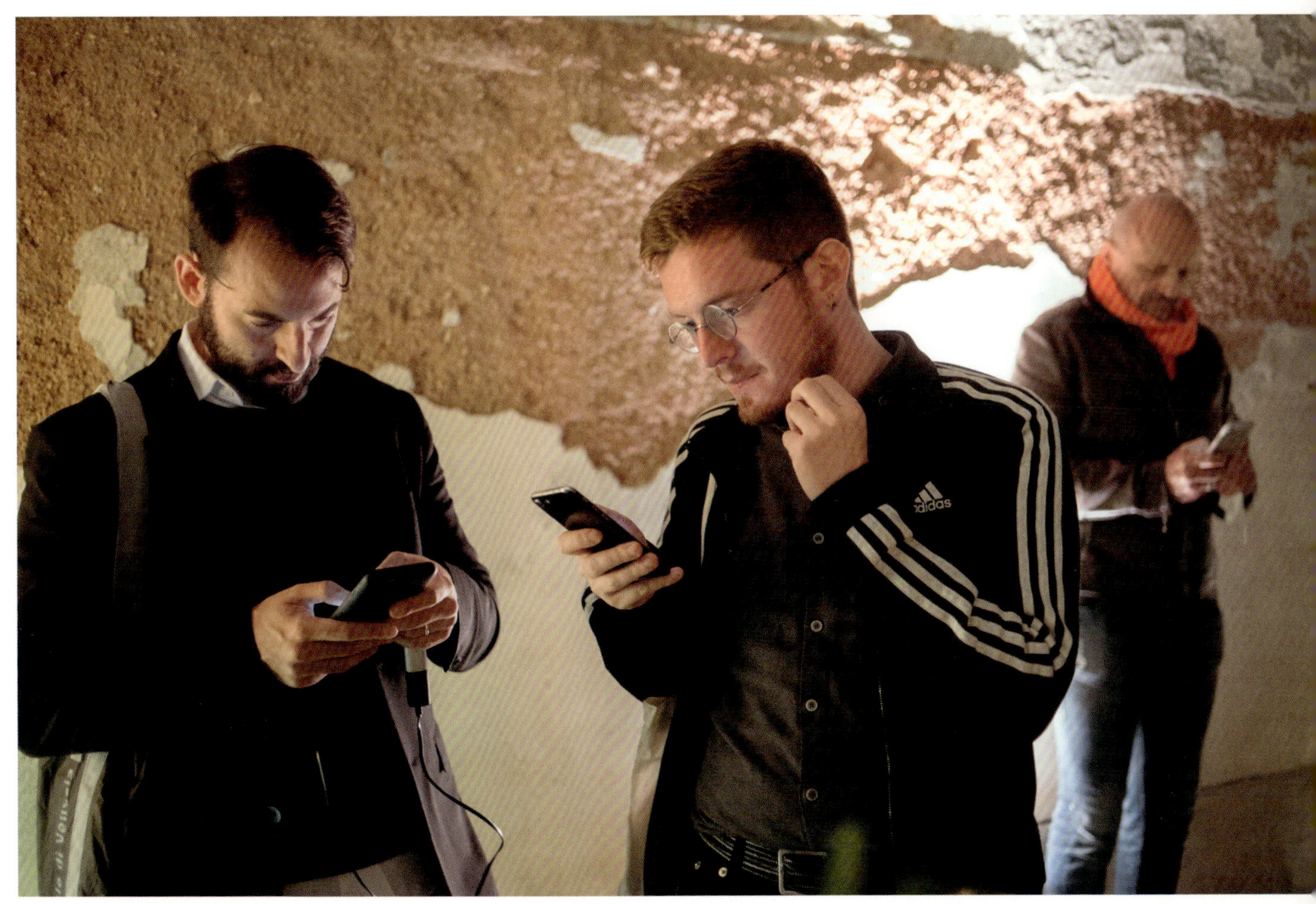

Palazzo Ca' Tron, Venice 2019

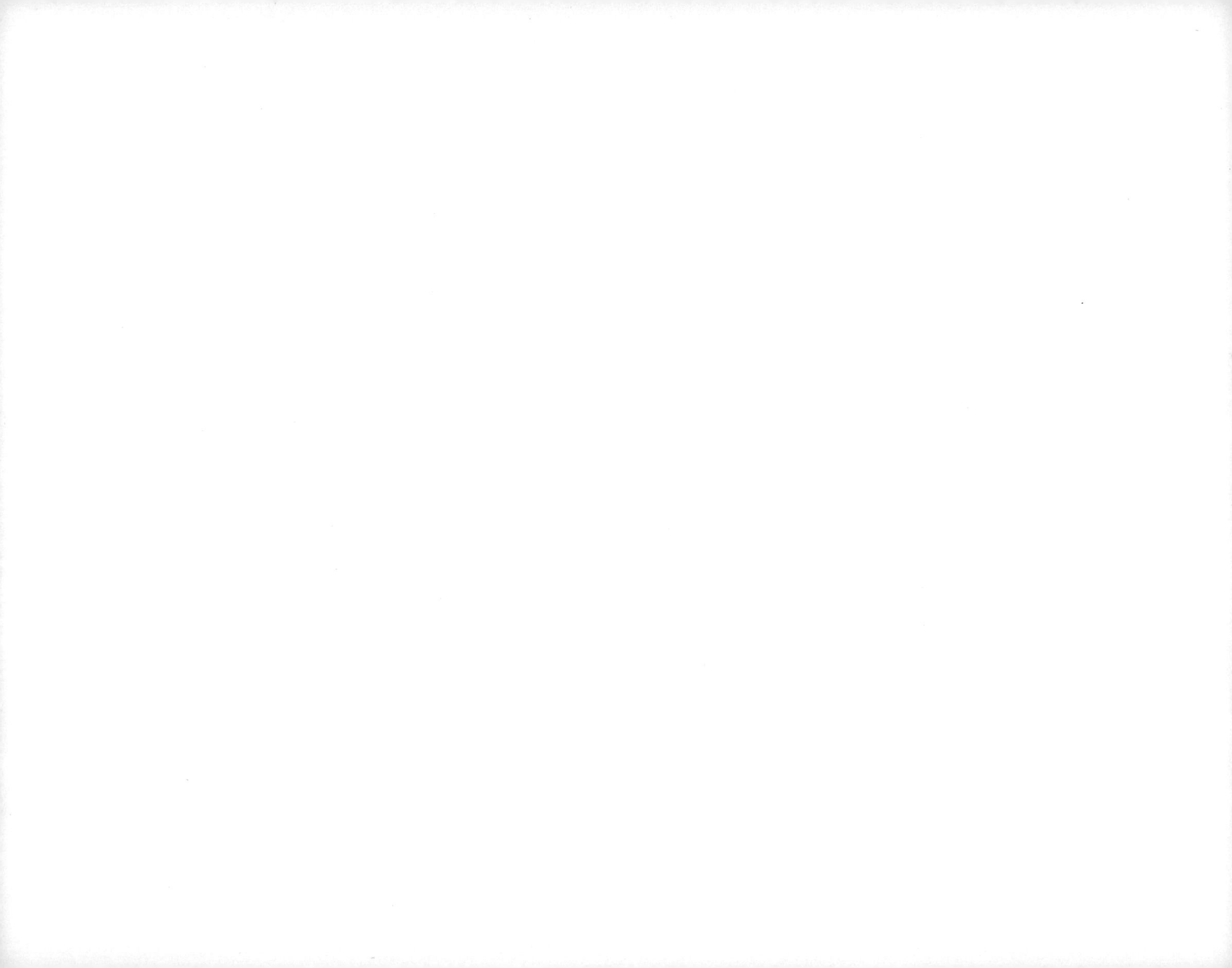

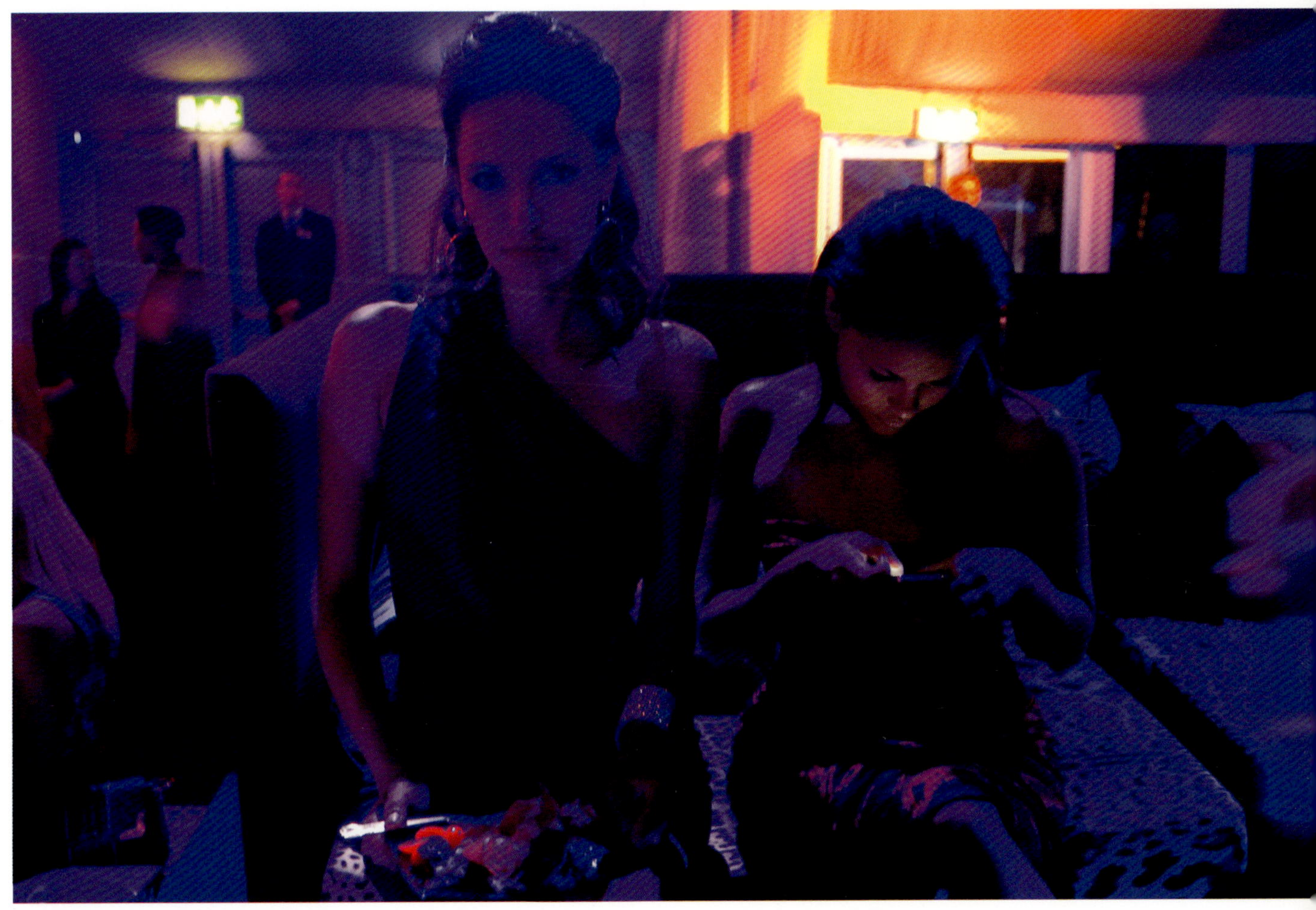

Battersea Power Station, London 2011

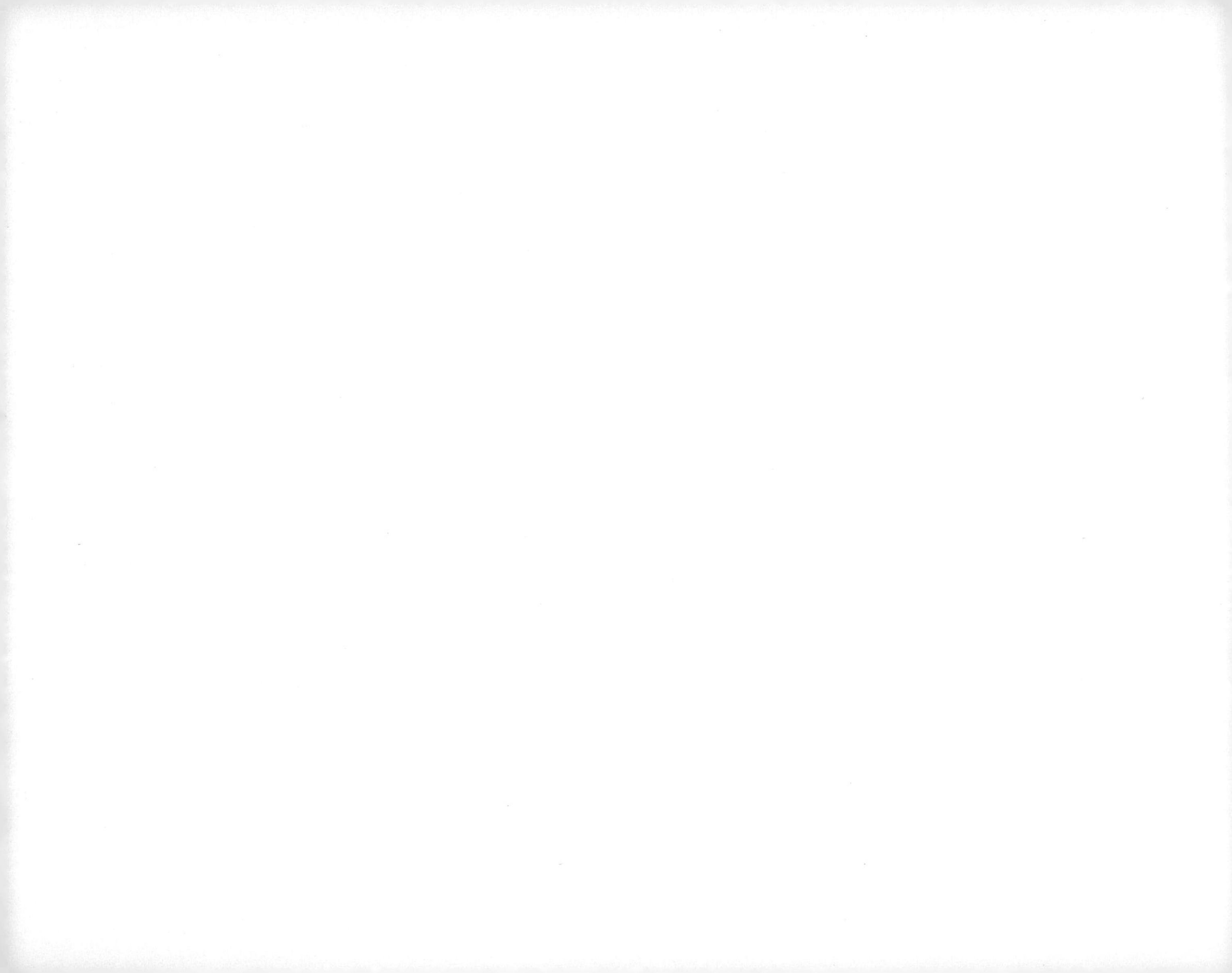

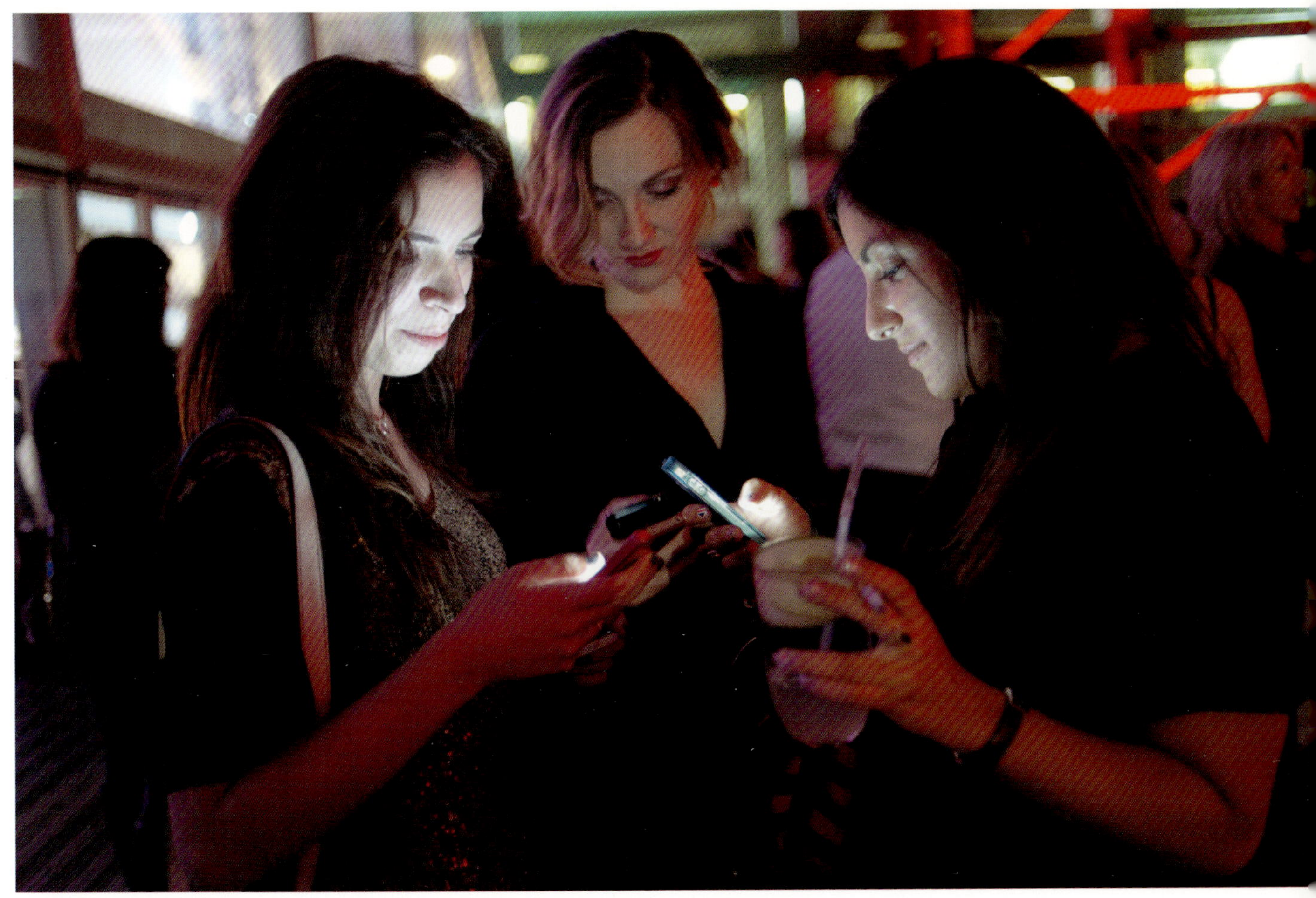

Battersea, London 2011

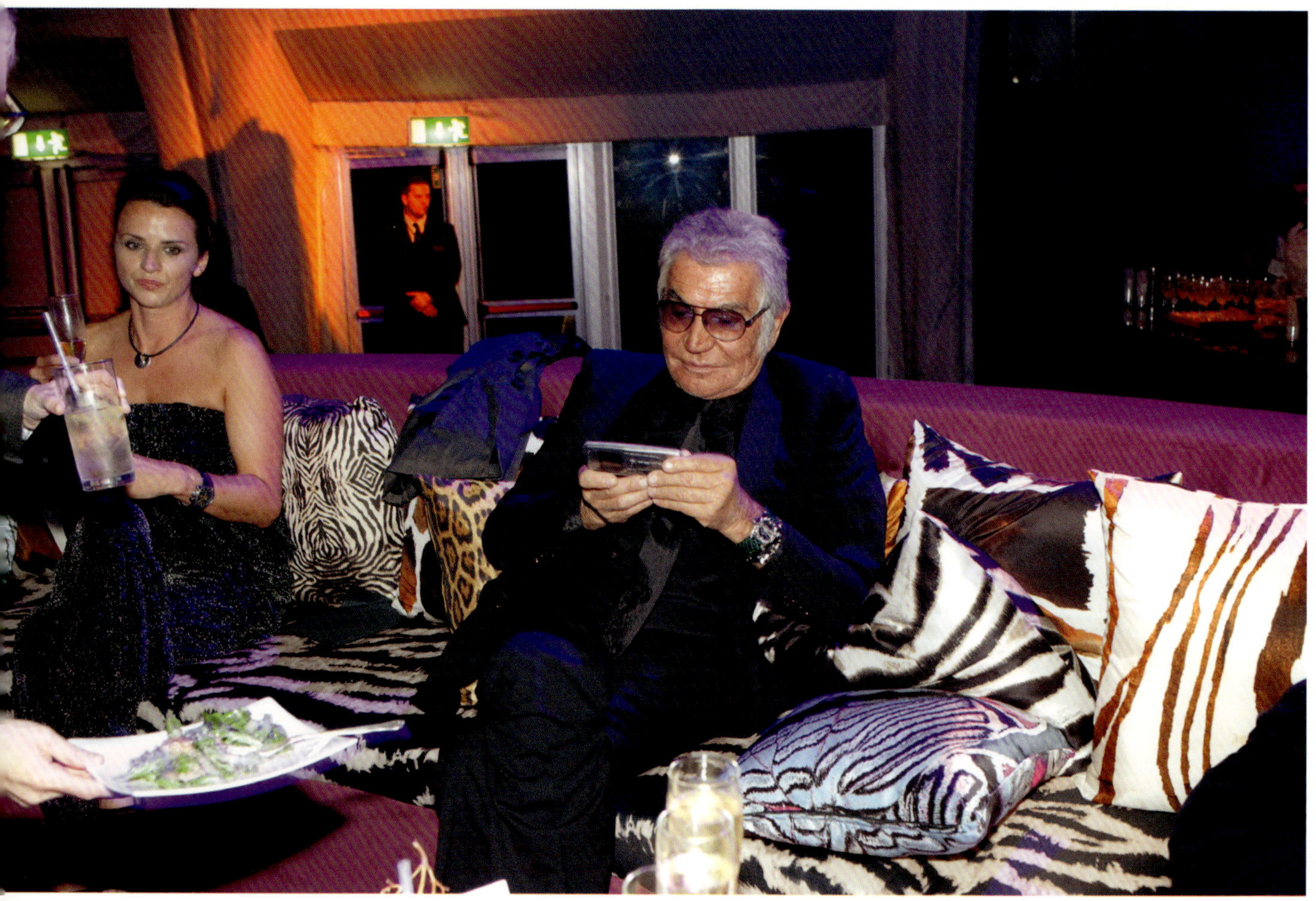

Battersea Power Station, London 2011

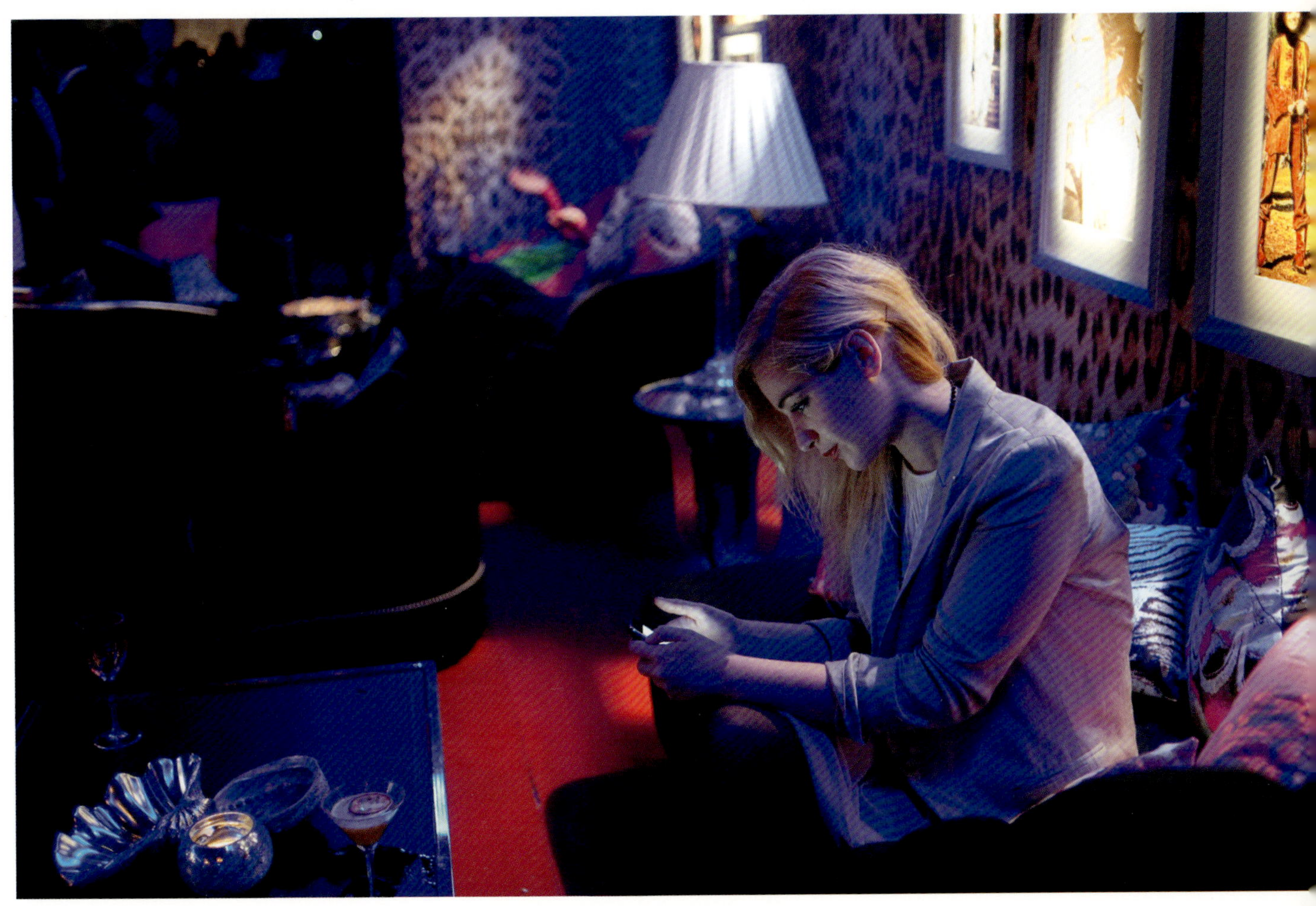

Battersea Power Station, London 2011

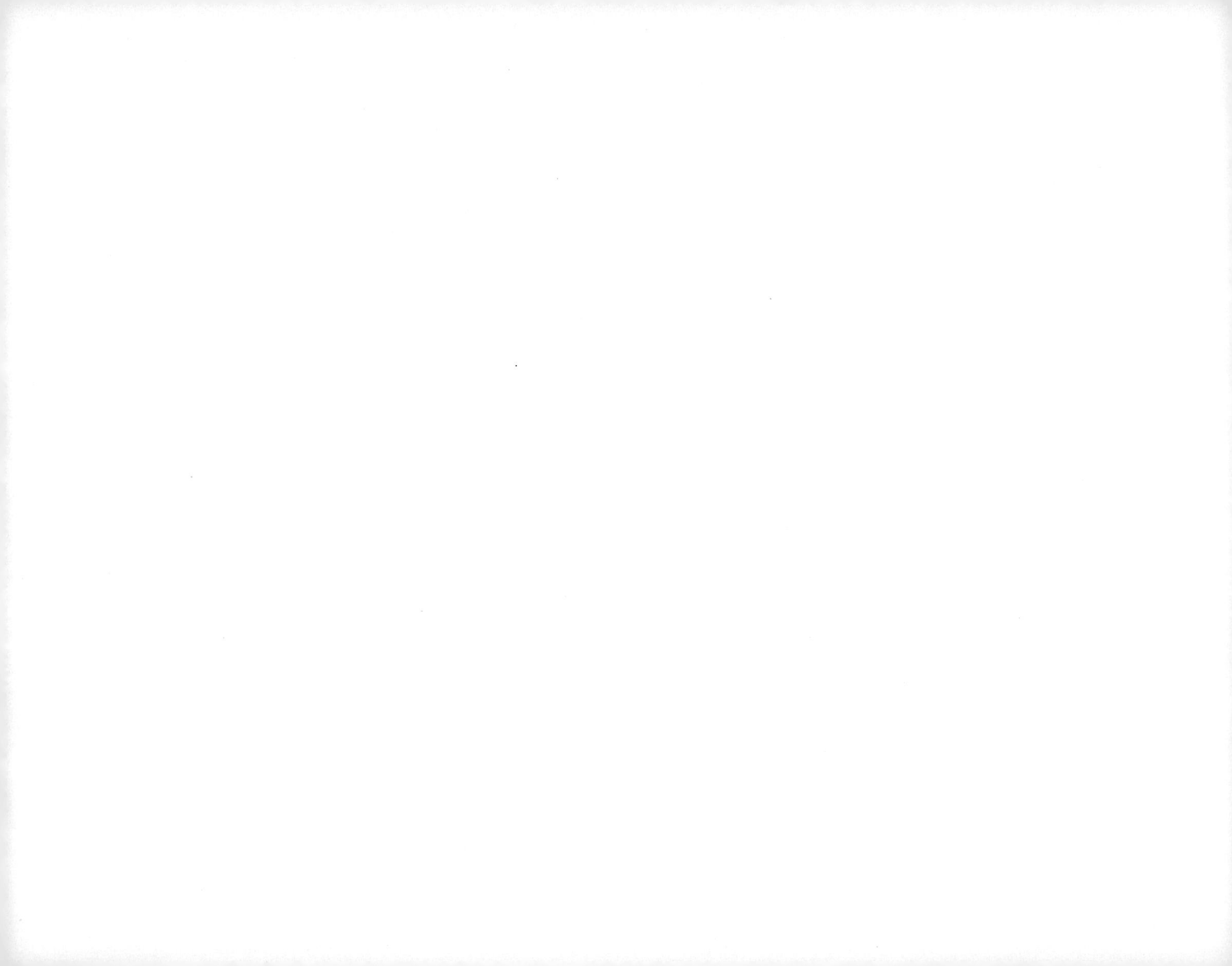

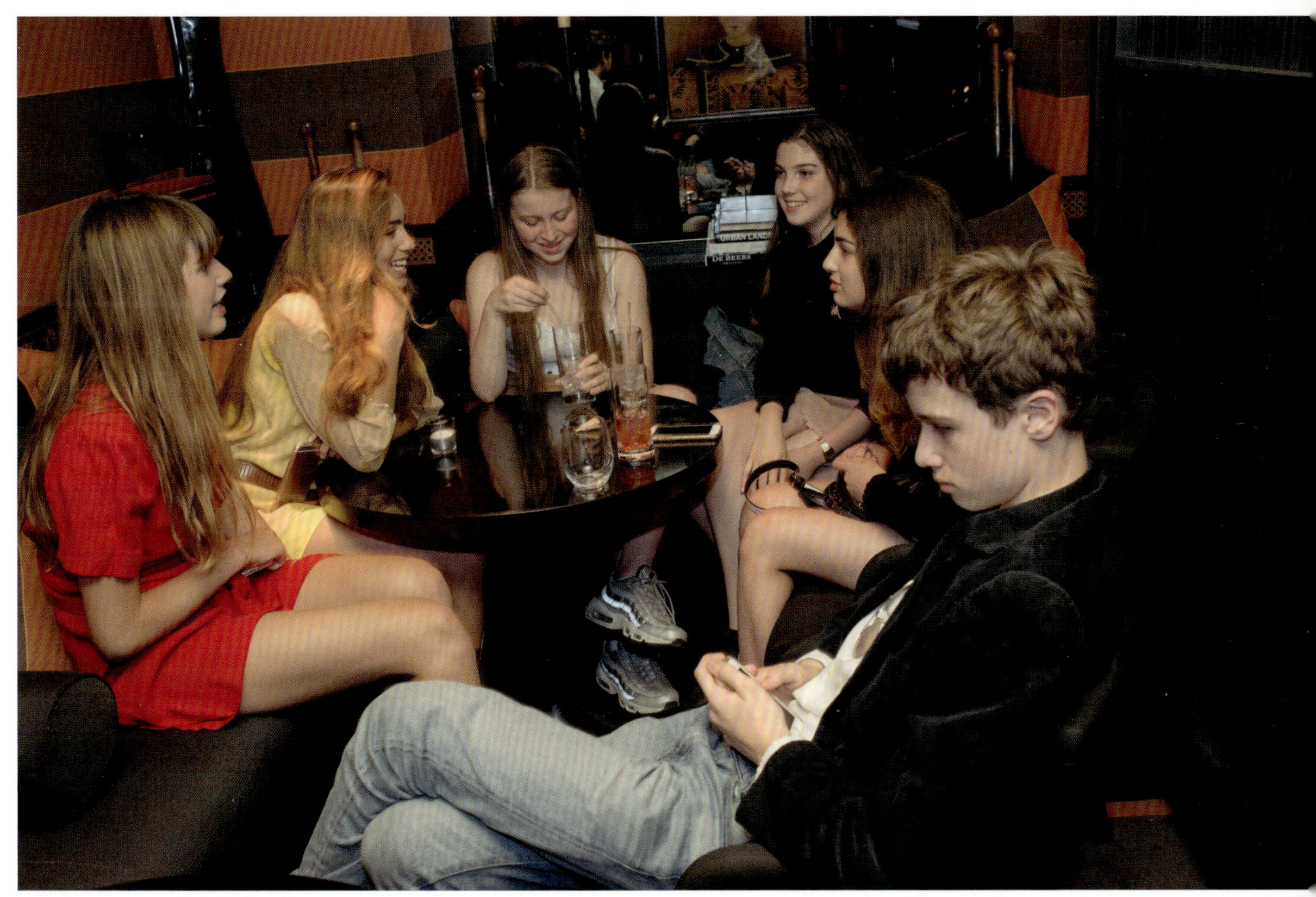

South Kensington, London 2017

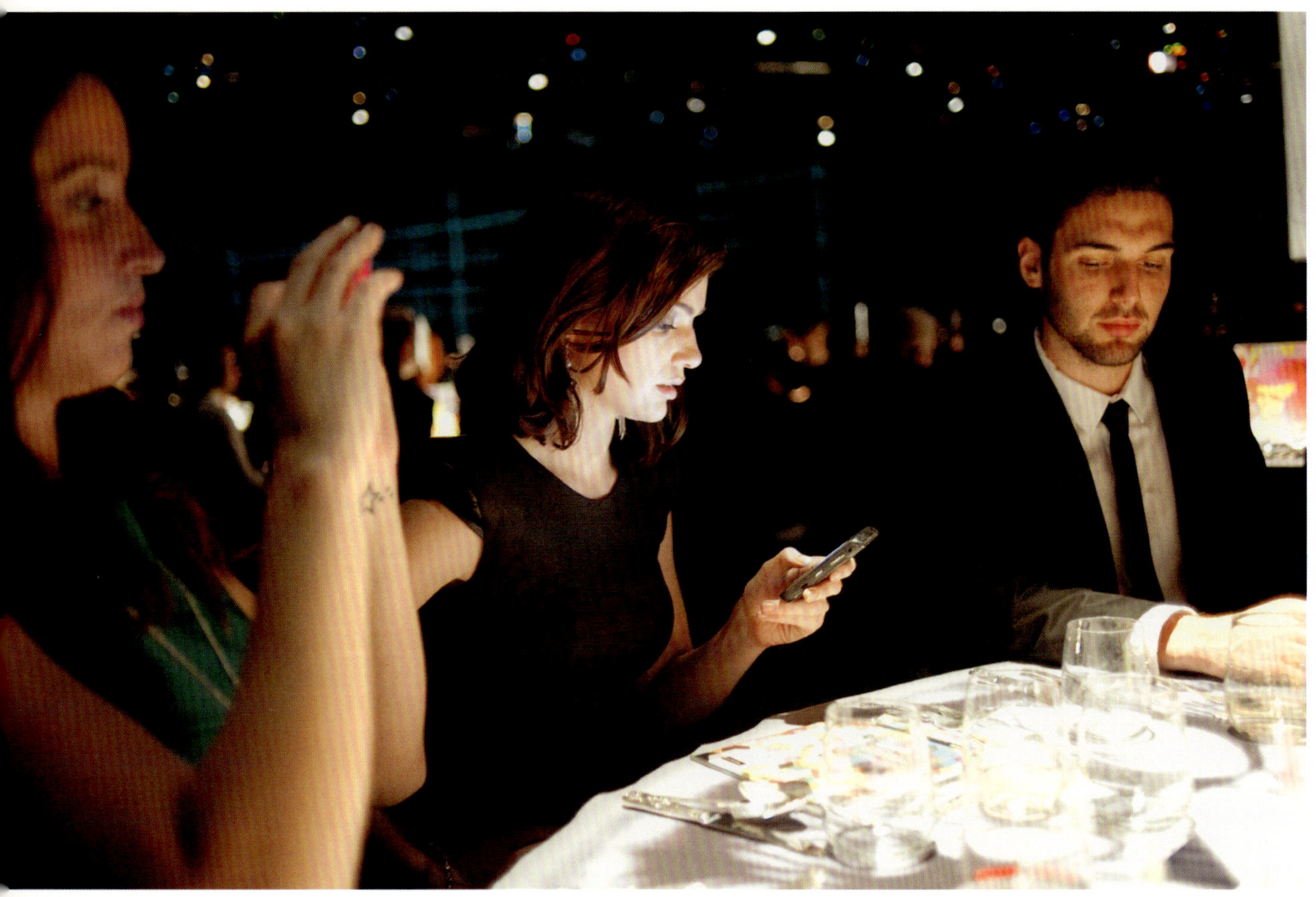

Battersea Park, London 2011

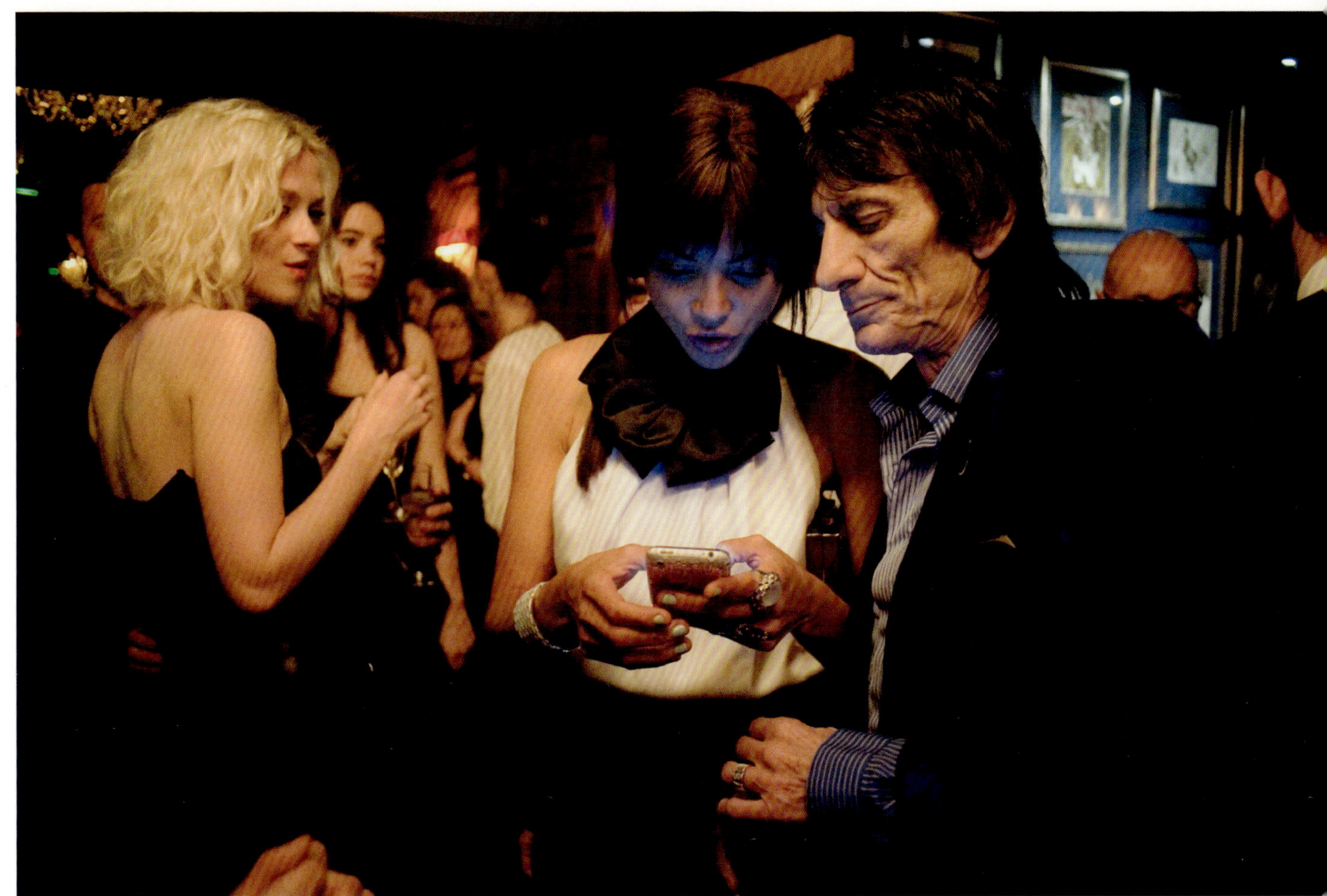

Tramp, London 2011

Whitehall, London 2011

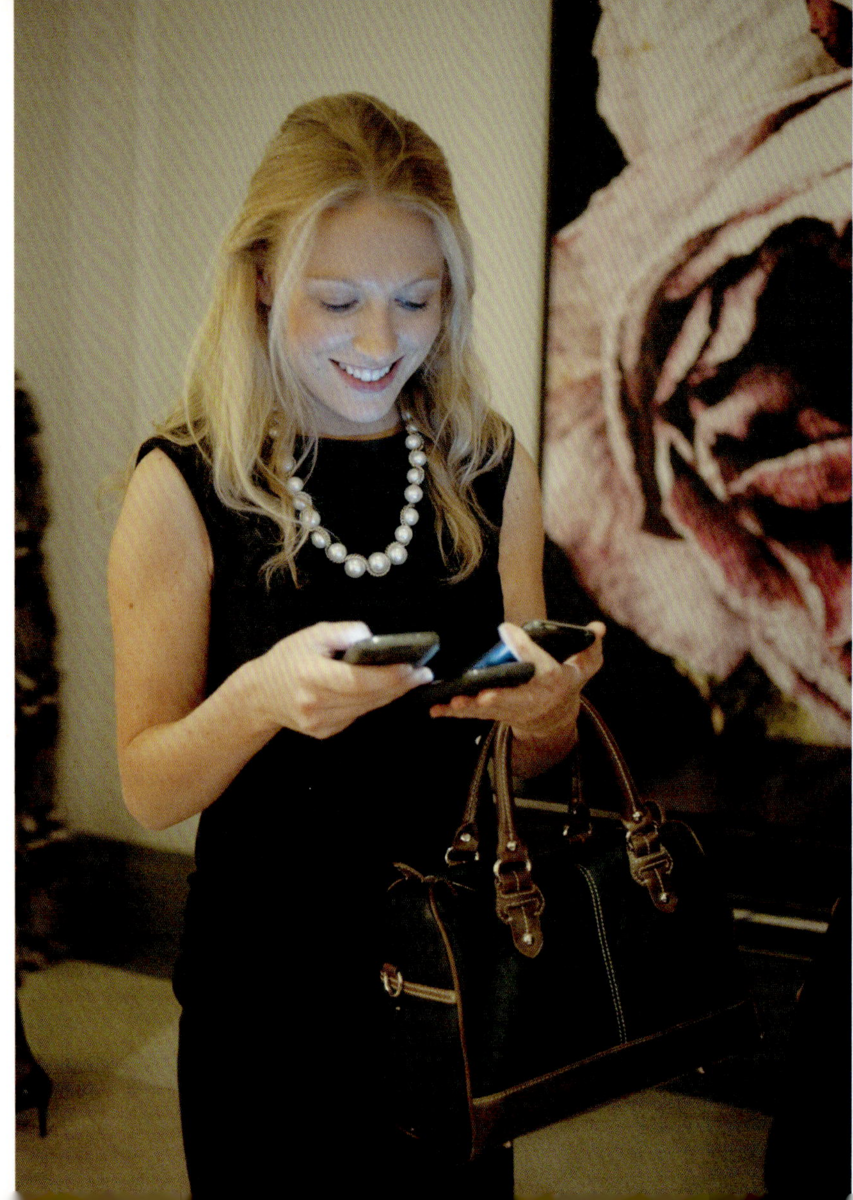

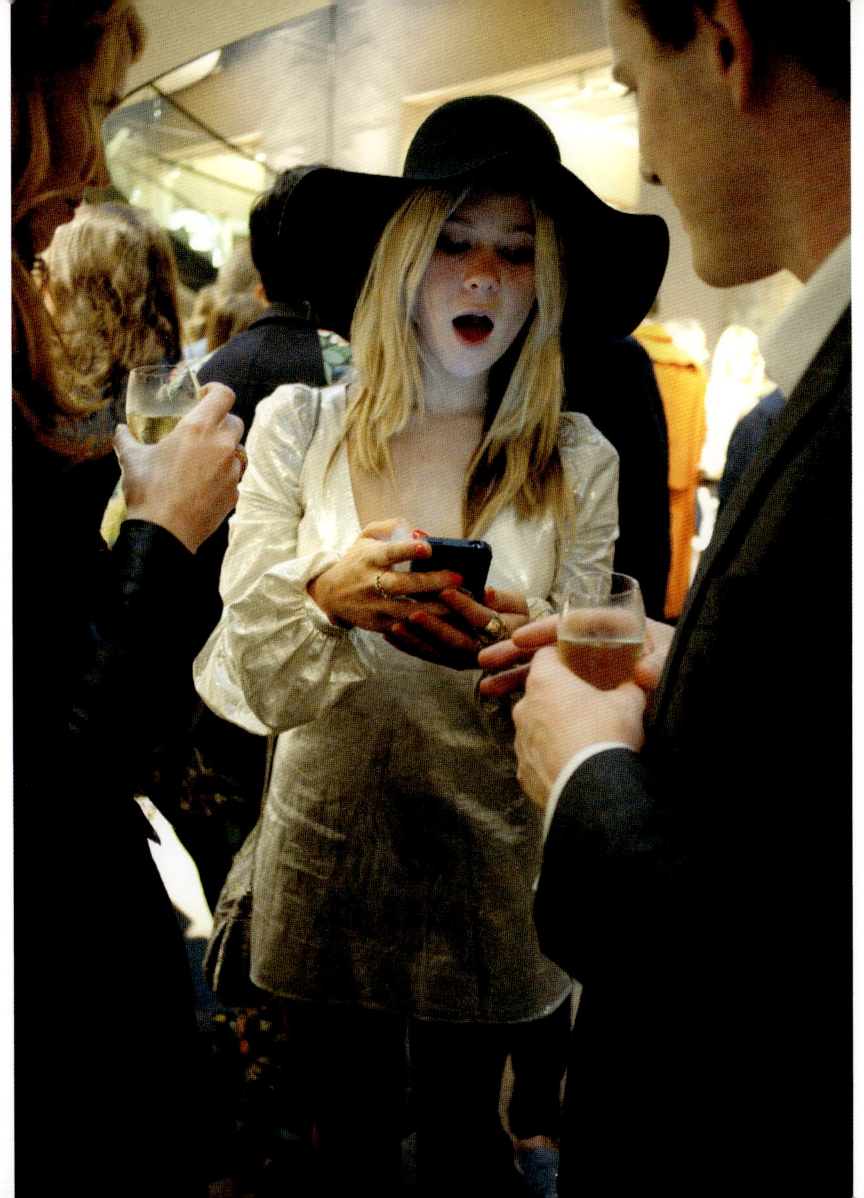

Mayfair, London 2011

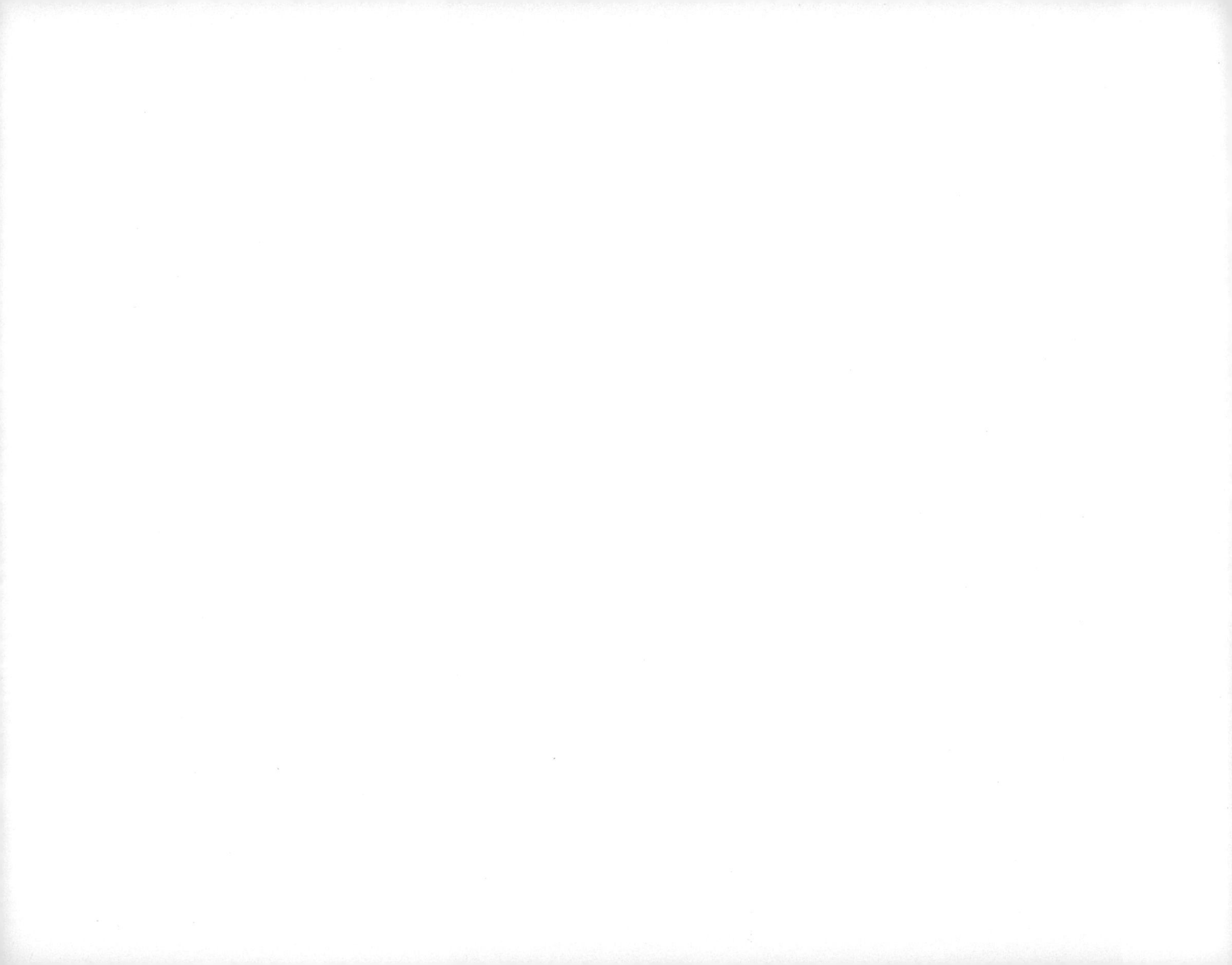

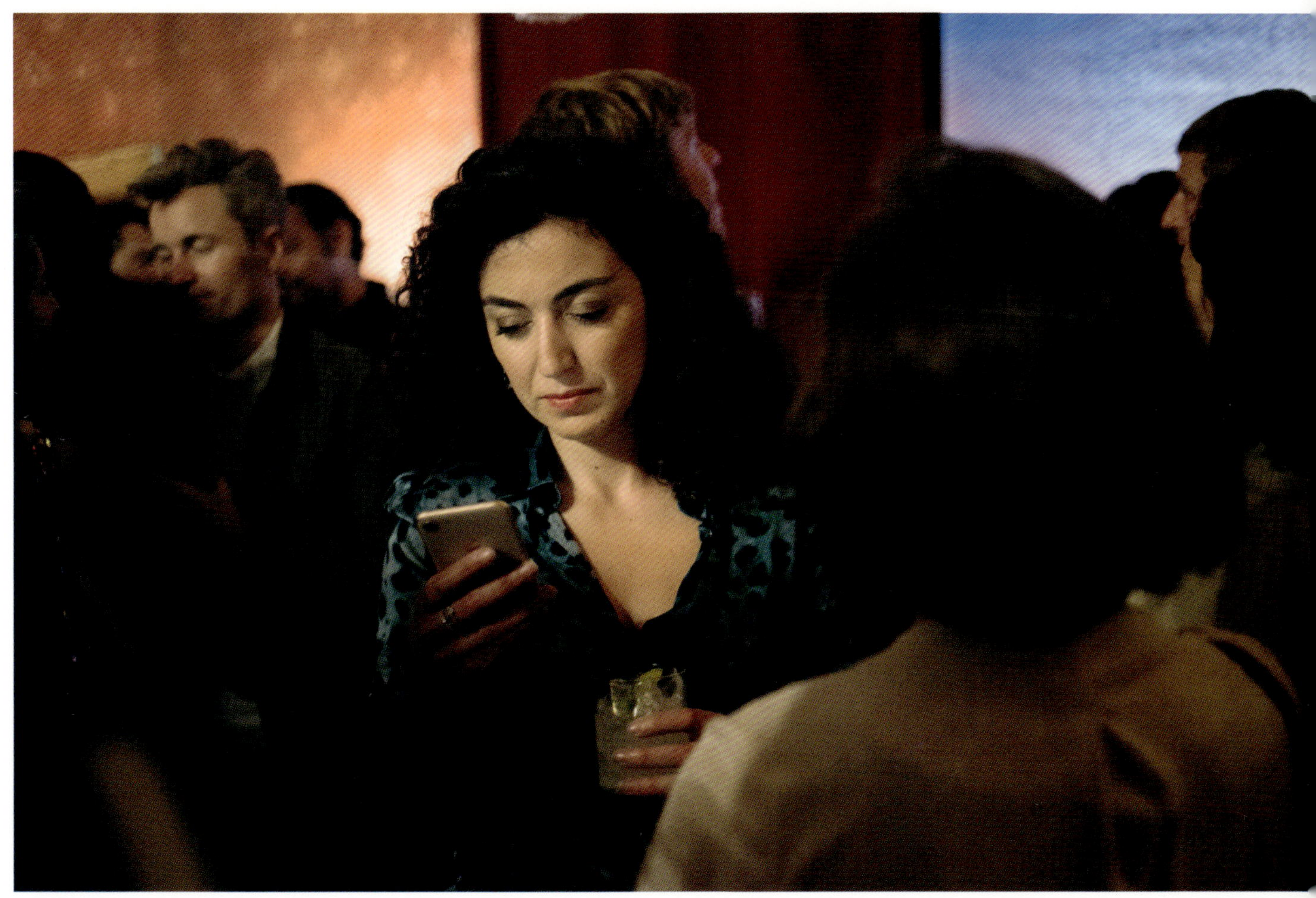

Palazzo Benzon, Venice 2019

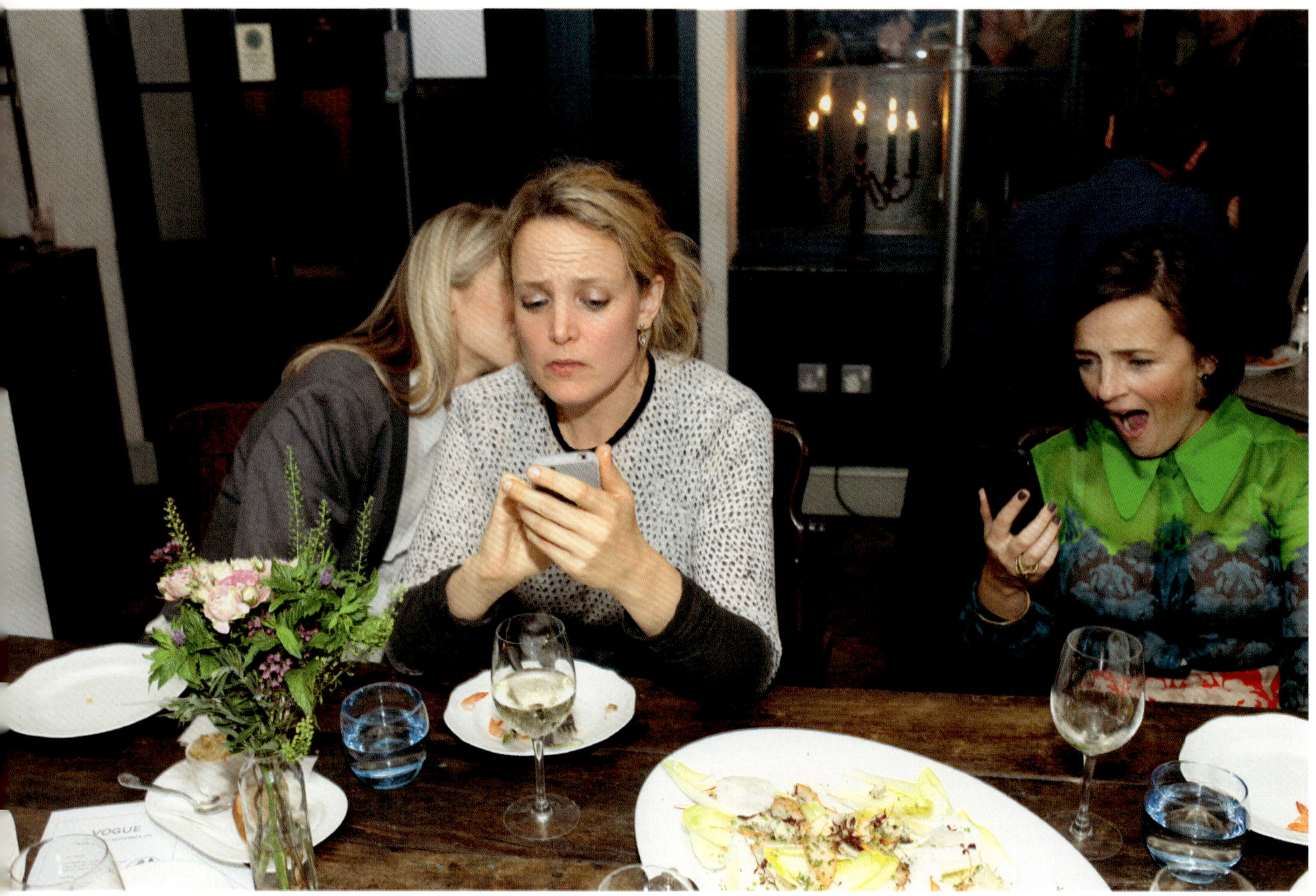

Fitzrovia, London 2011

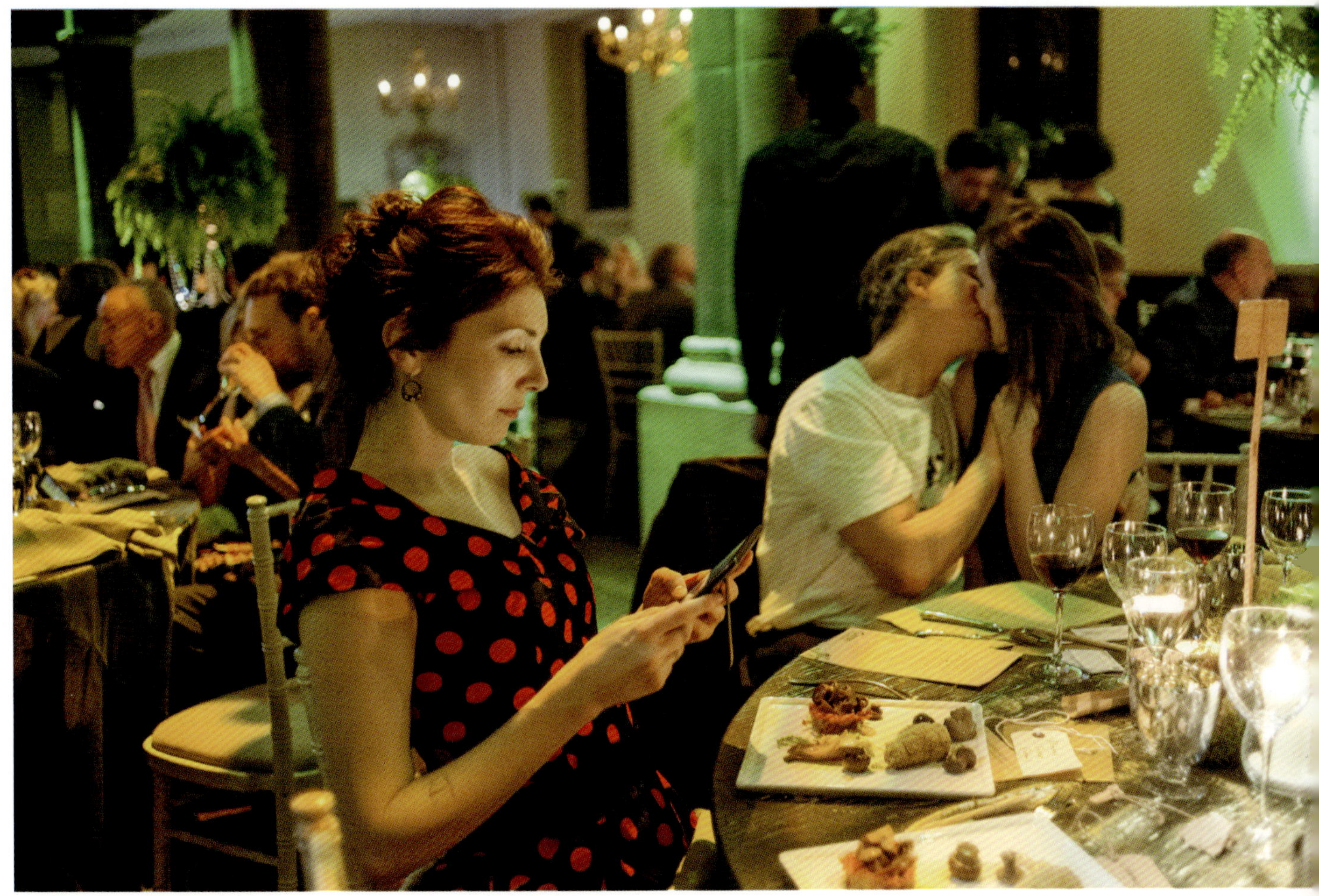

Mayfair, London 2014

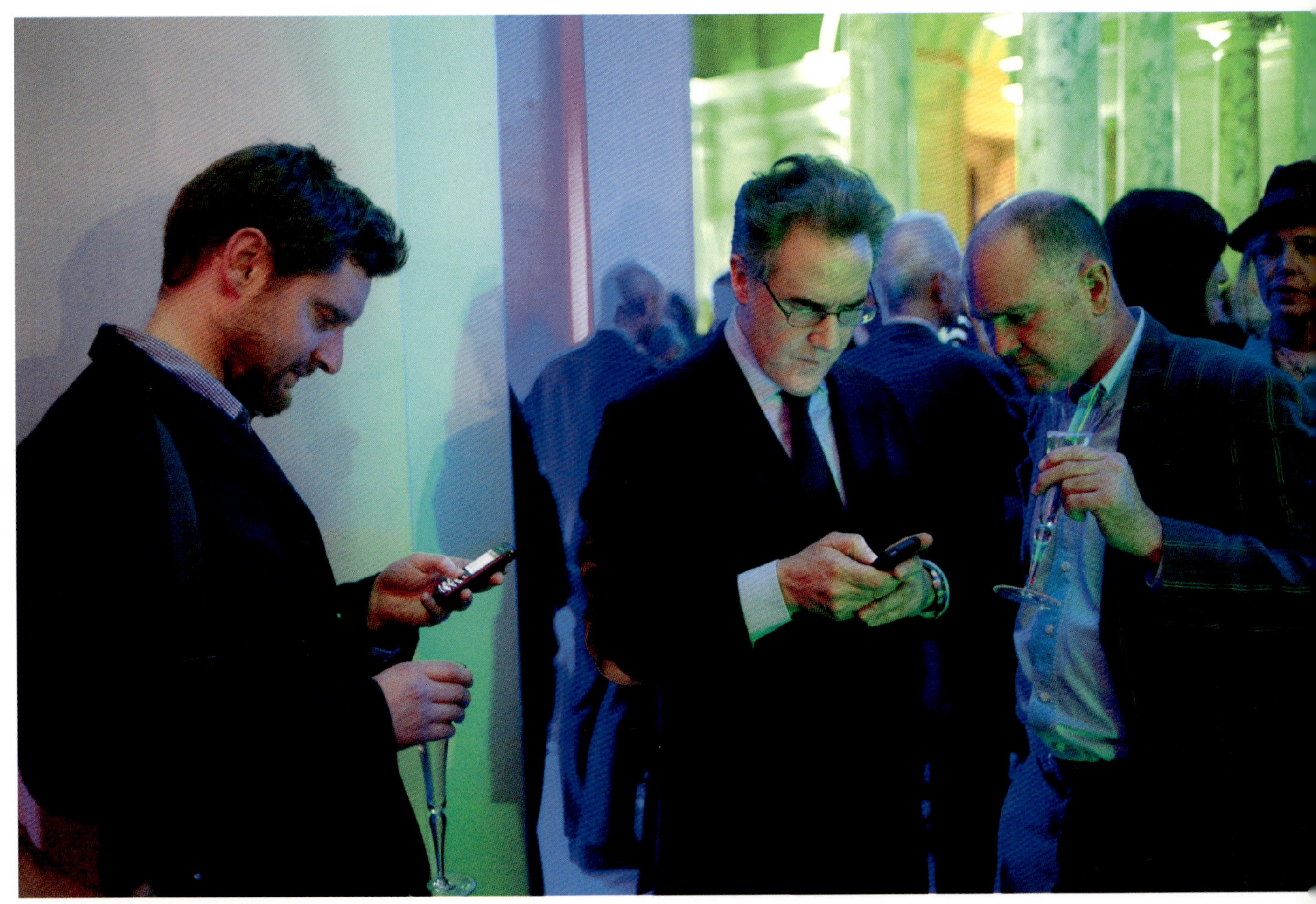

V&A, London 2011

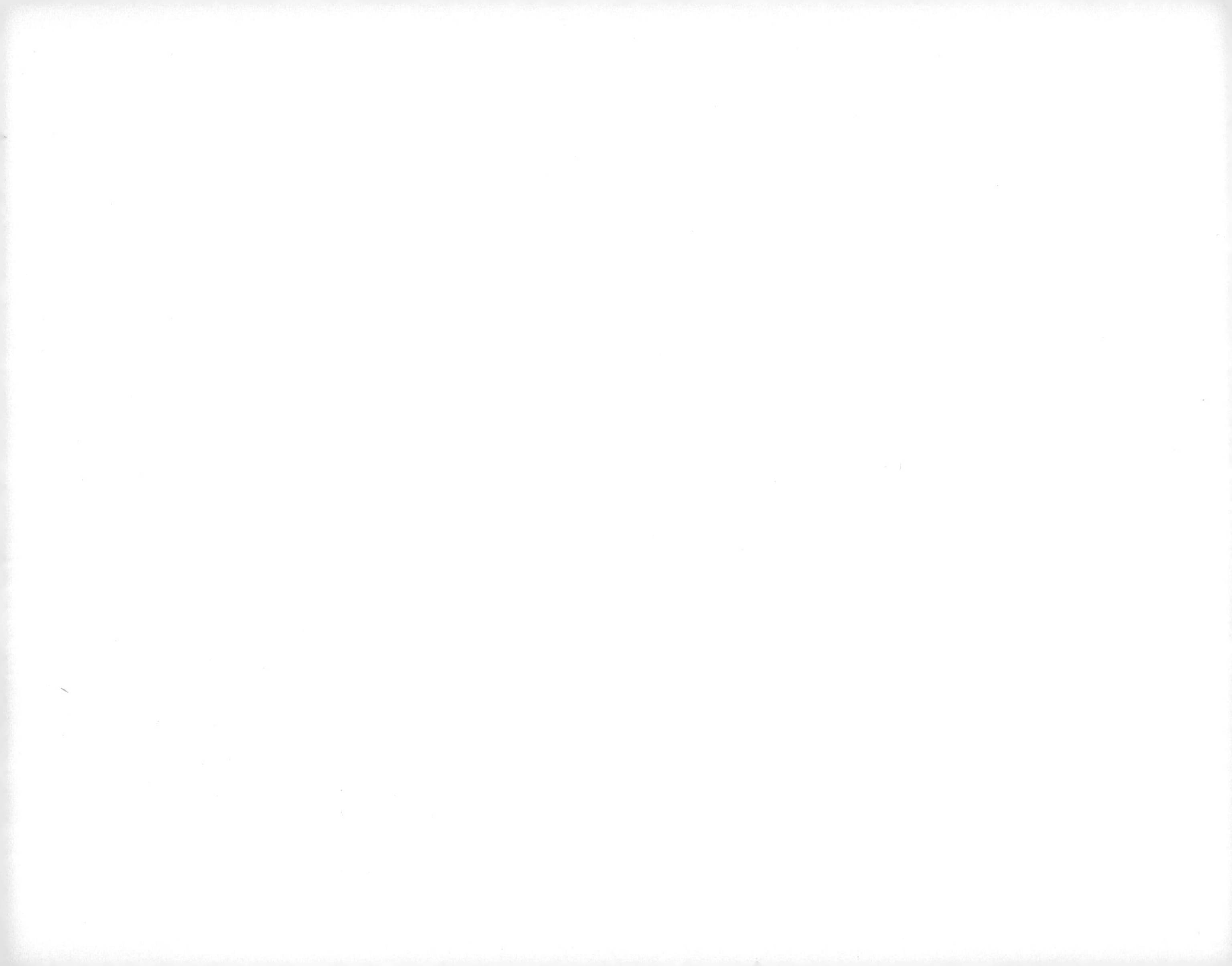

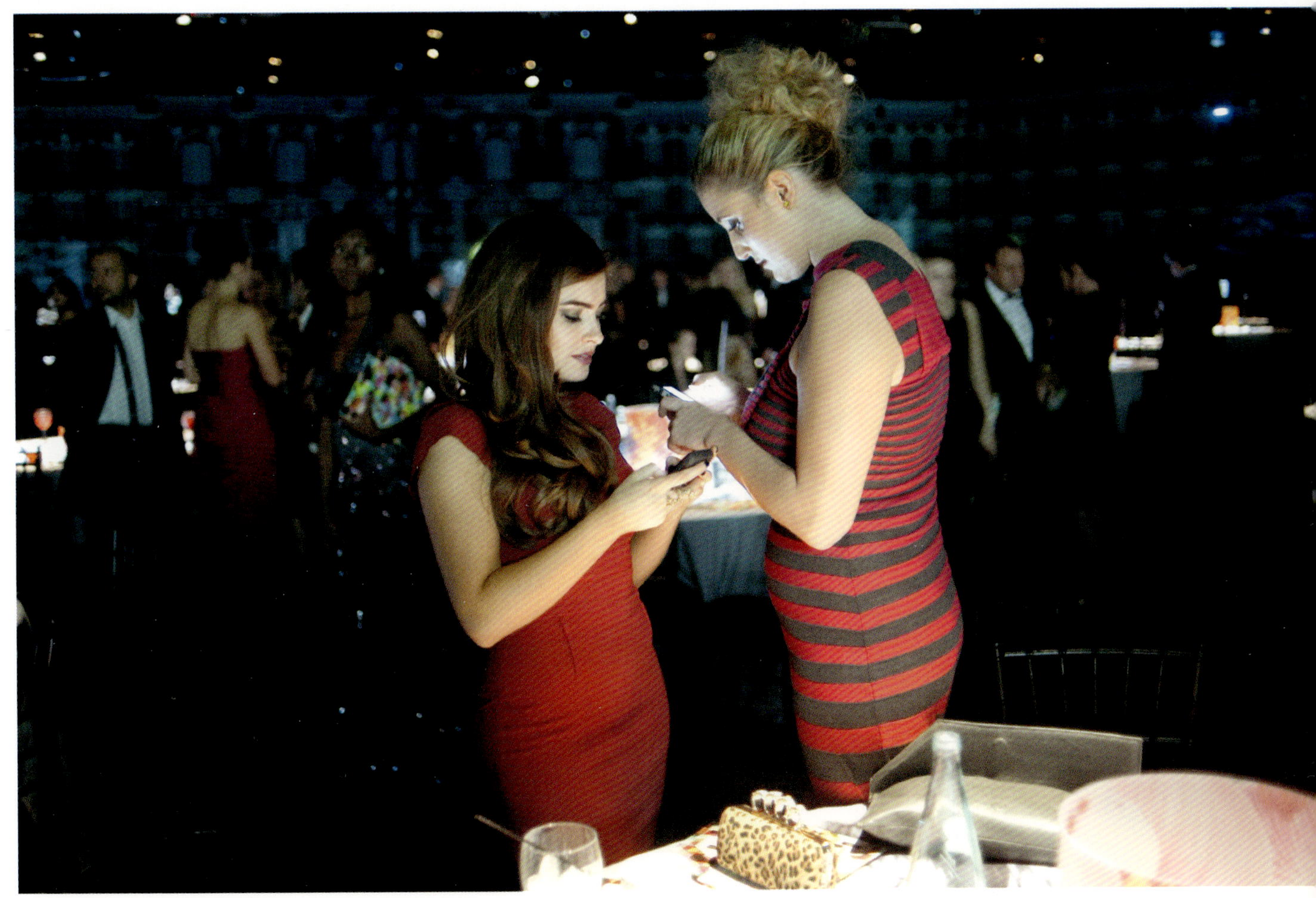

Battersea Park, London 2011

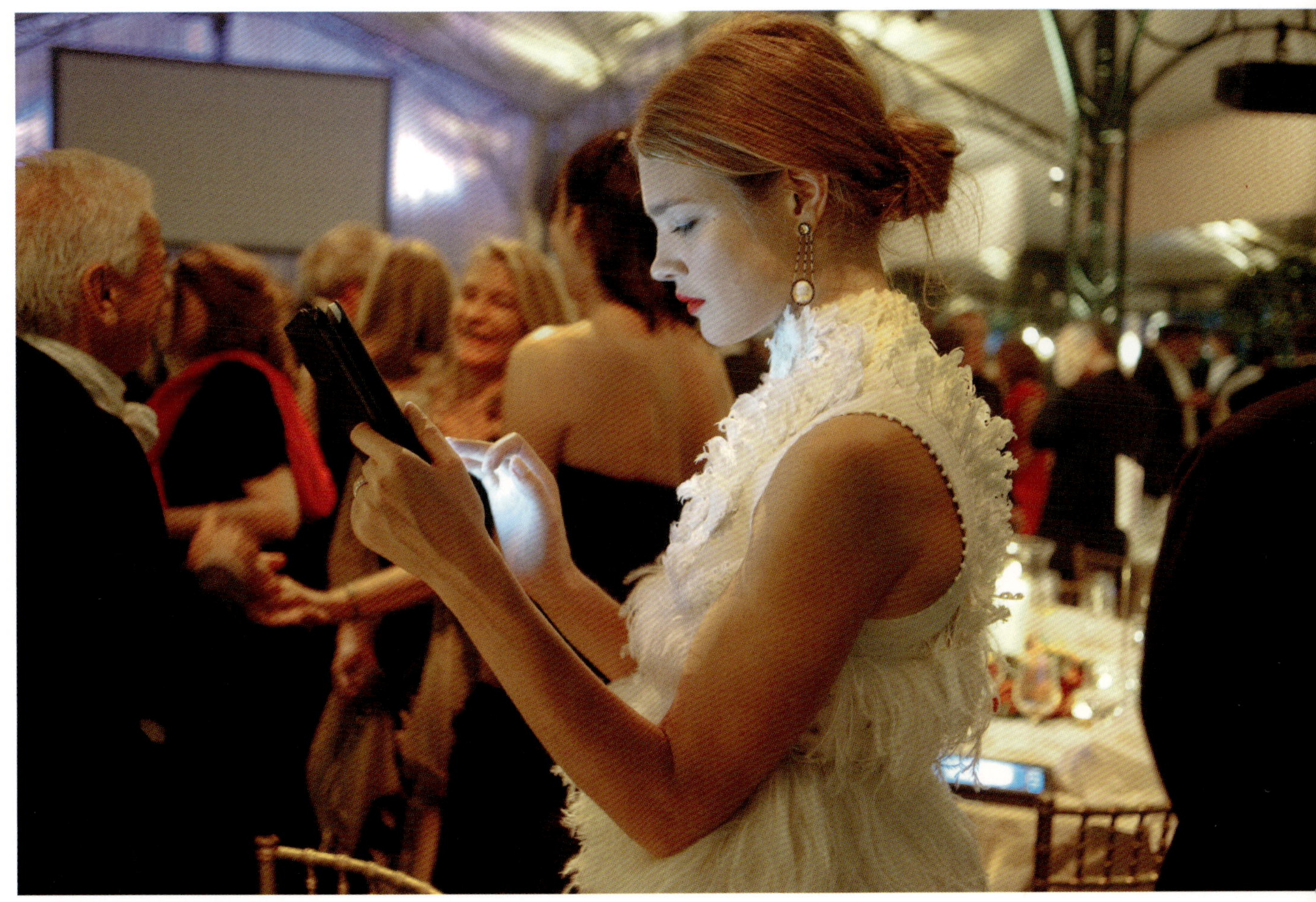

Hampton Court, London 2011

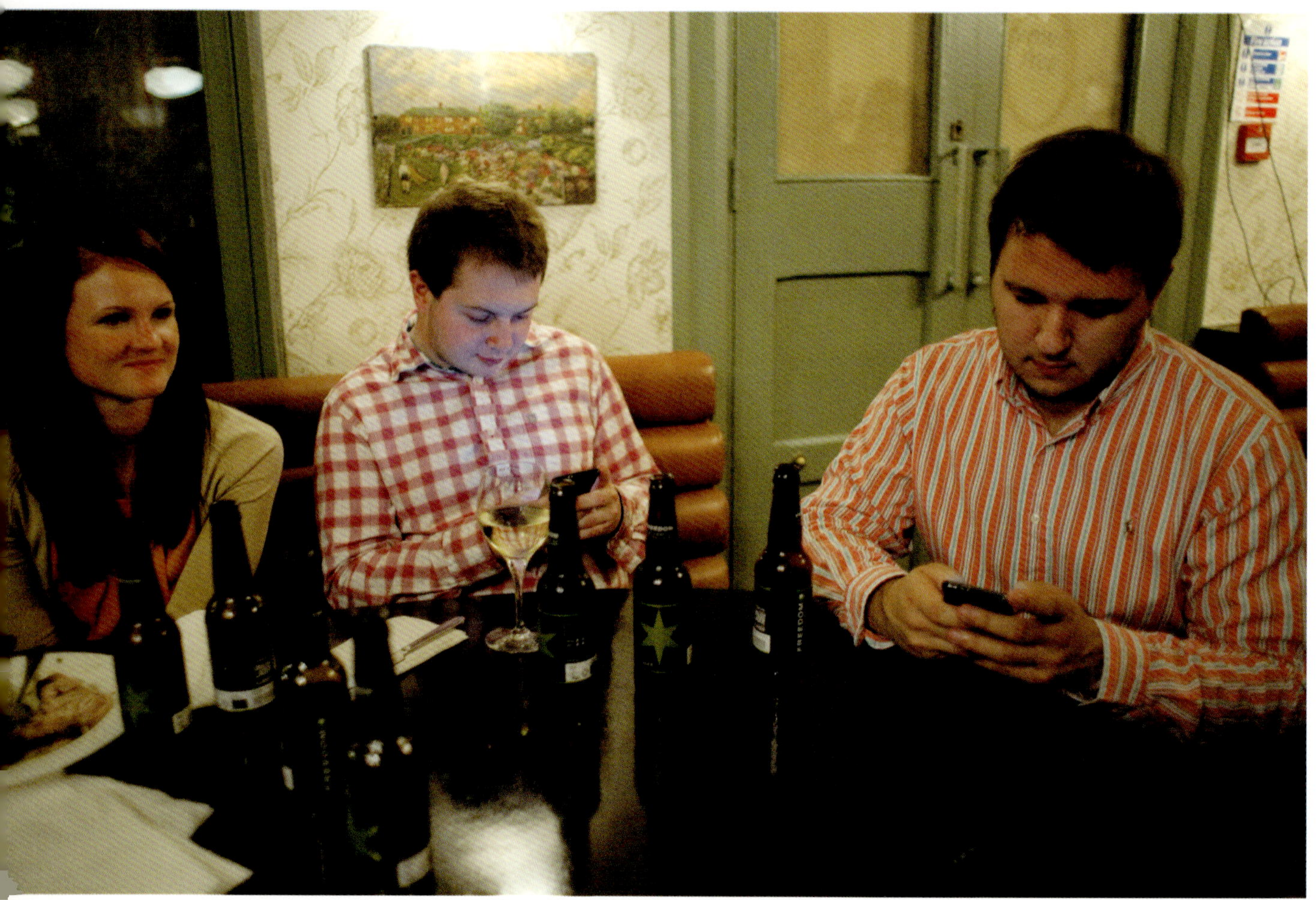

Notting Hill, London 2011

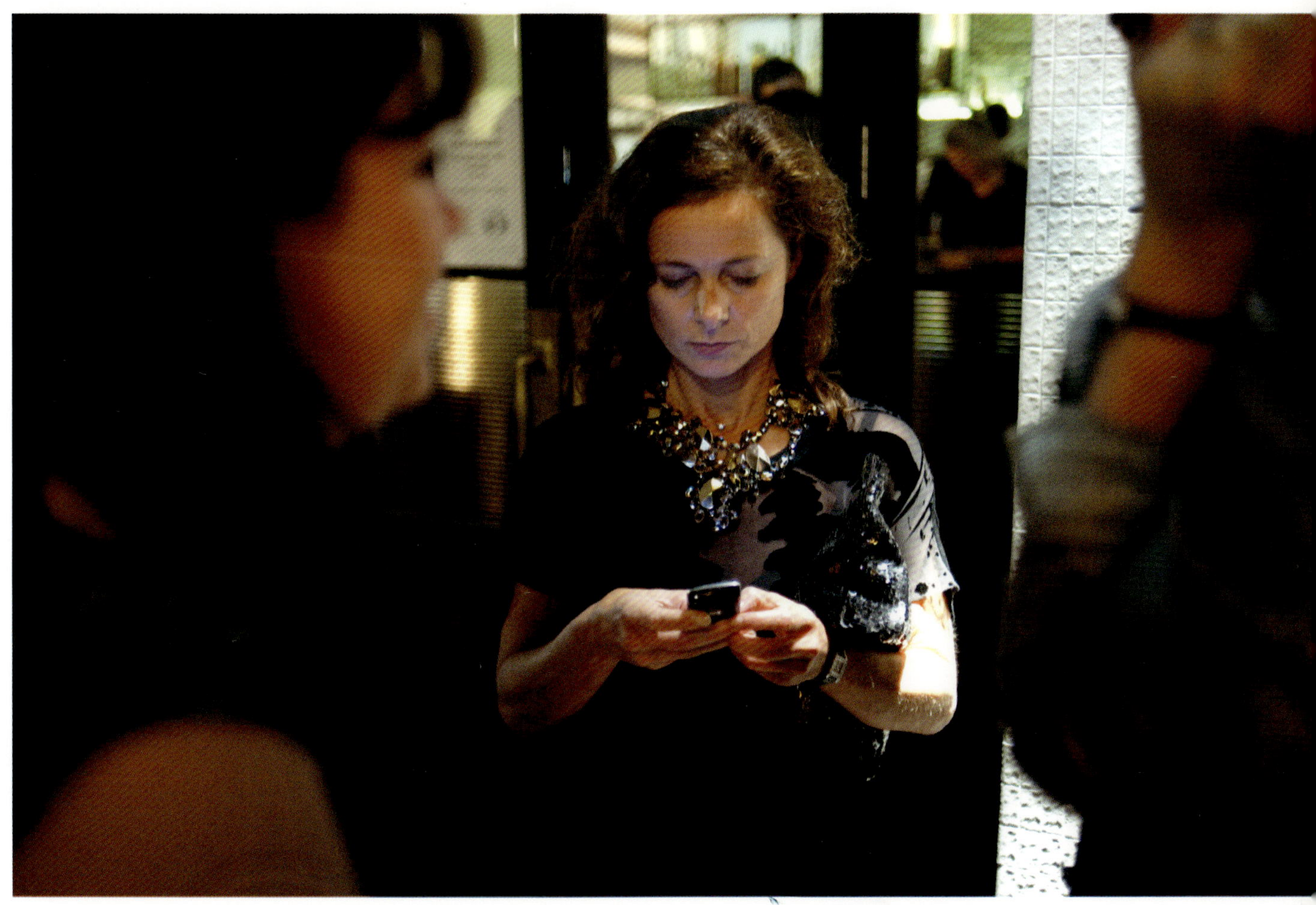

Fitzrovia, London 2011

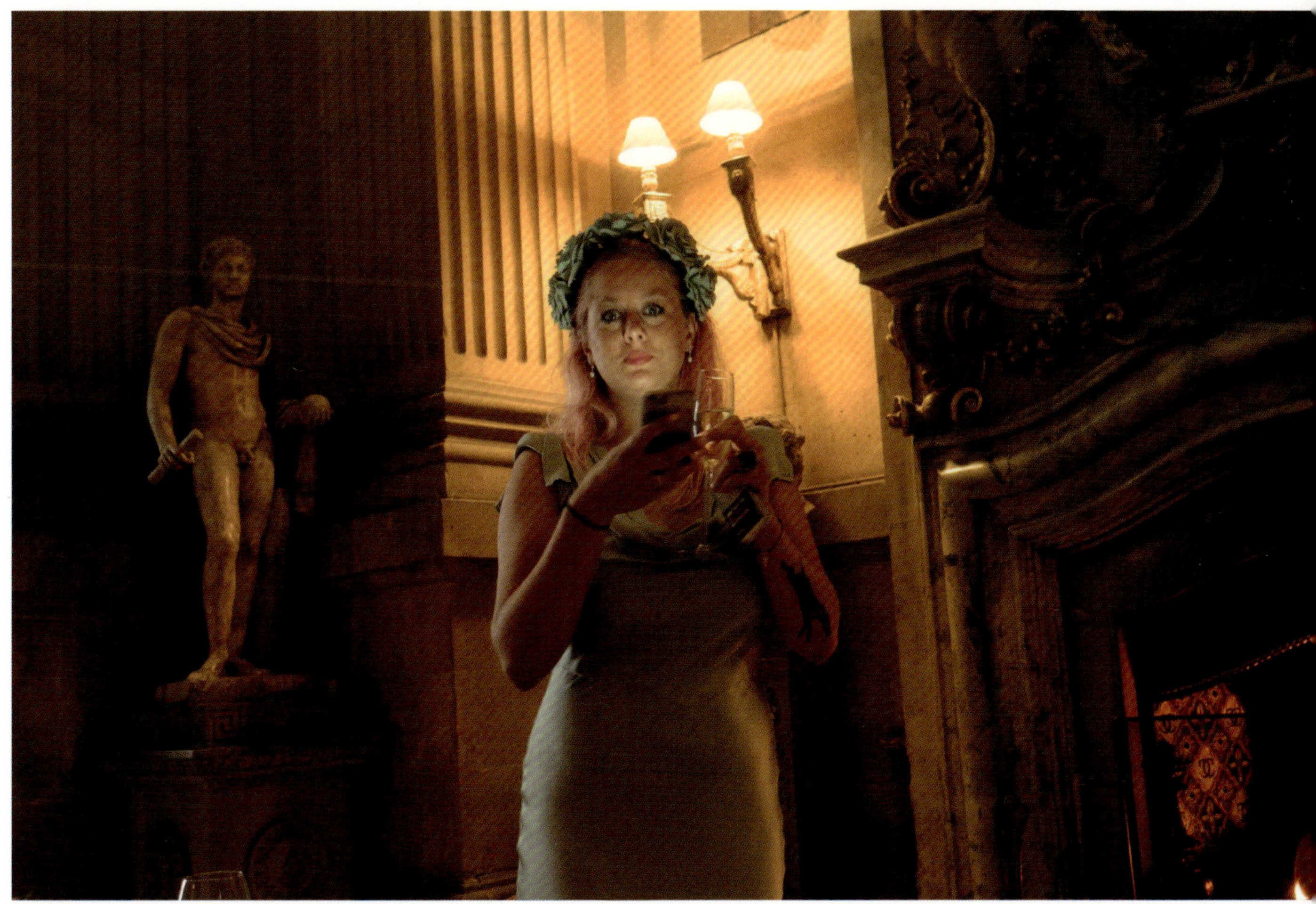

Castle Howard, Yorkshire 2016

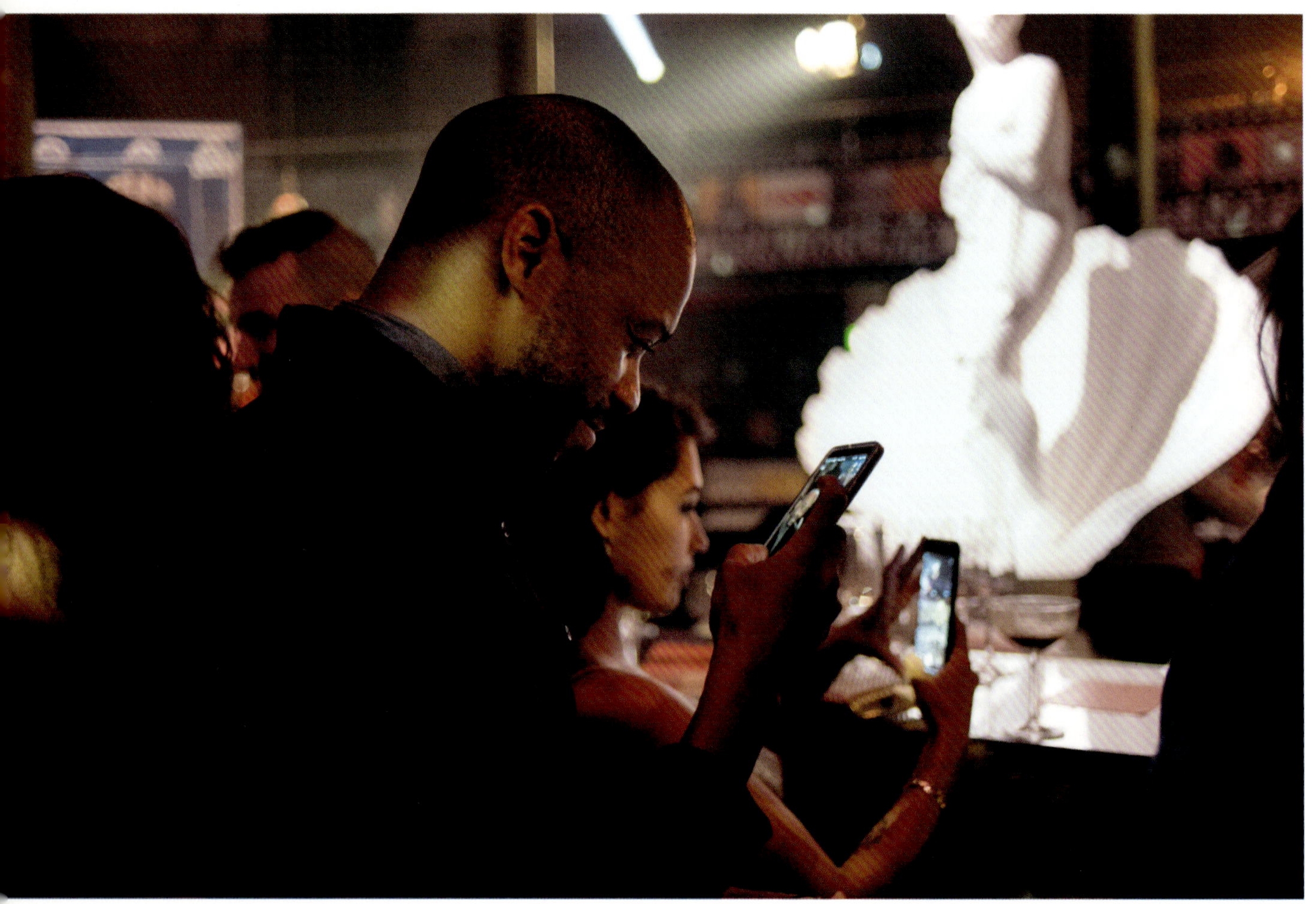

Roundhouse, London 2019

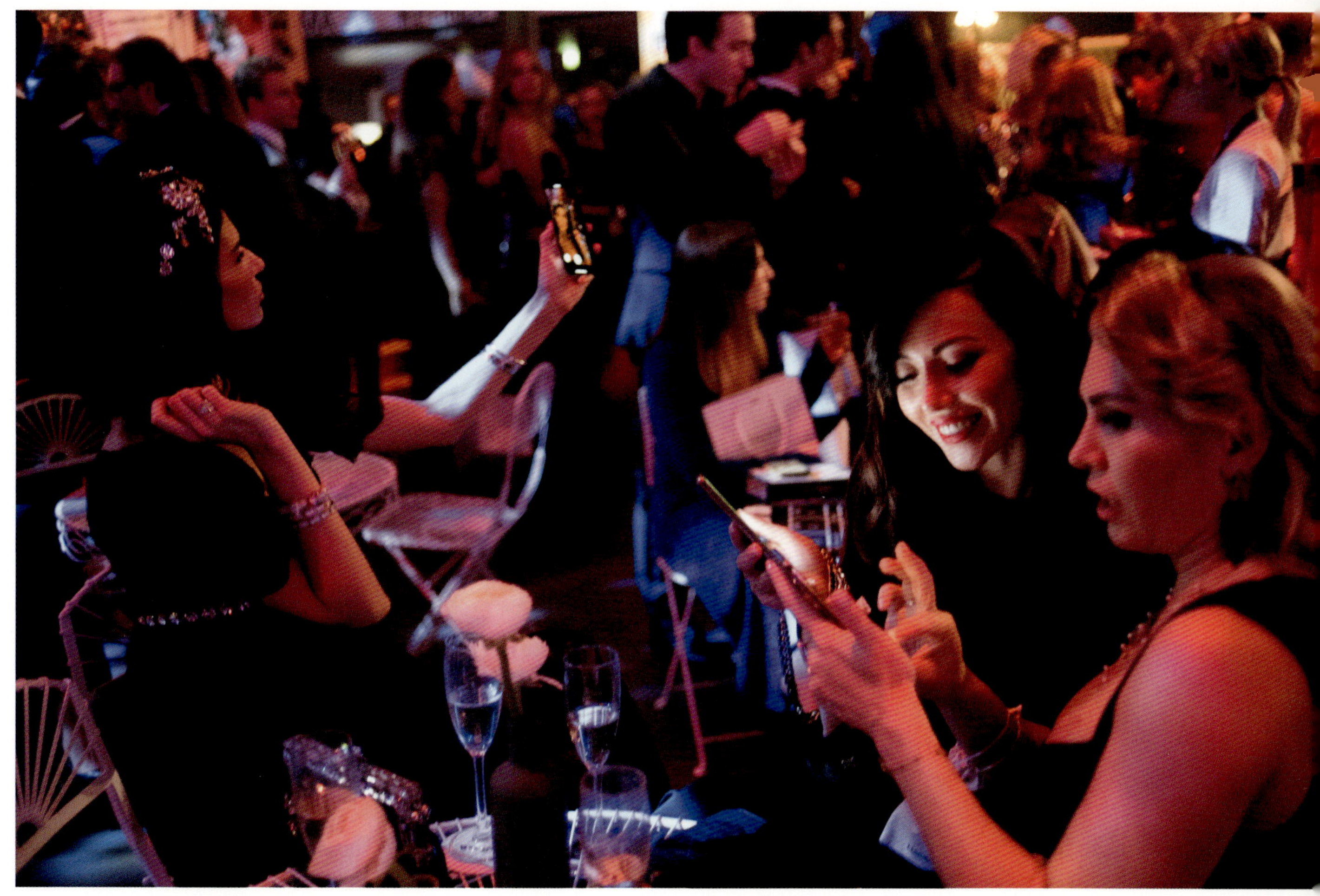

Roundhouse, London 2019

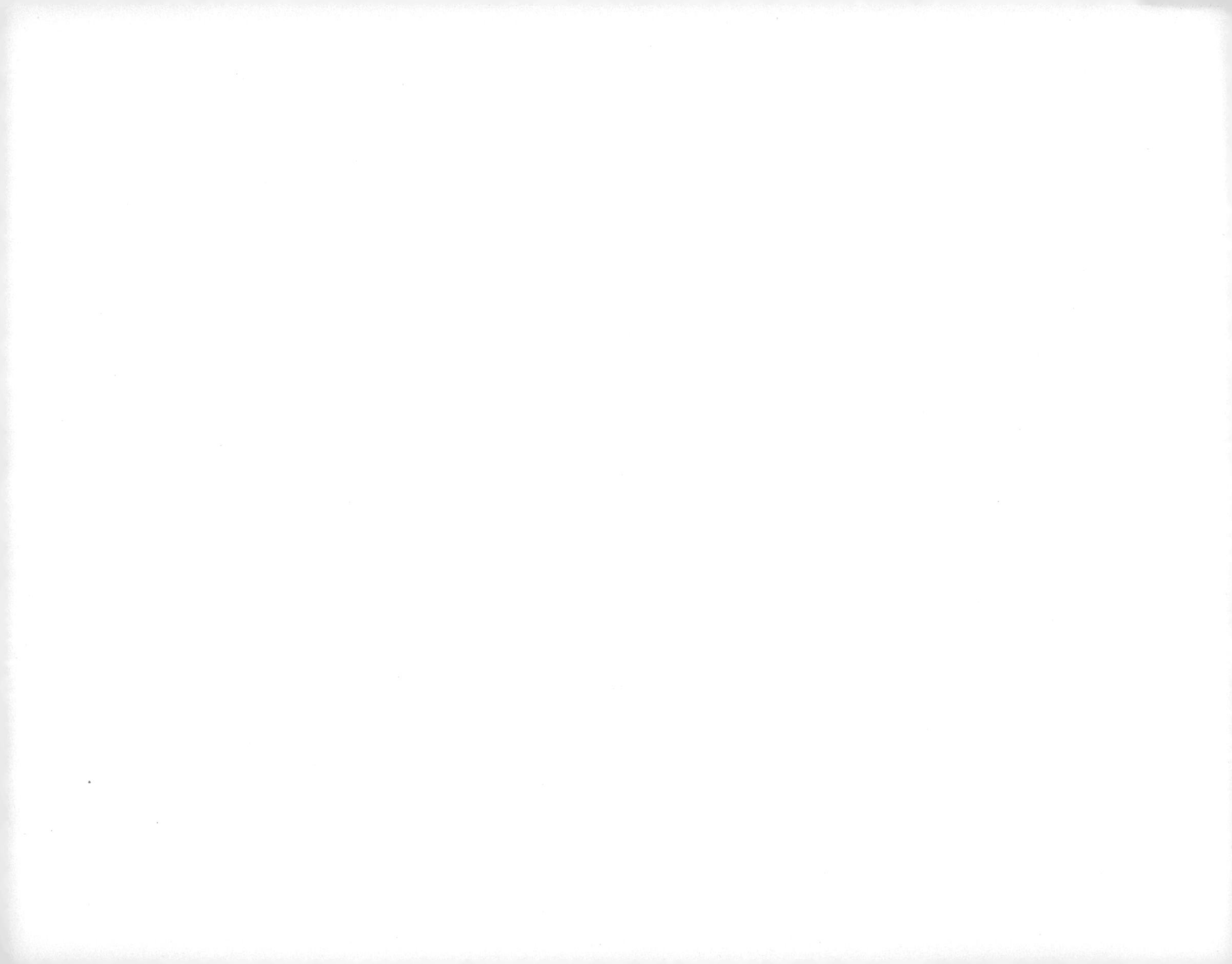

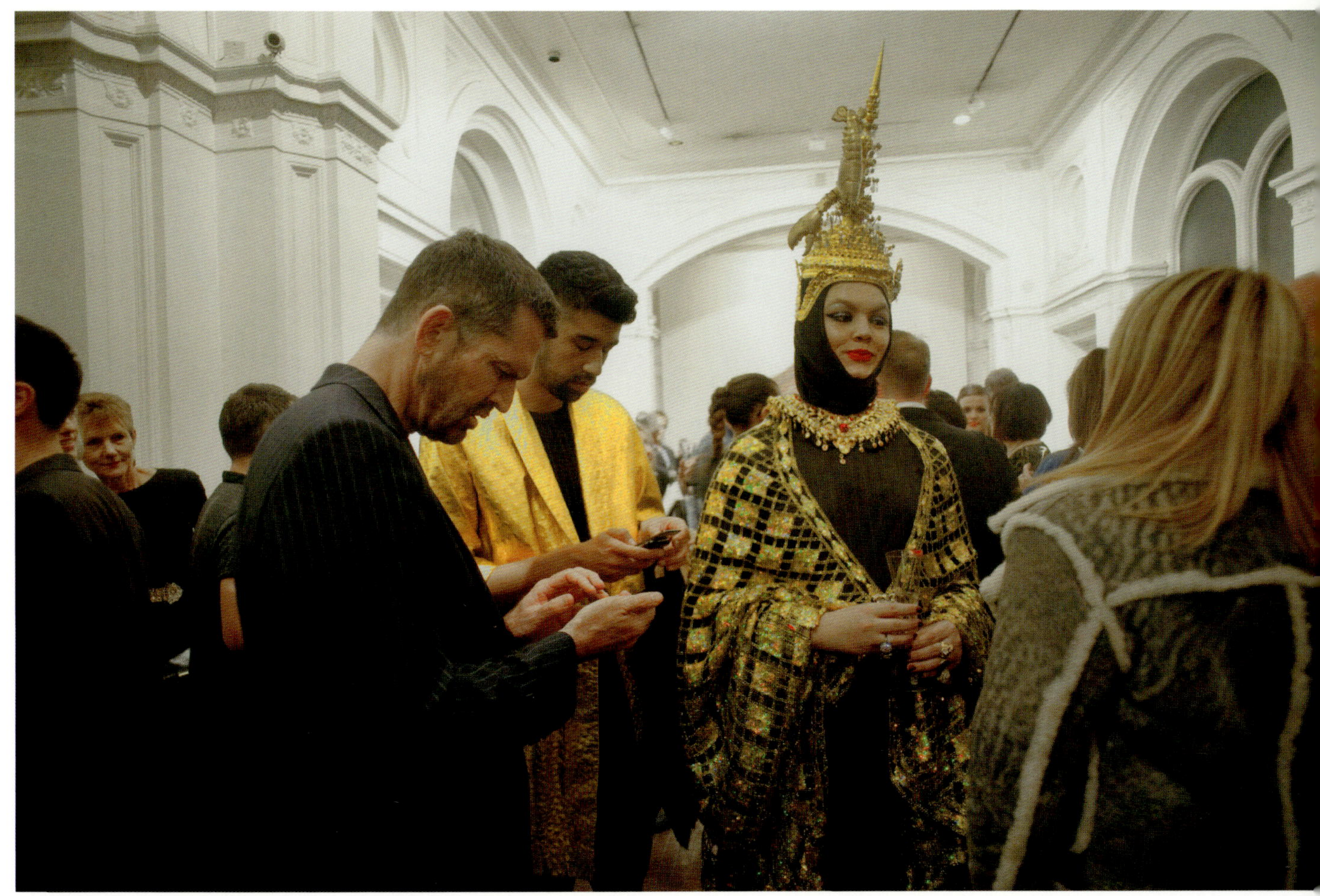

Burlington House, London 2010

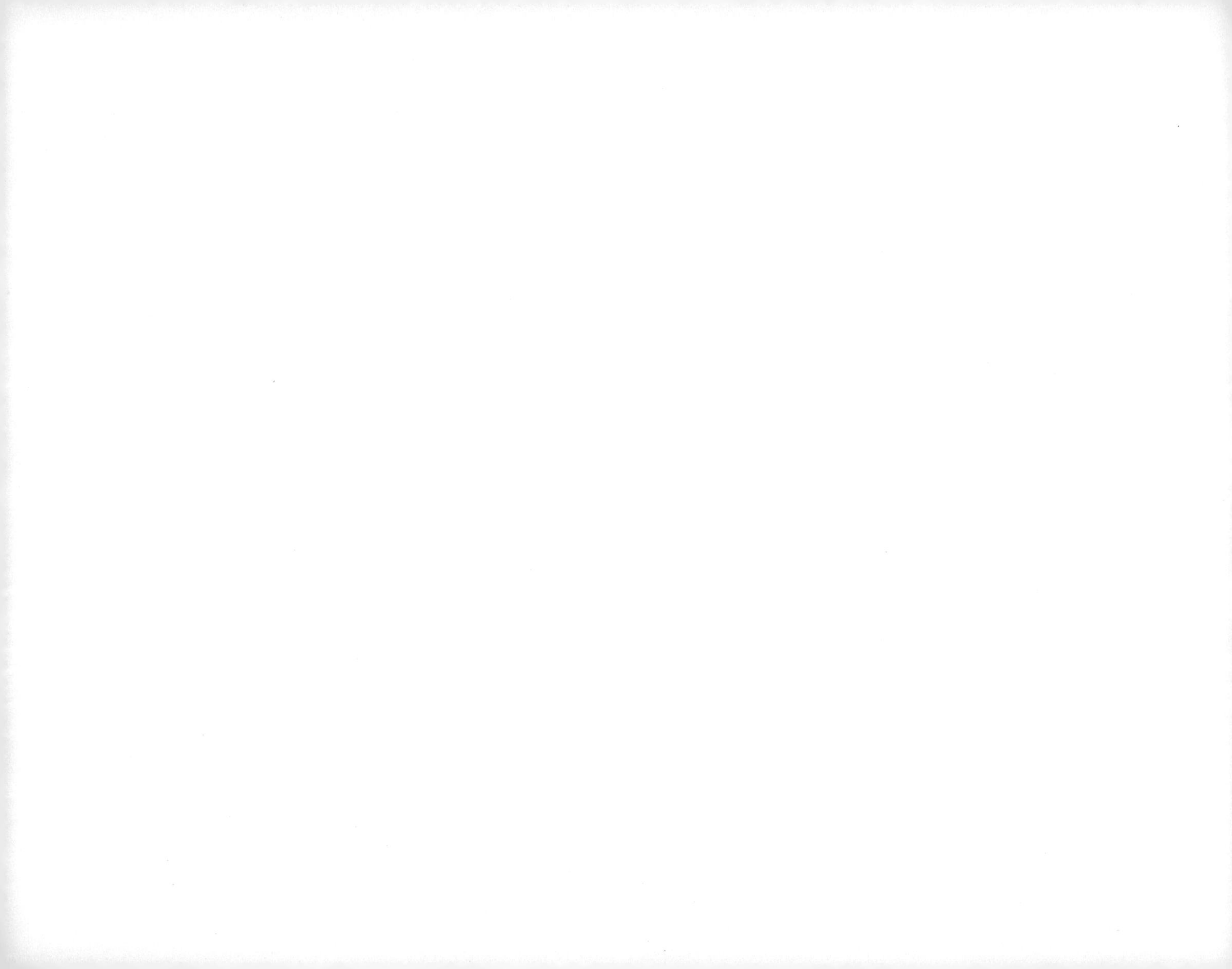

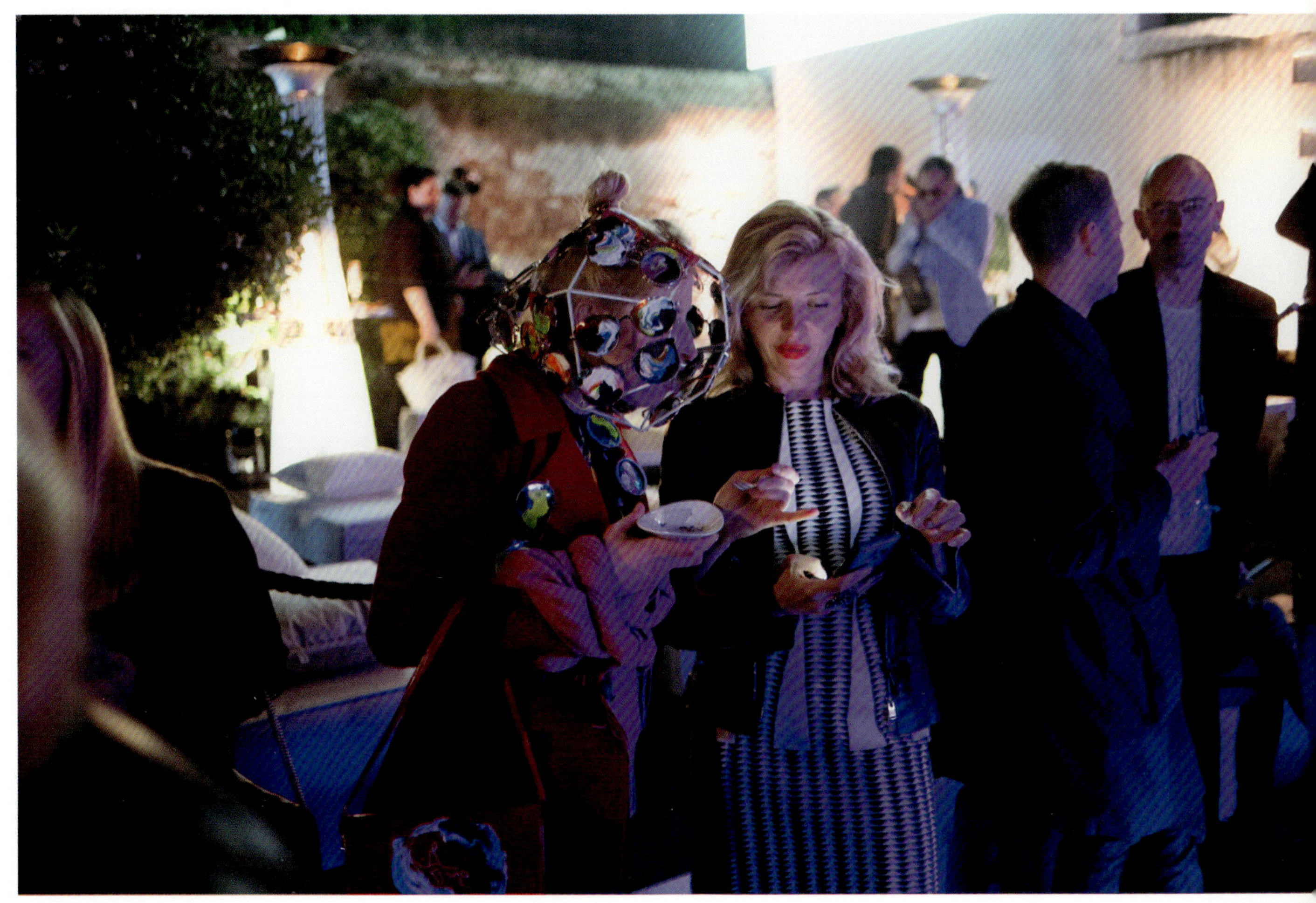

Palazzo Ca' Tron, Venice 2019

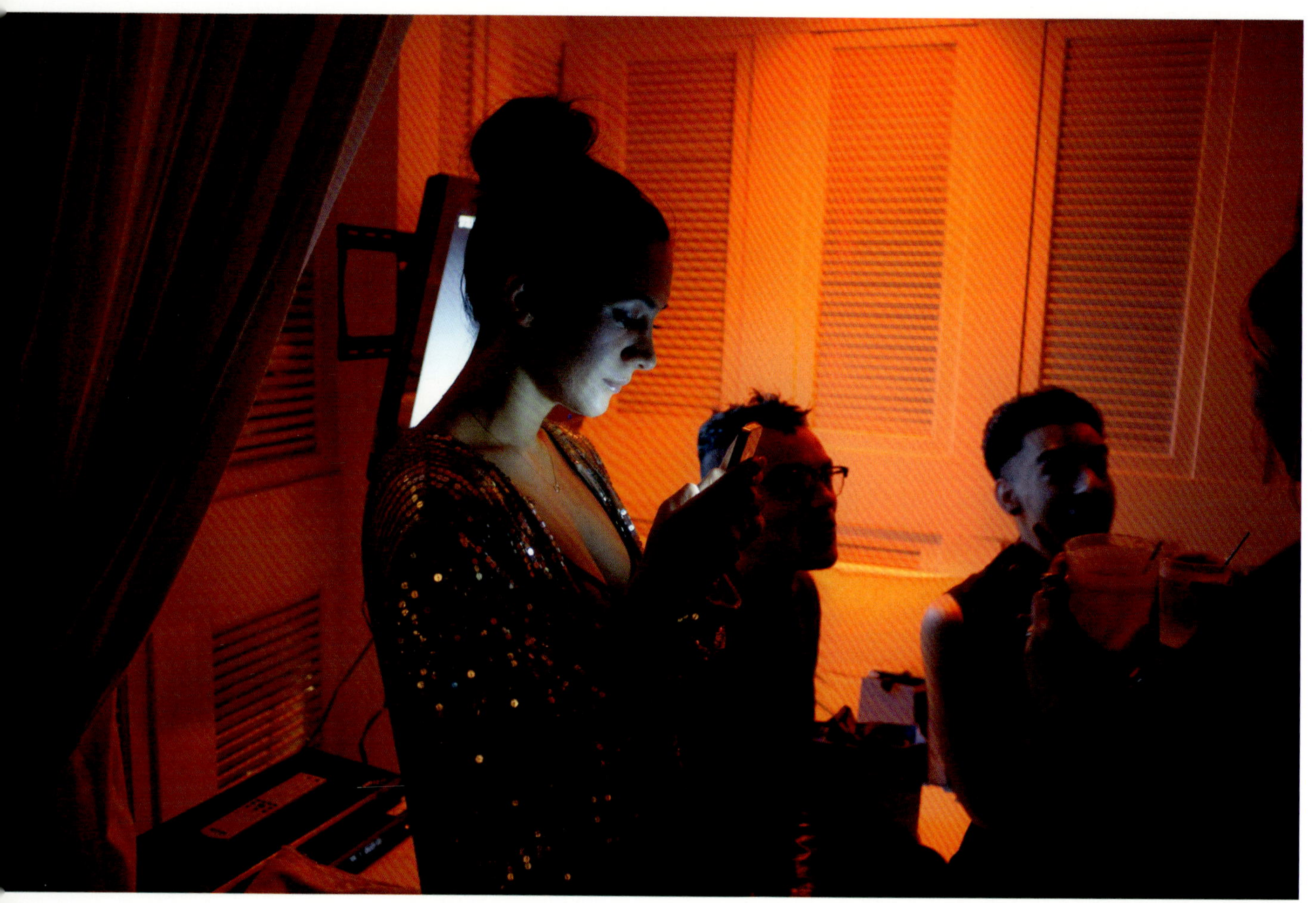

Art Basel, Miami 2011

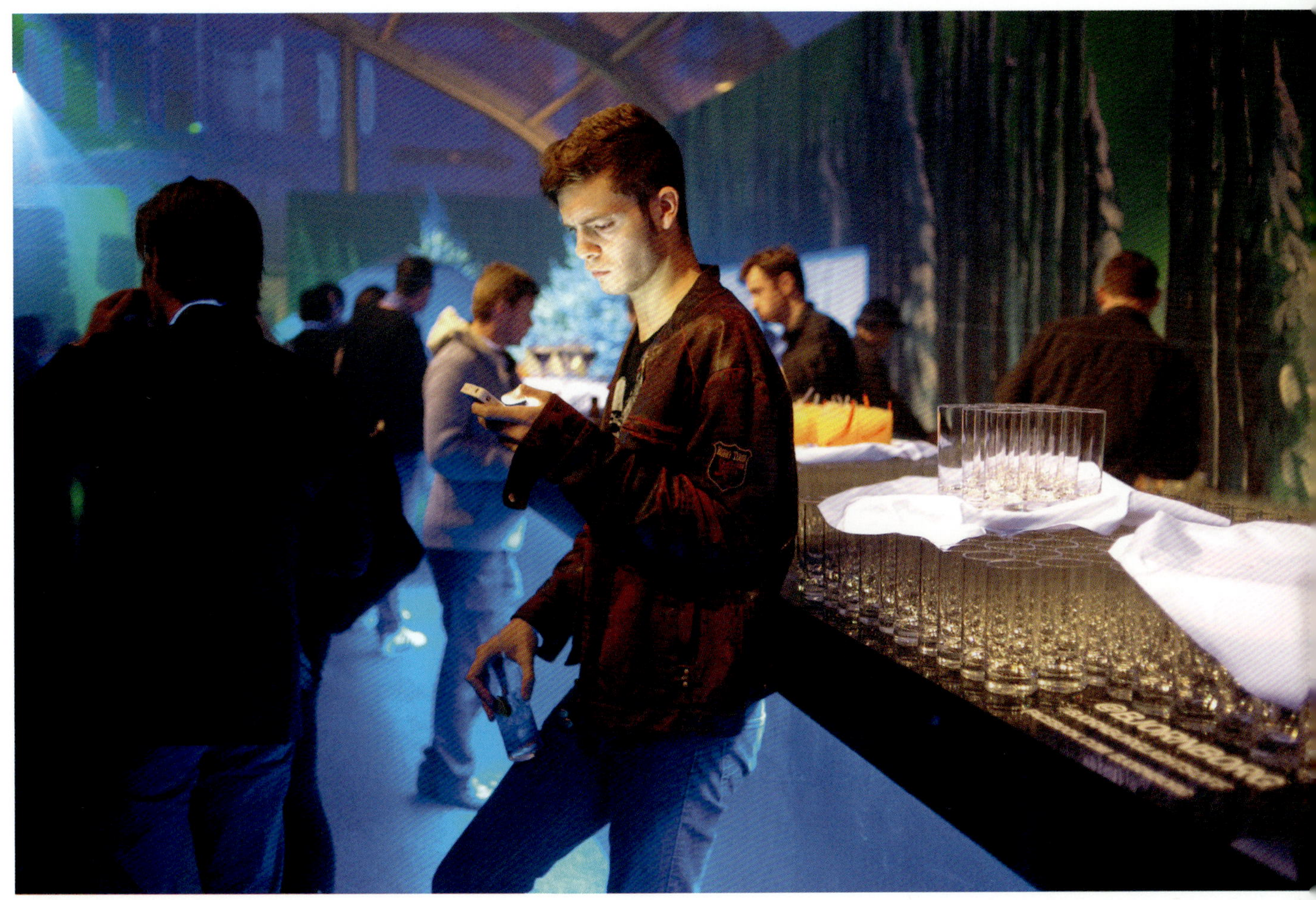

Battersea, London 2012

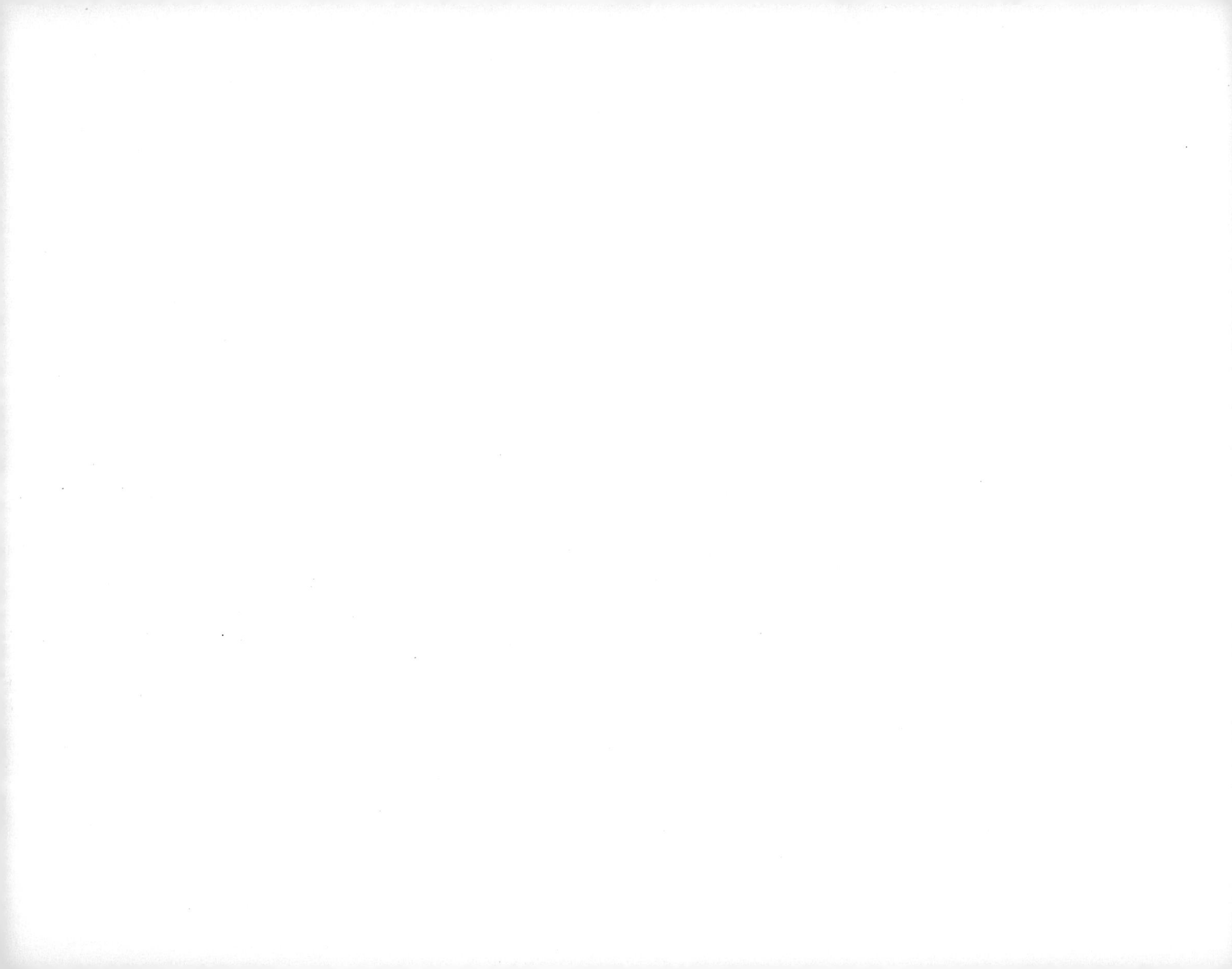

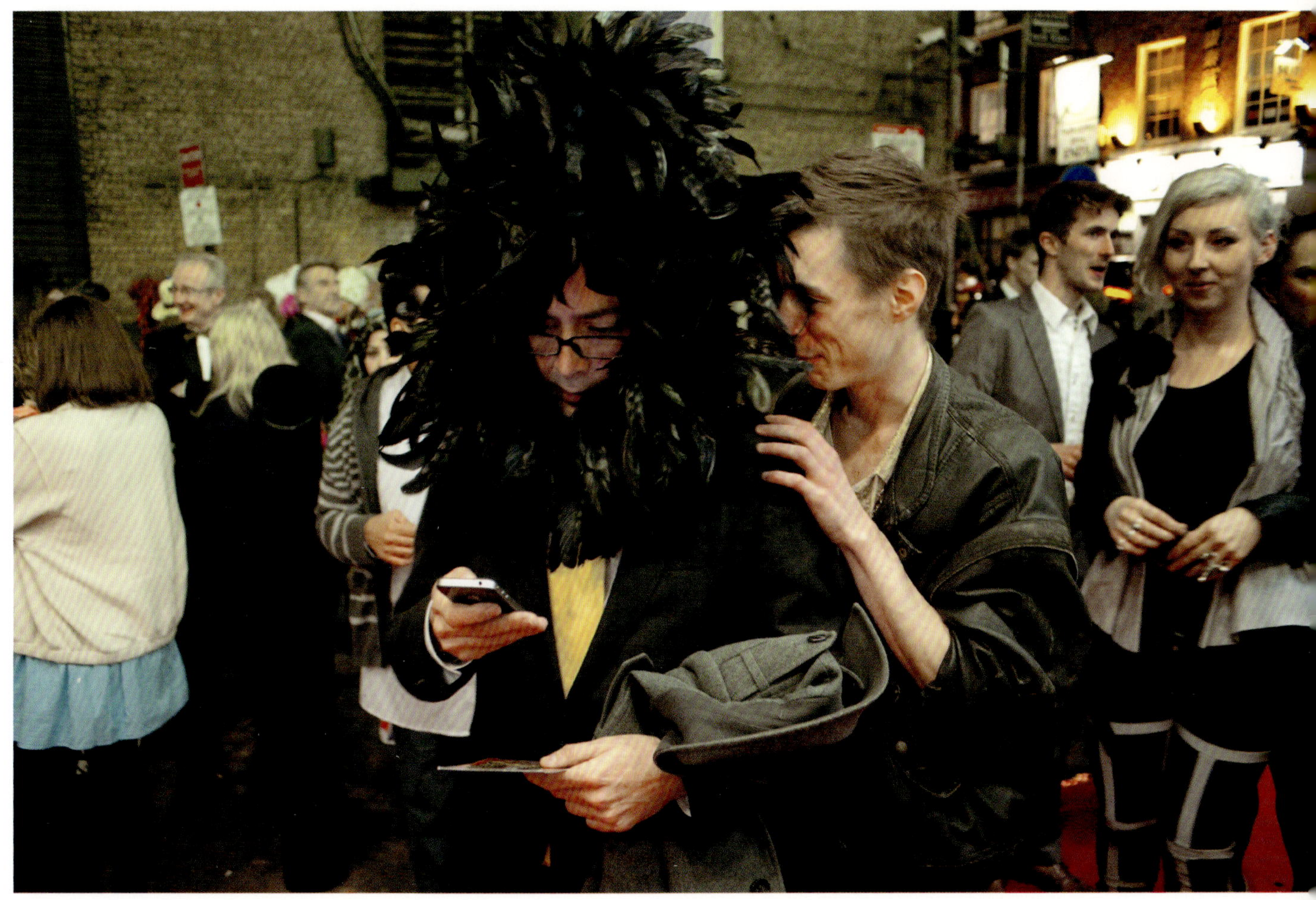

Soho, London 2011

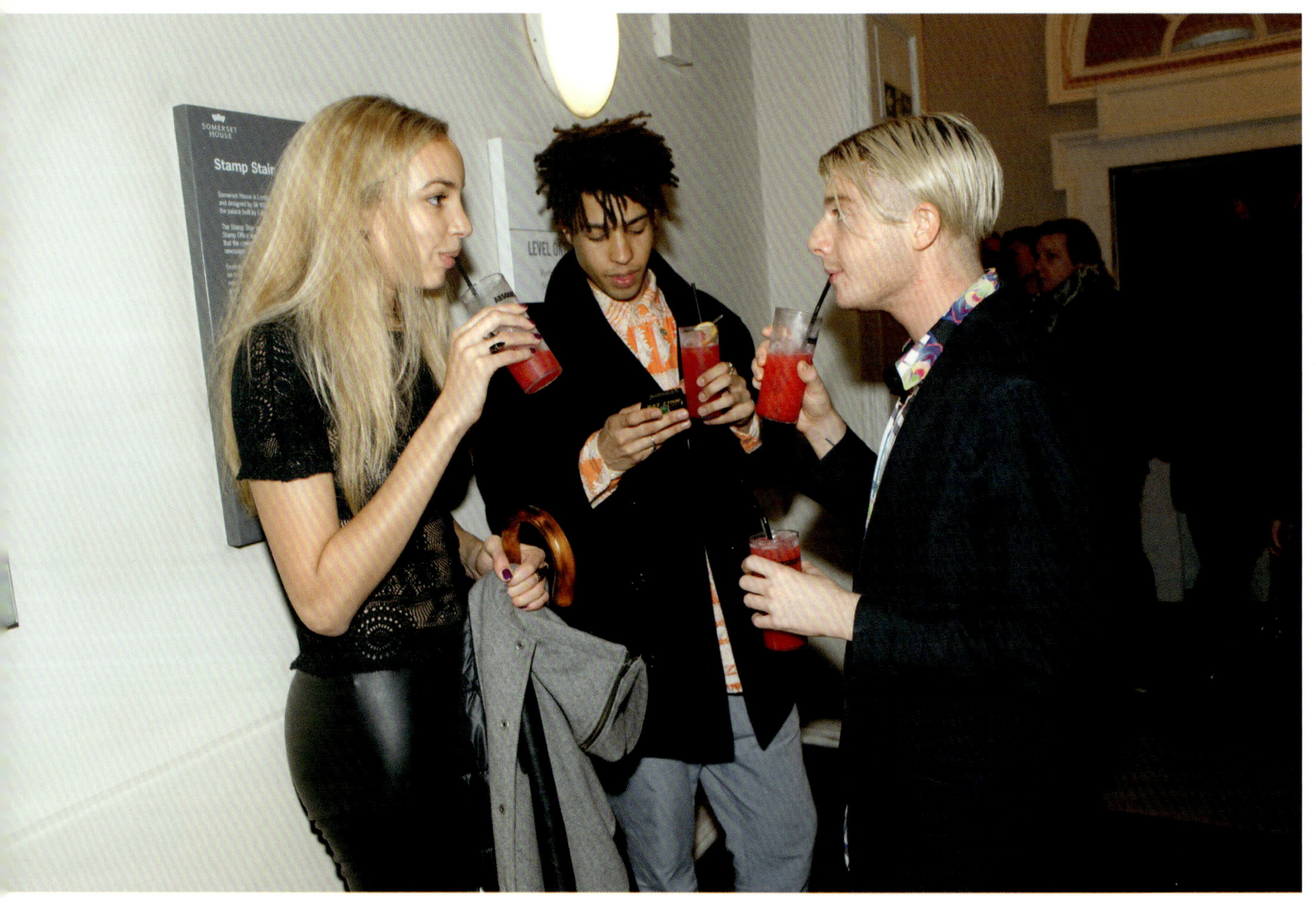

Somerset House, London 2011

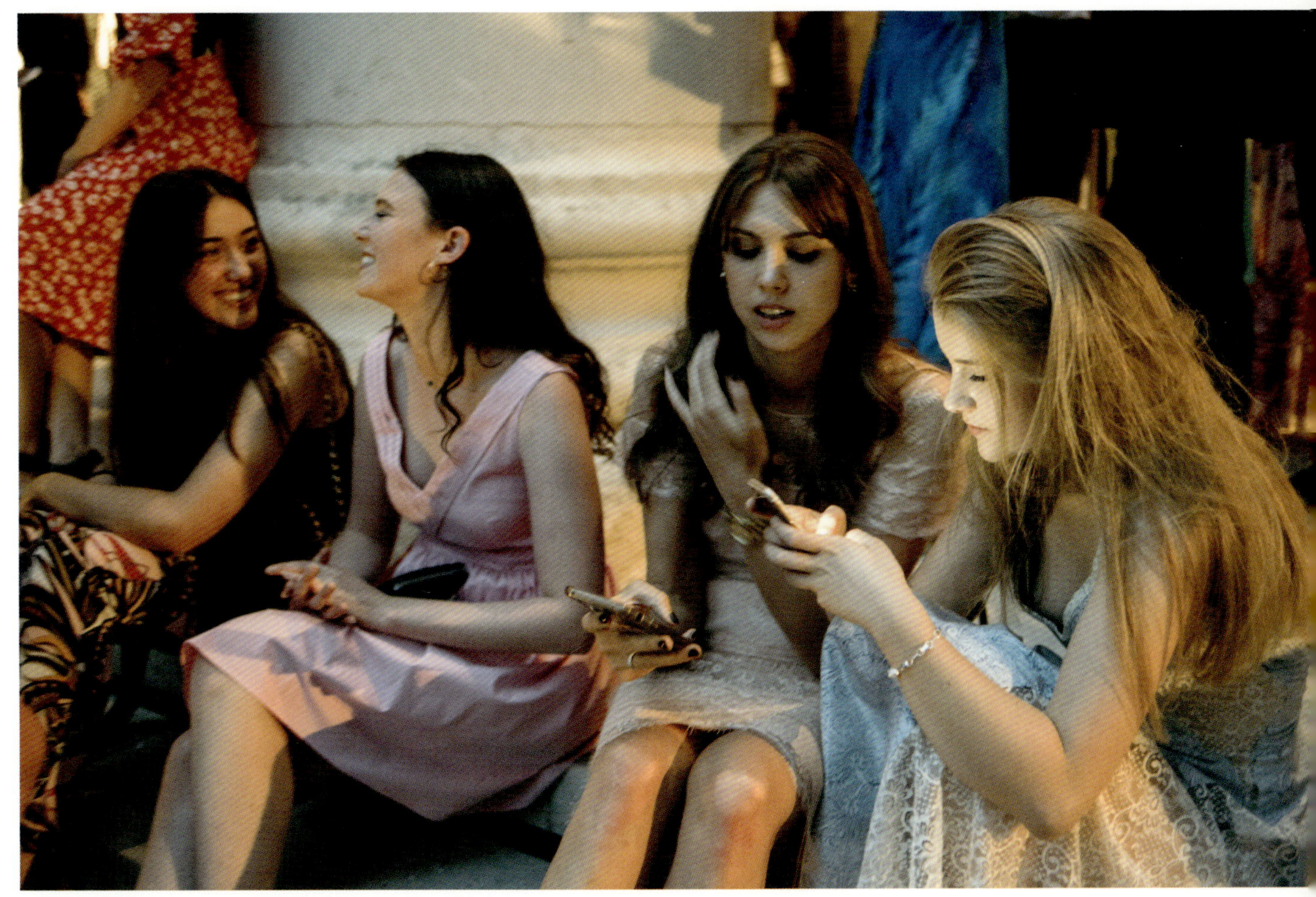

Saatchi Gallery, London 2017

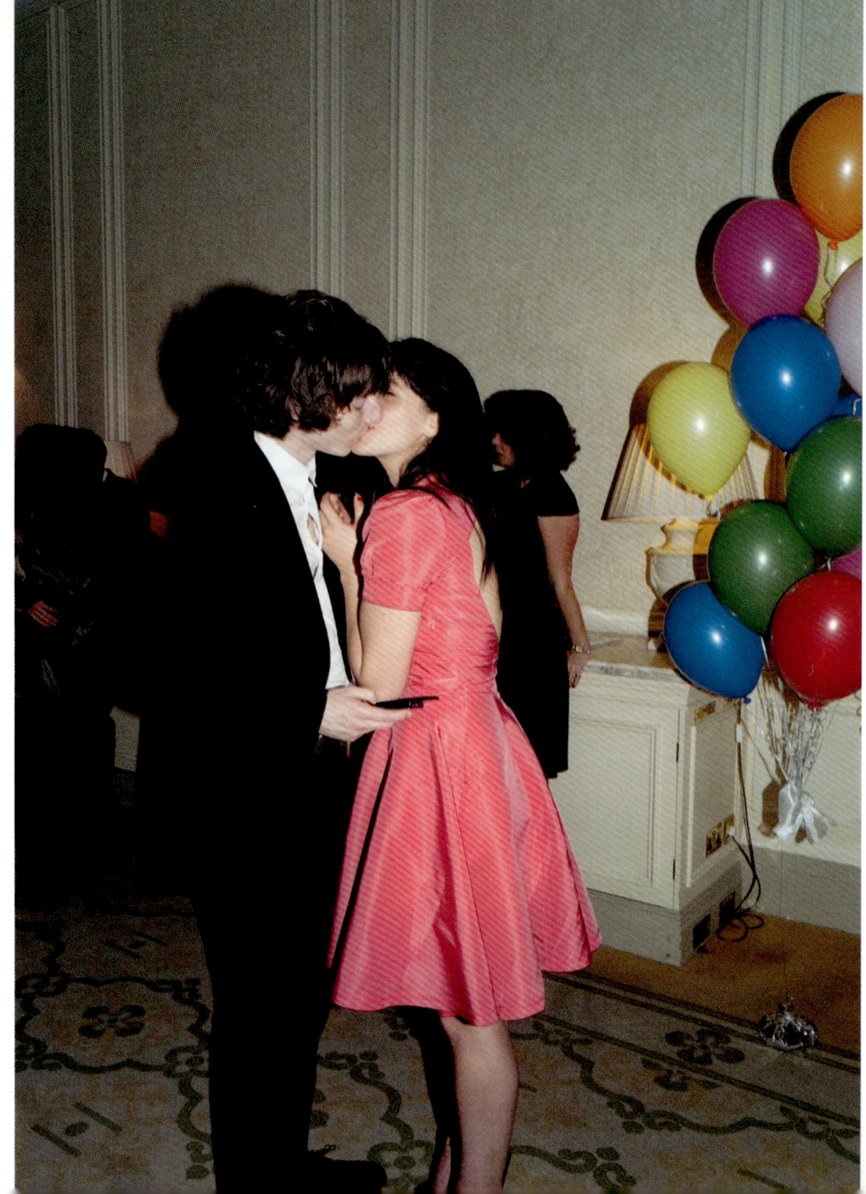

Belgravia. London 2010

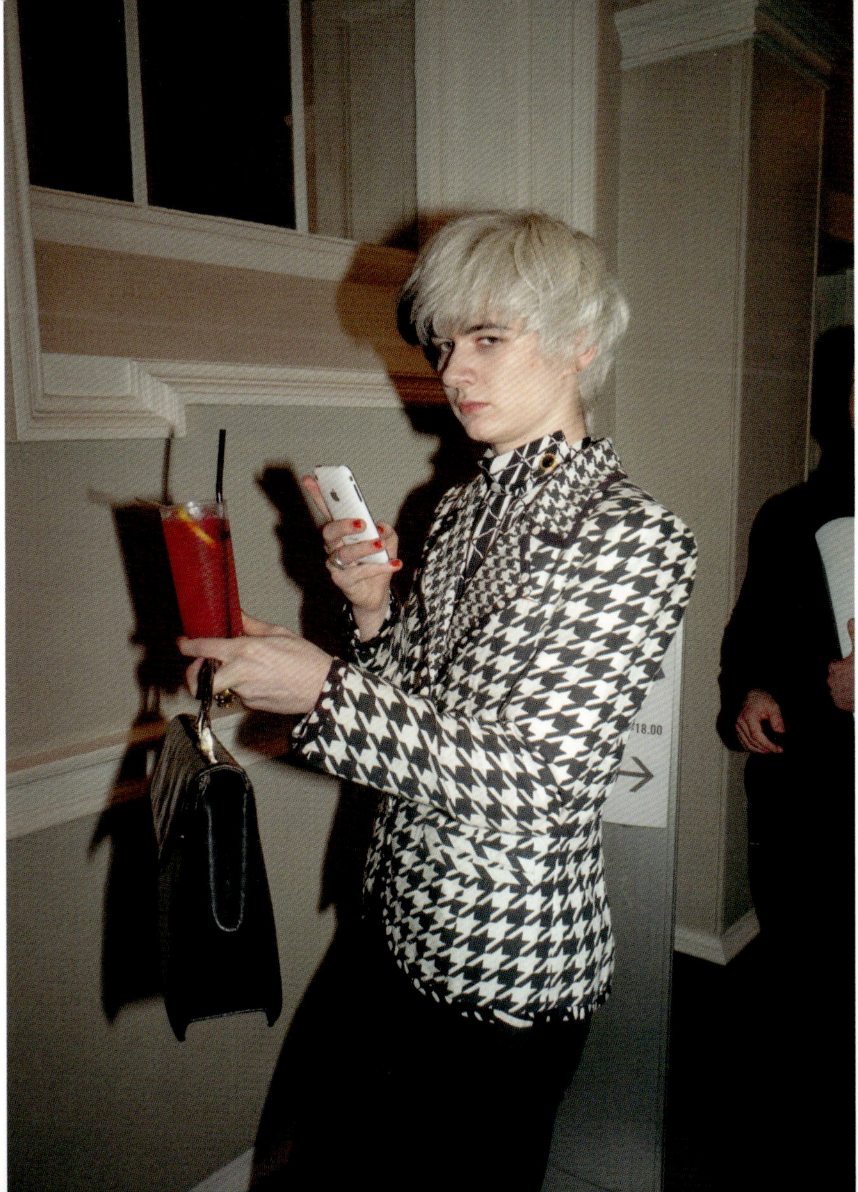

Somerset House, London 2011

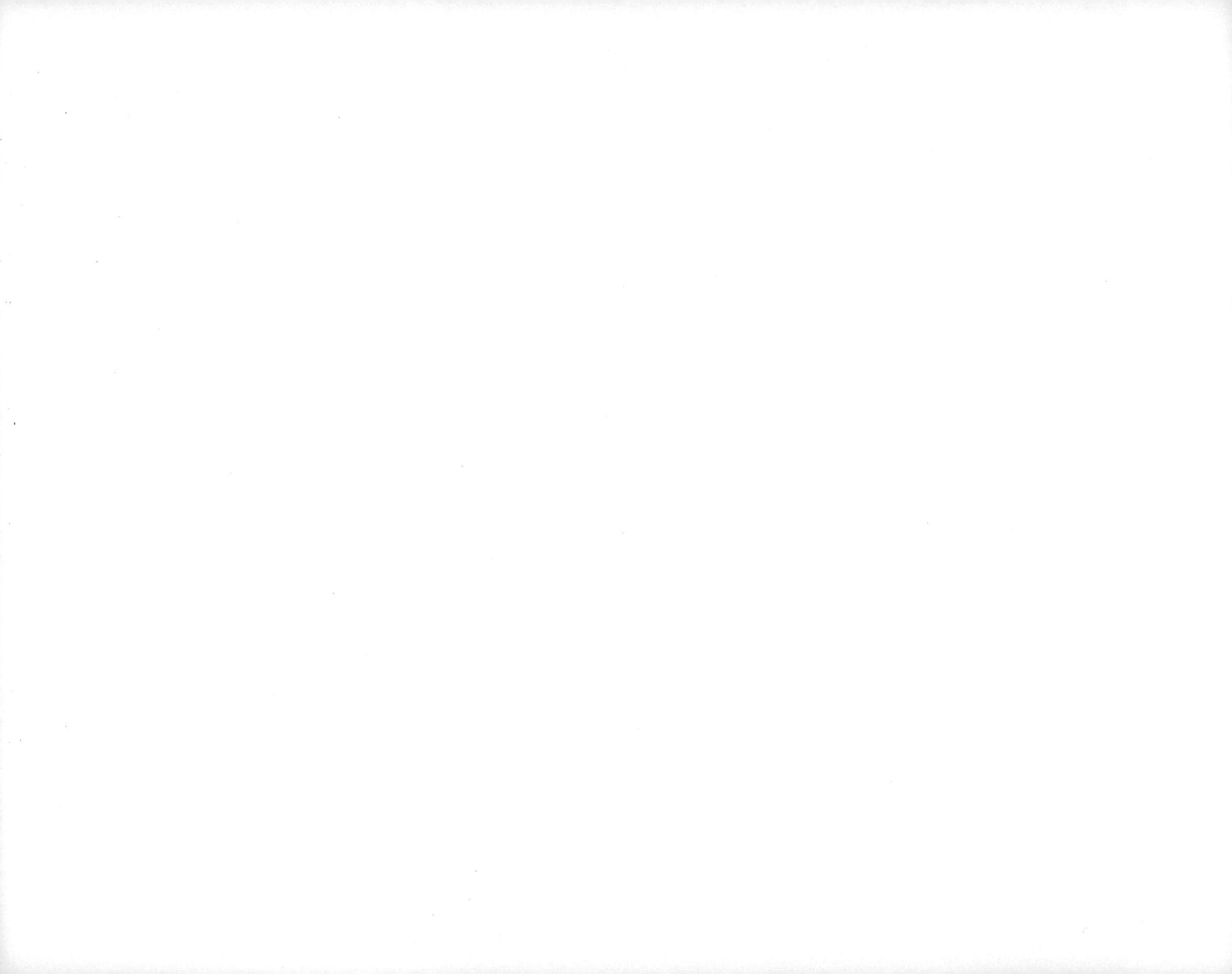

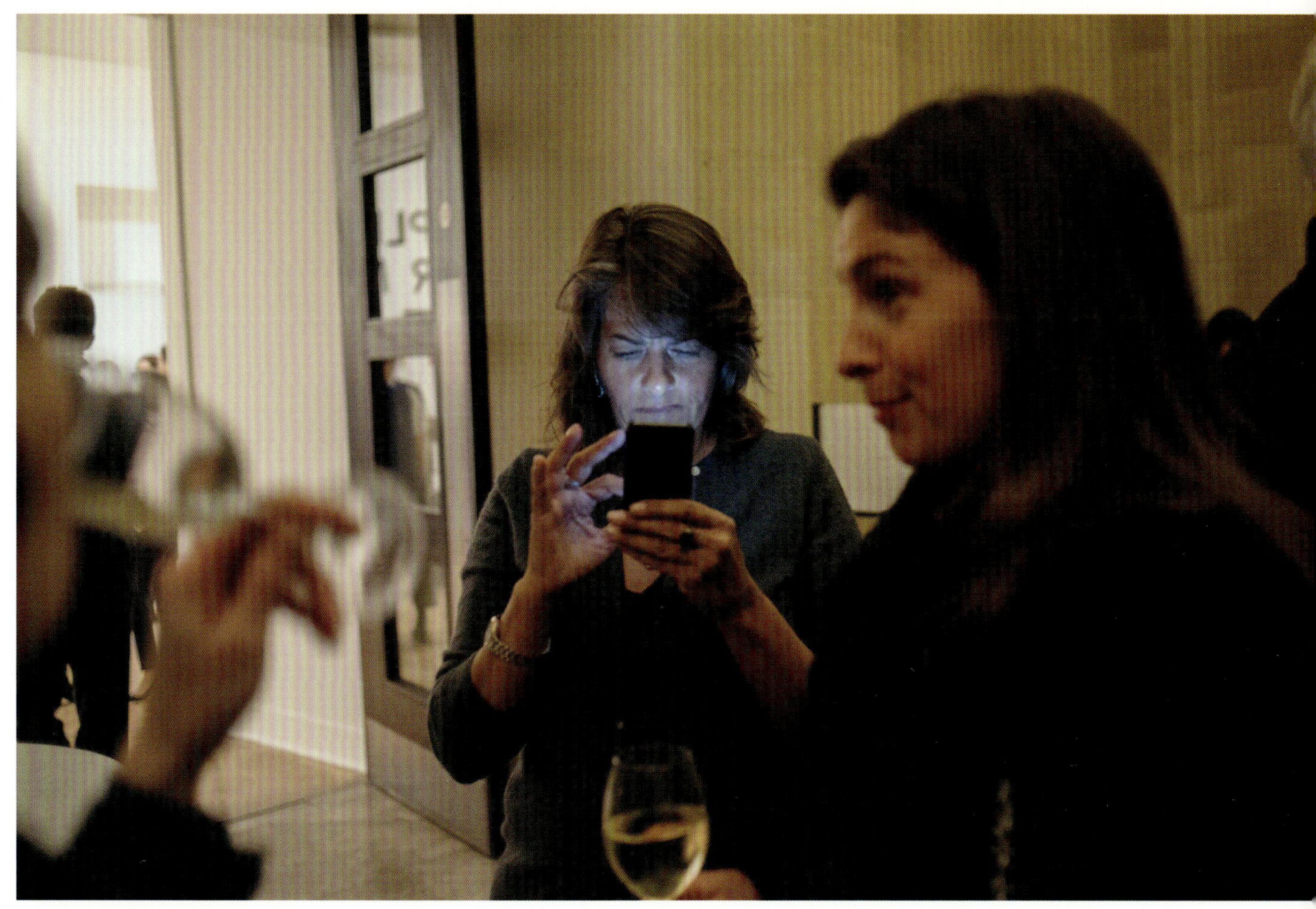

Tate Britain, London 2015

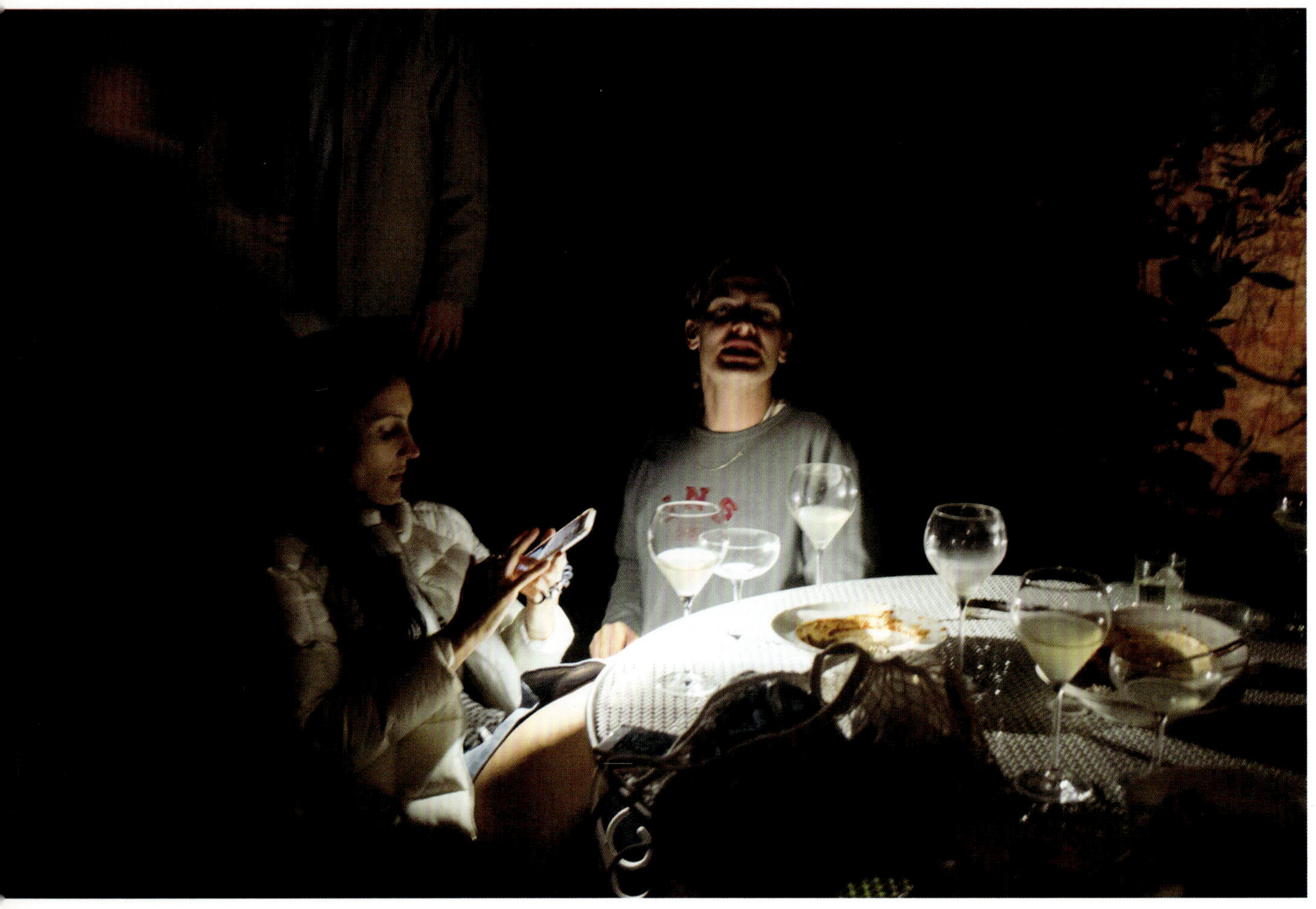

Palazzo Benzon, Venice 2019

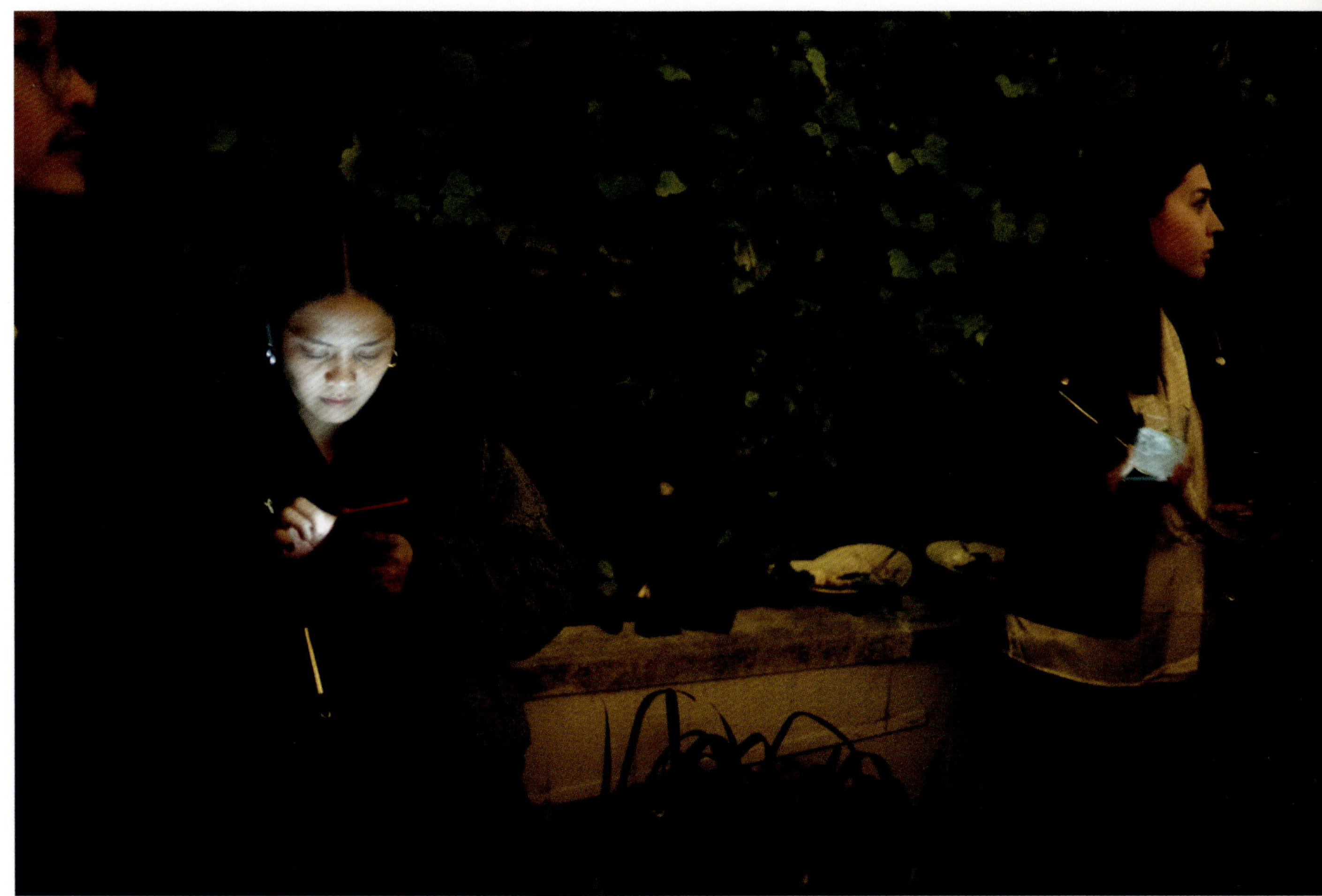

Palazzo Benzon, Venice 2019

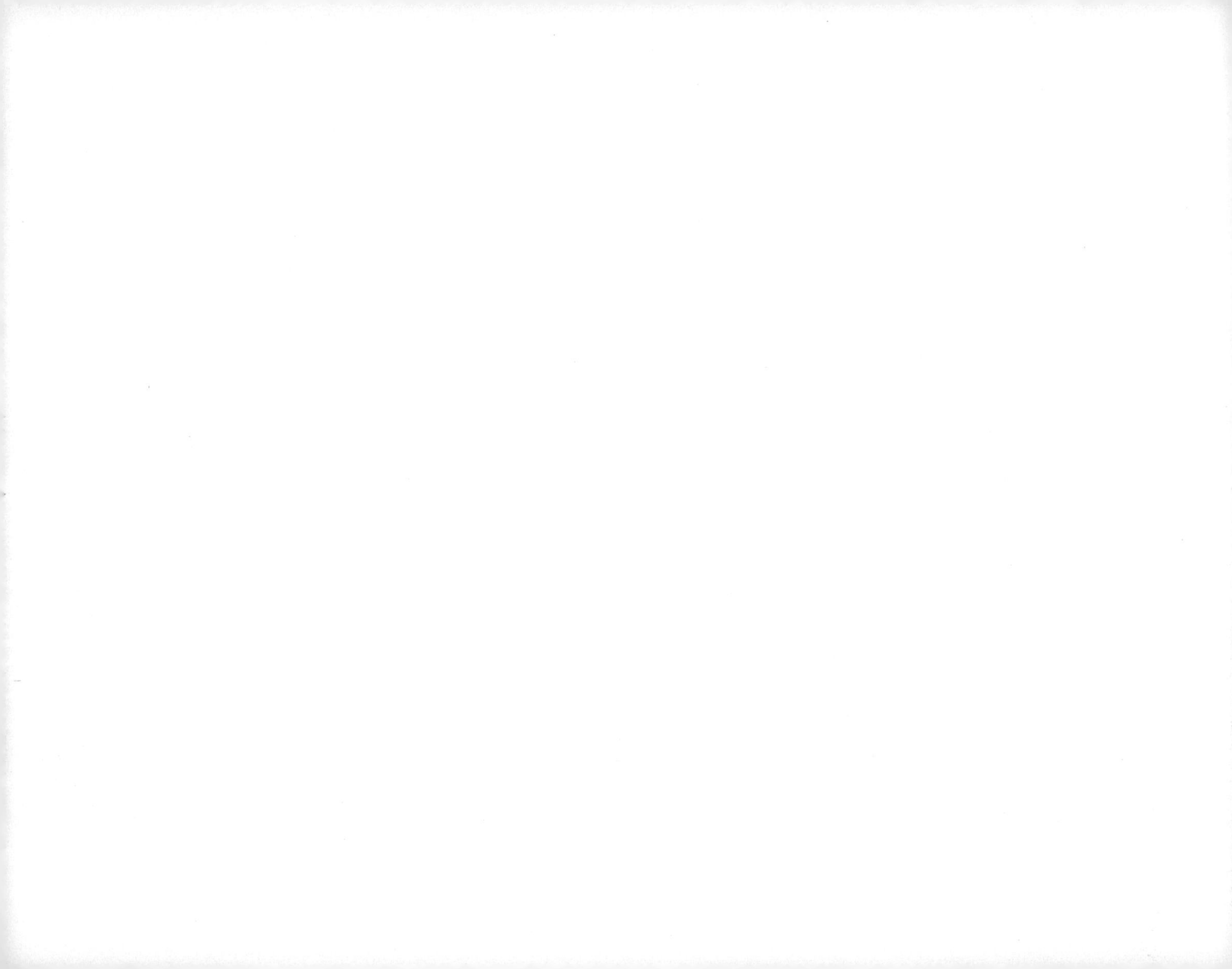

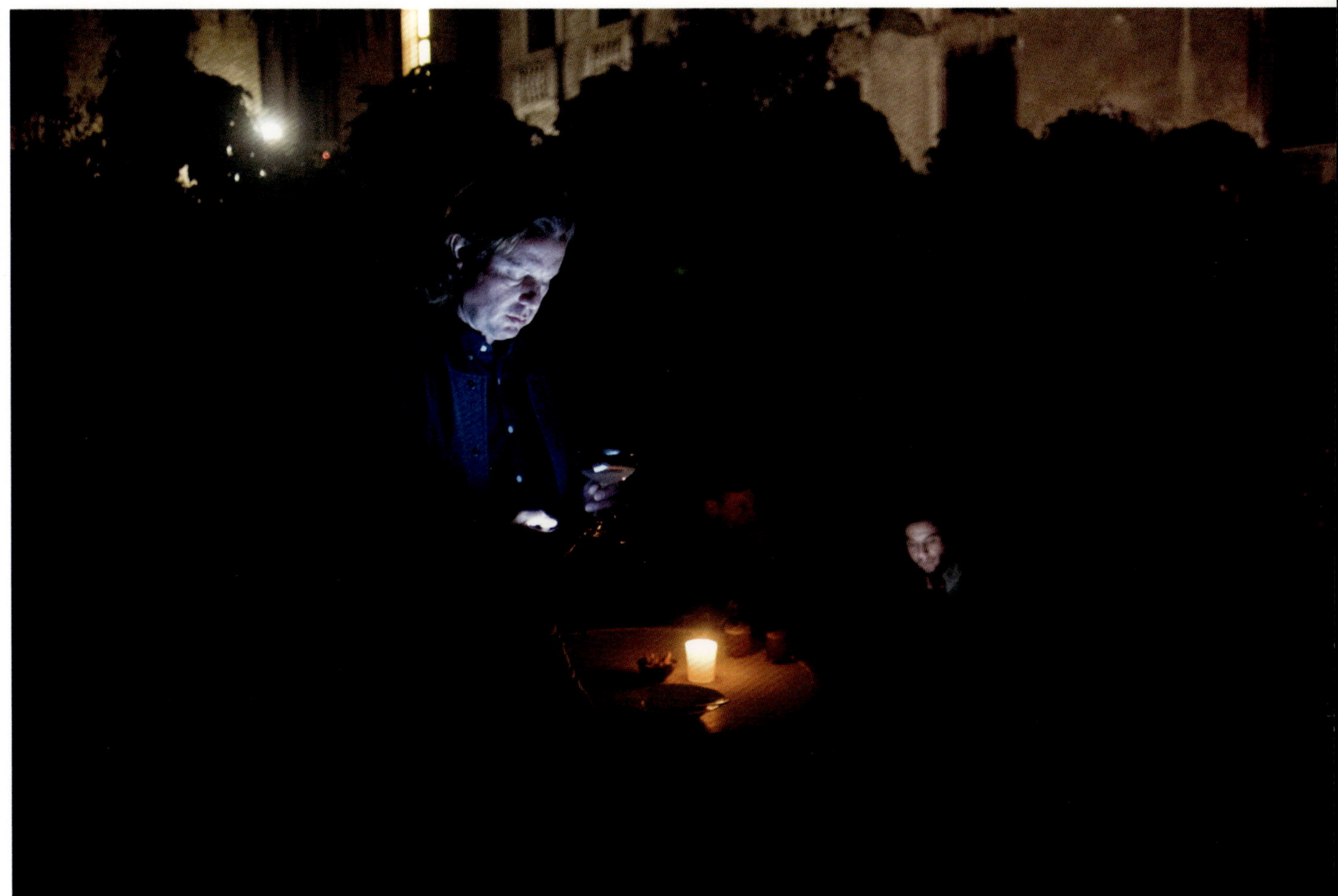

Palazzo Benzon, Venice 2019

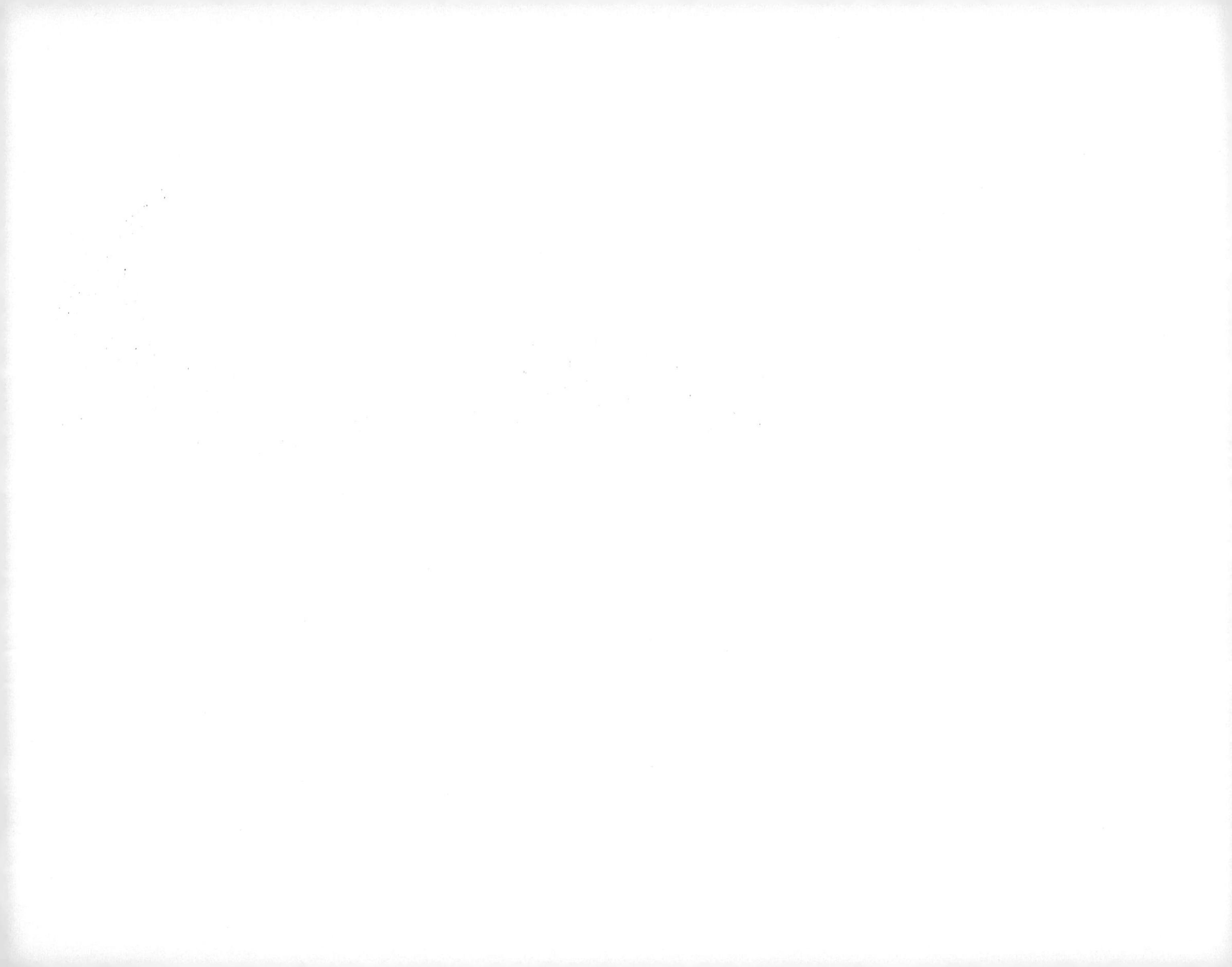

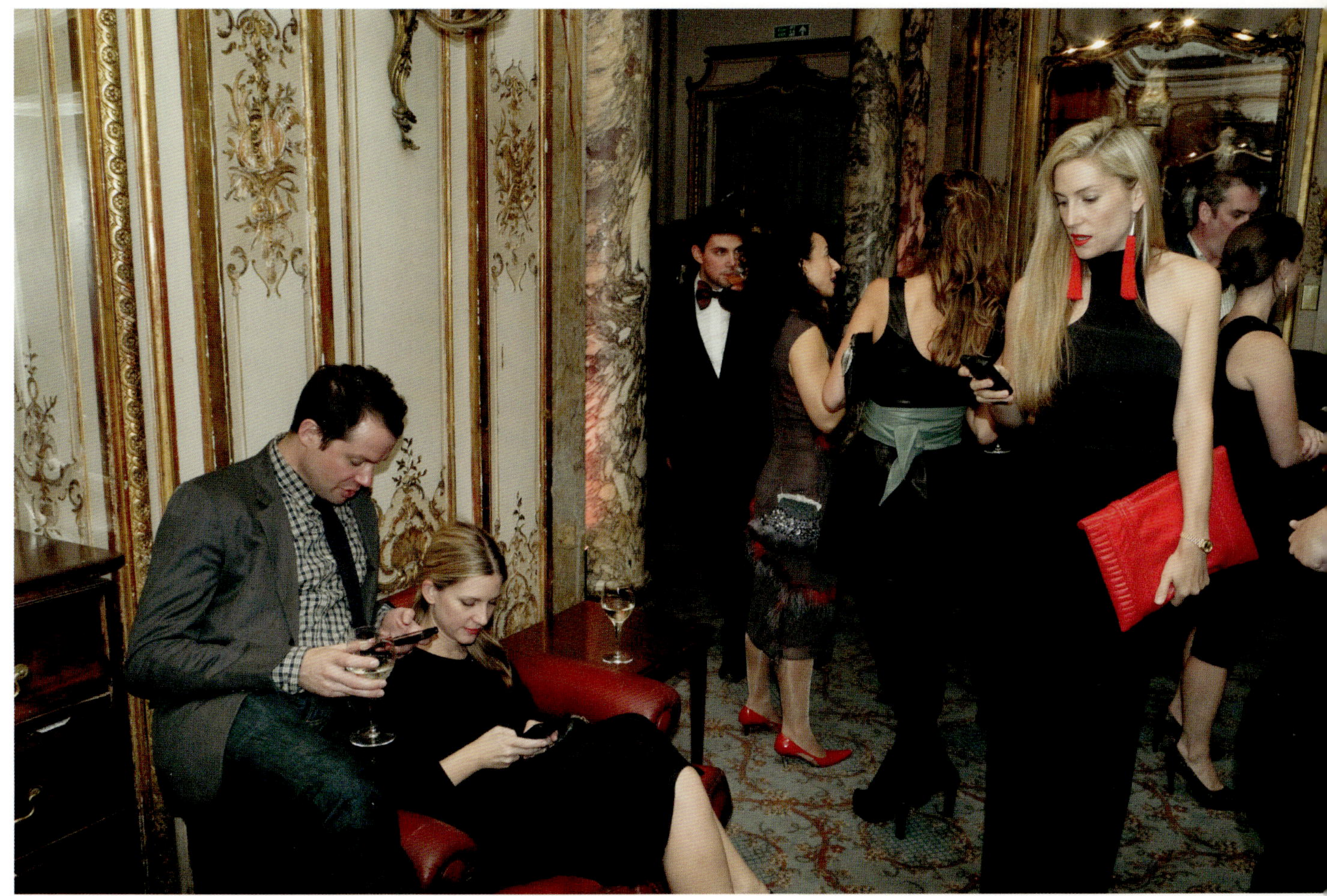

Savile Club, London 2011

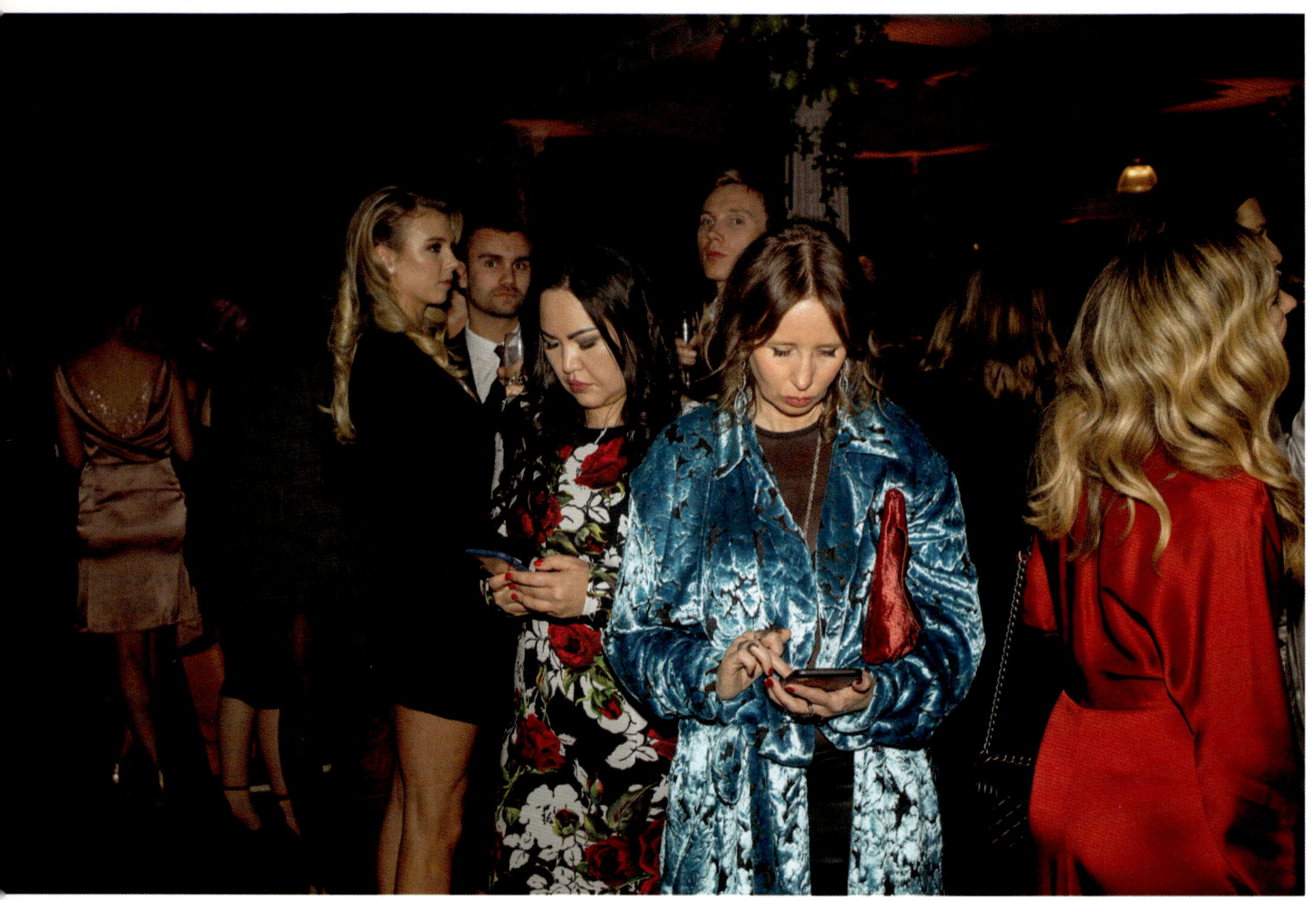

Roundhouse, London 2019

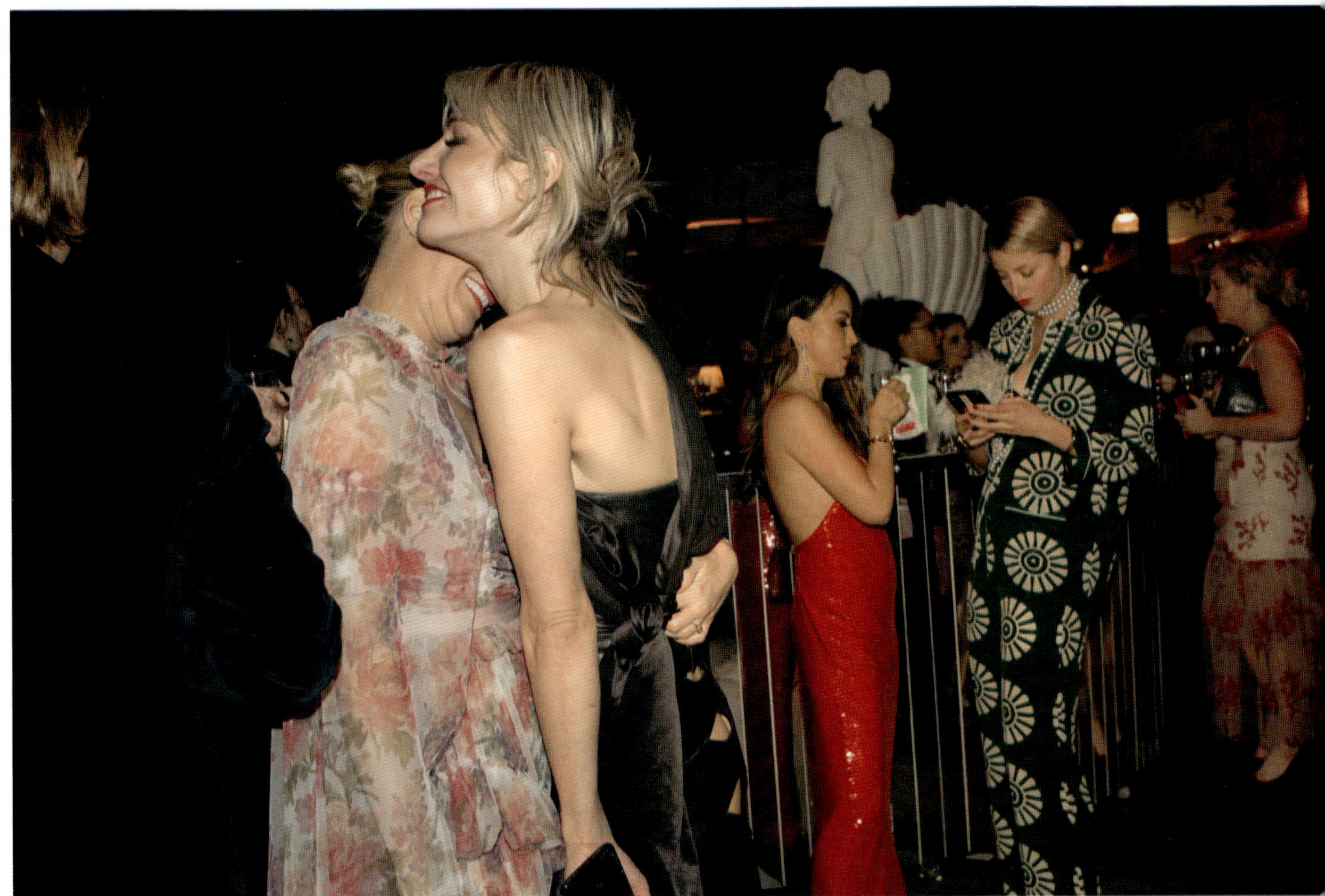

Roundhouse, London 2019

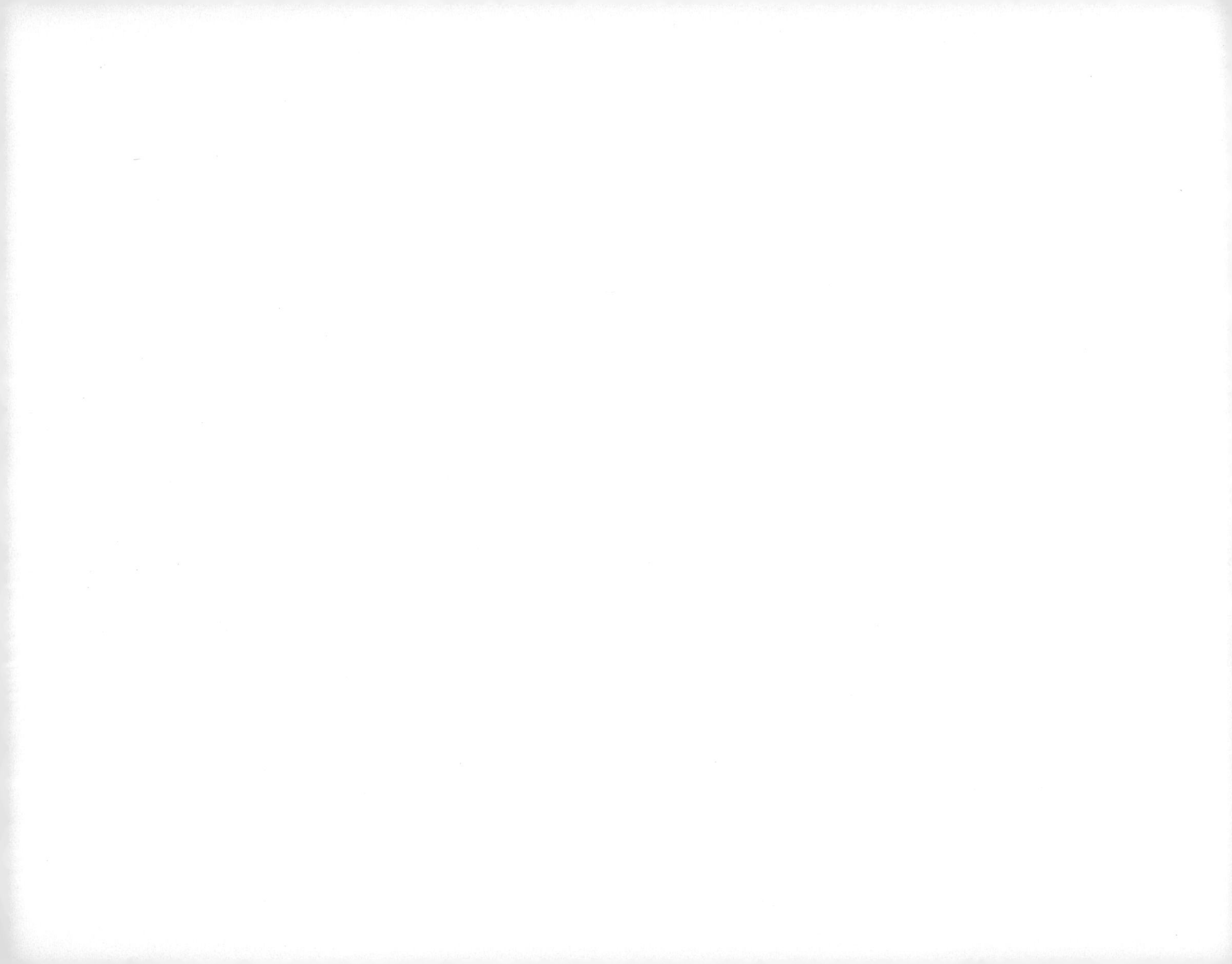

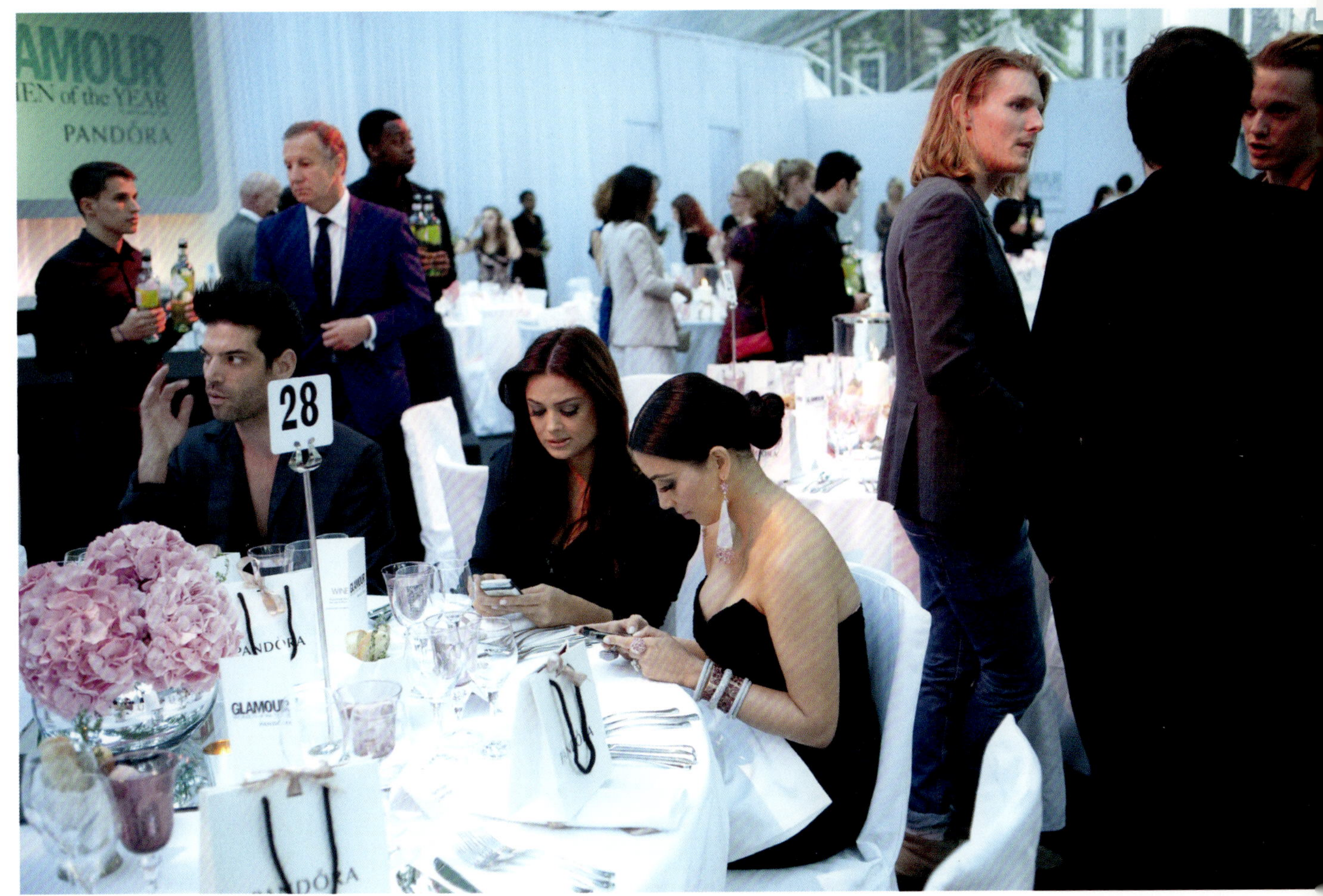

Mayfair, London 2011

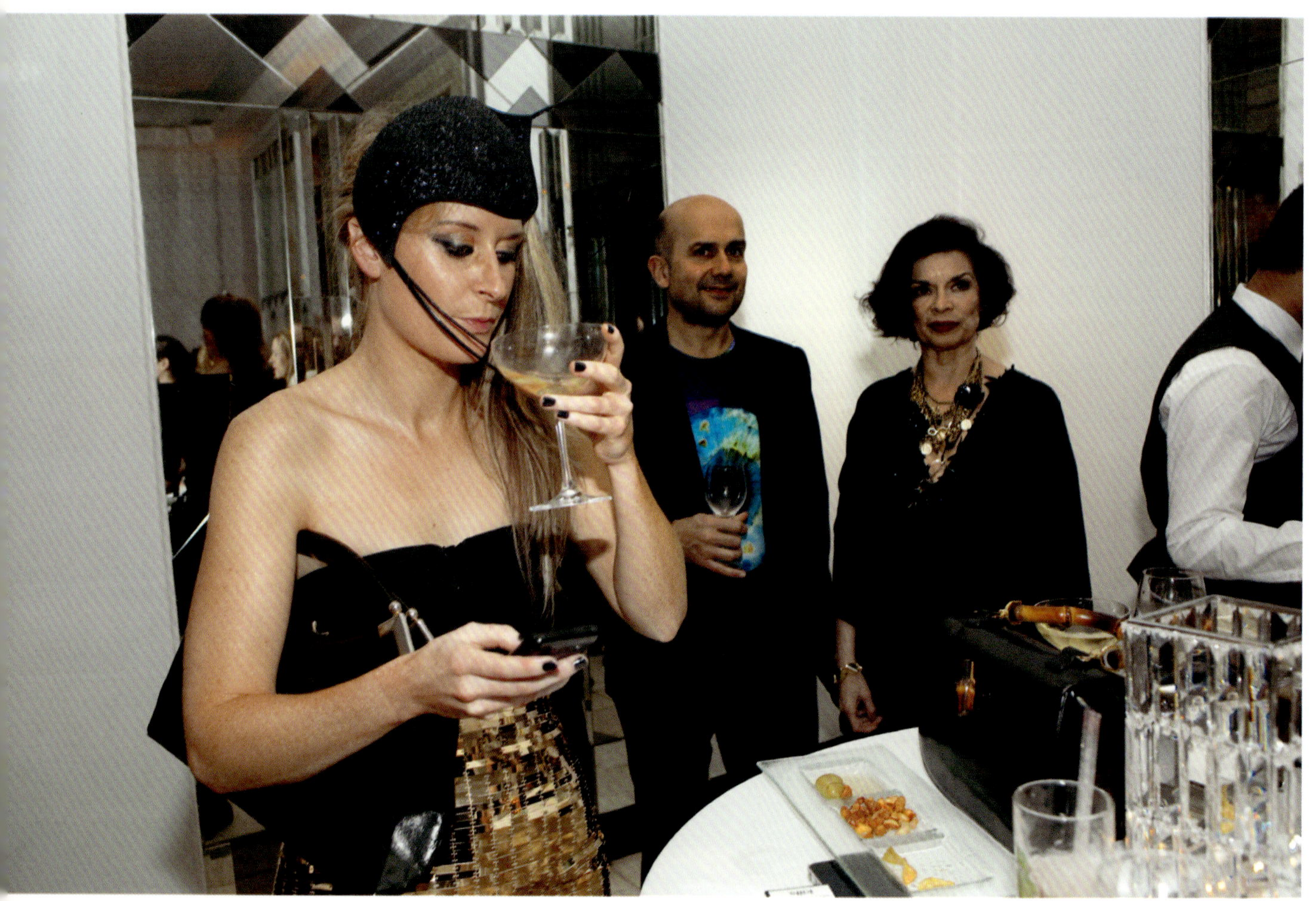

Mayfair, London 2011

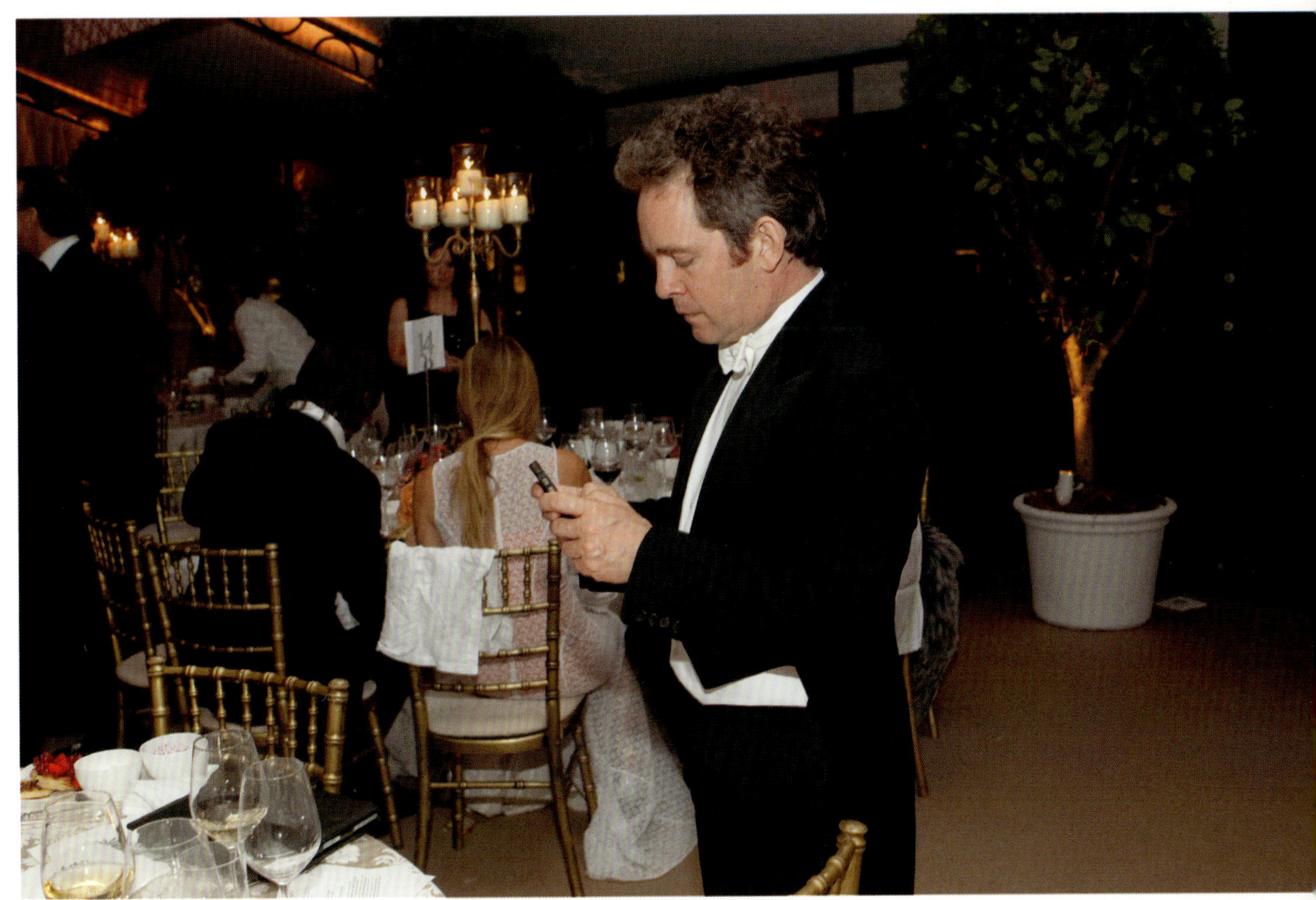

Hampton Court, London 2011

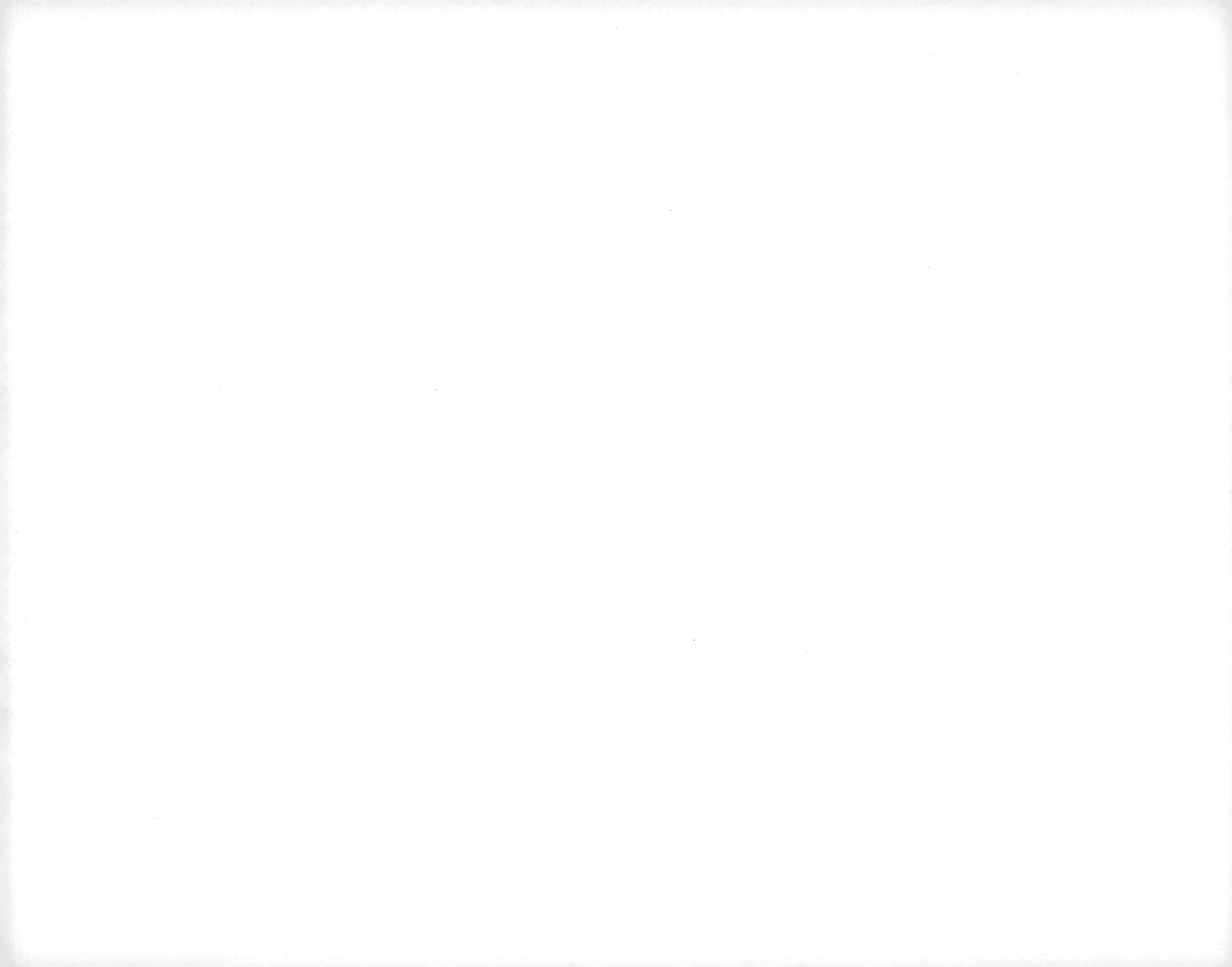

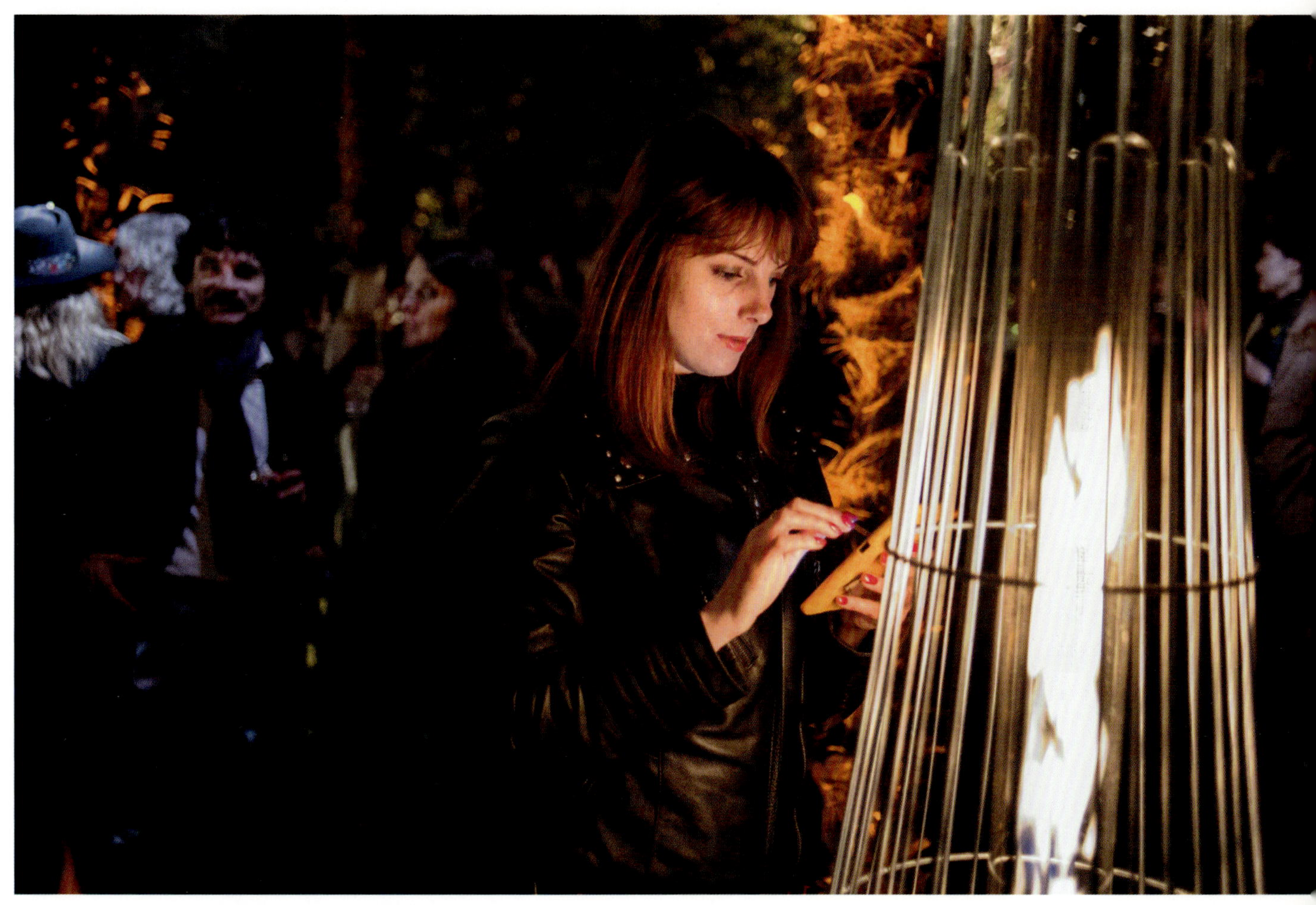

Palazzo Ca' Tron, Venice 2019

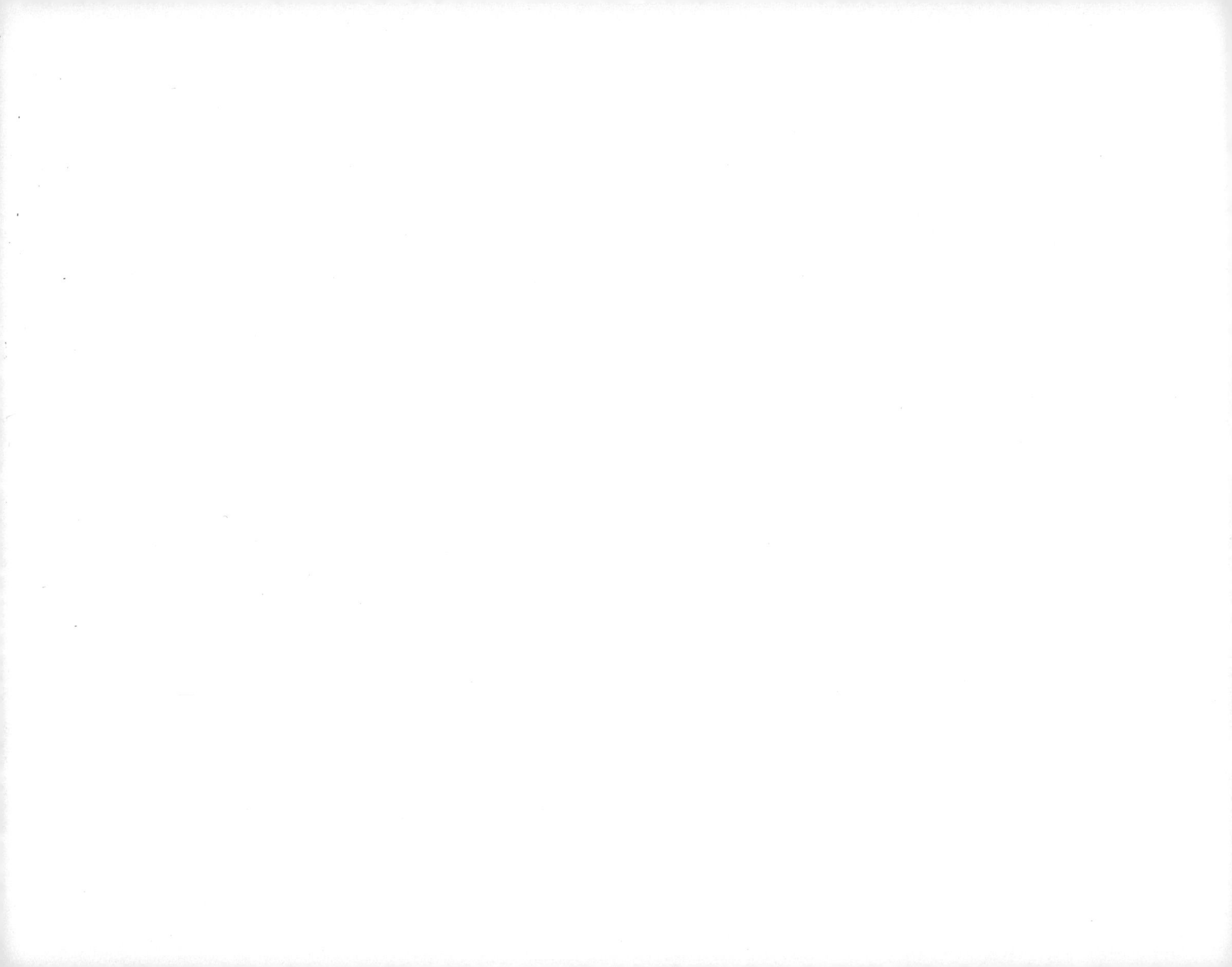

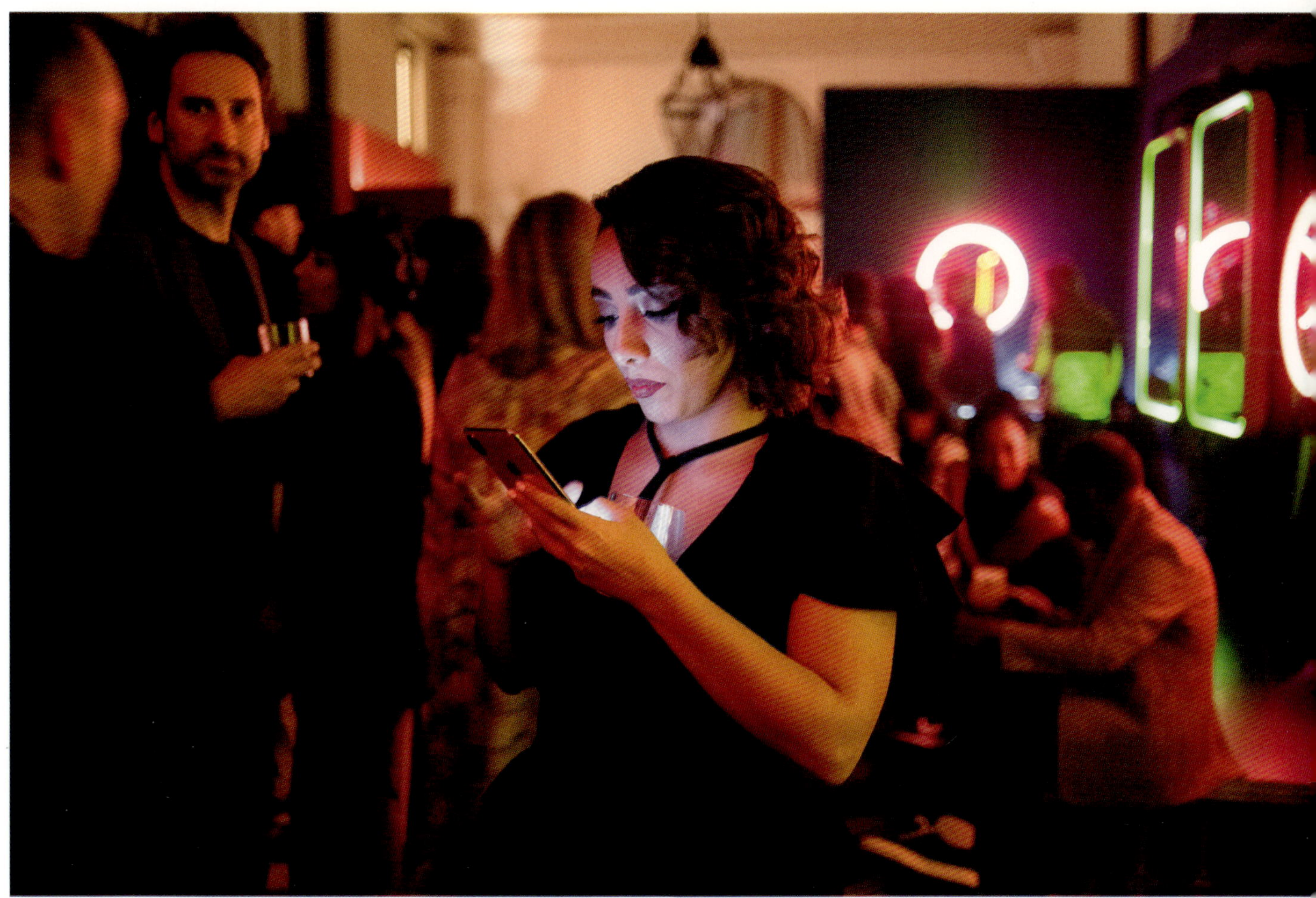

Palazzo Benzon, Venice 2019

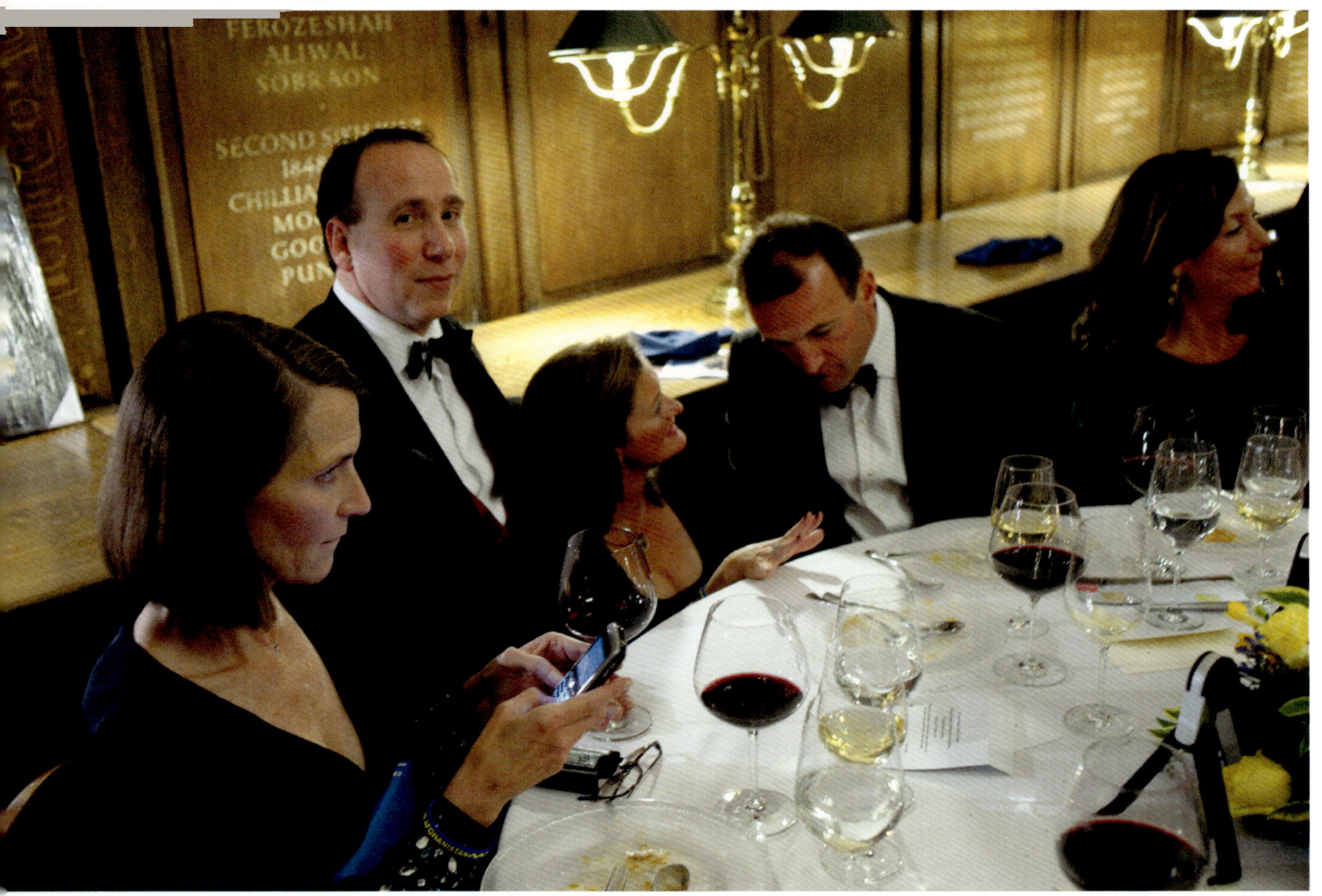

Chelsea, London 2011

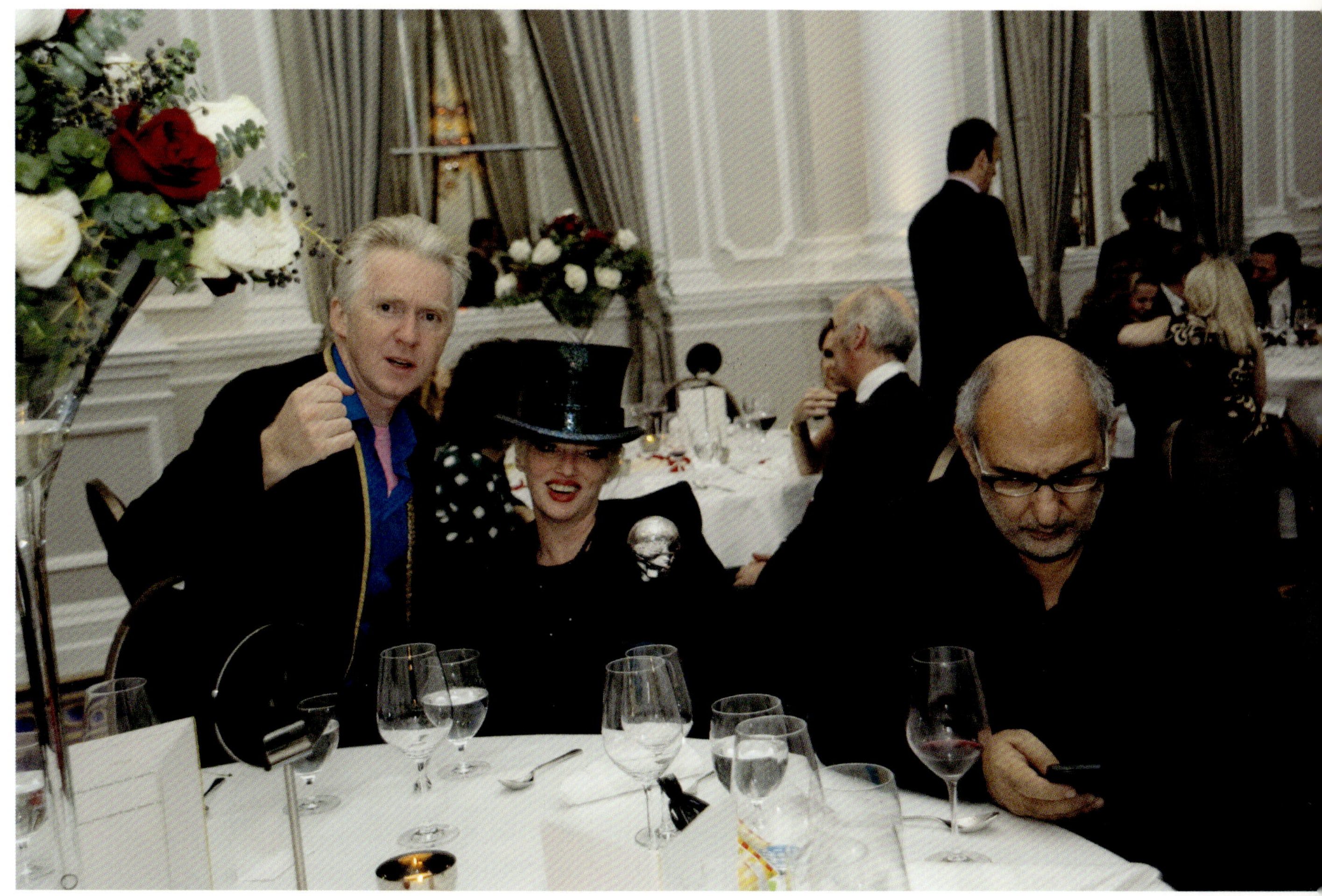

Whitehall, London 2011

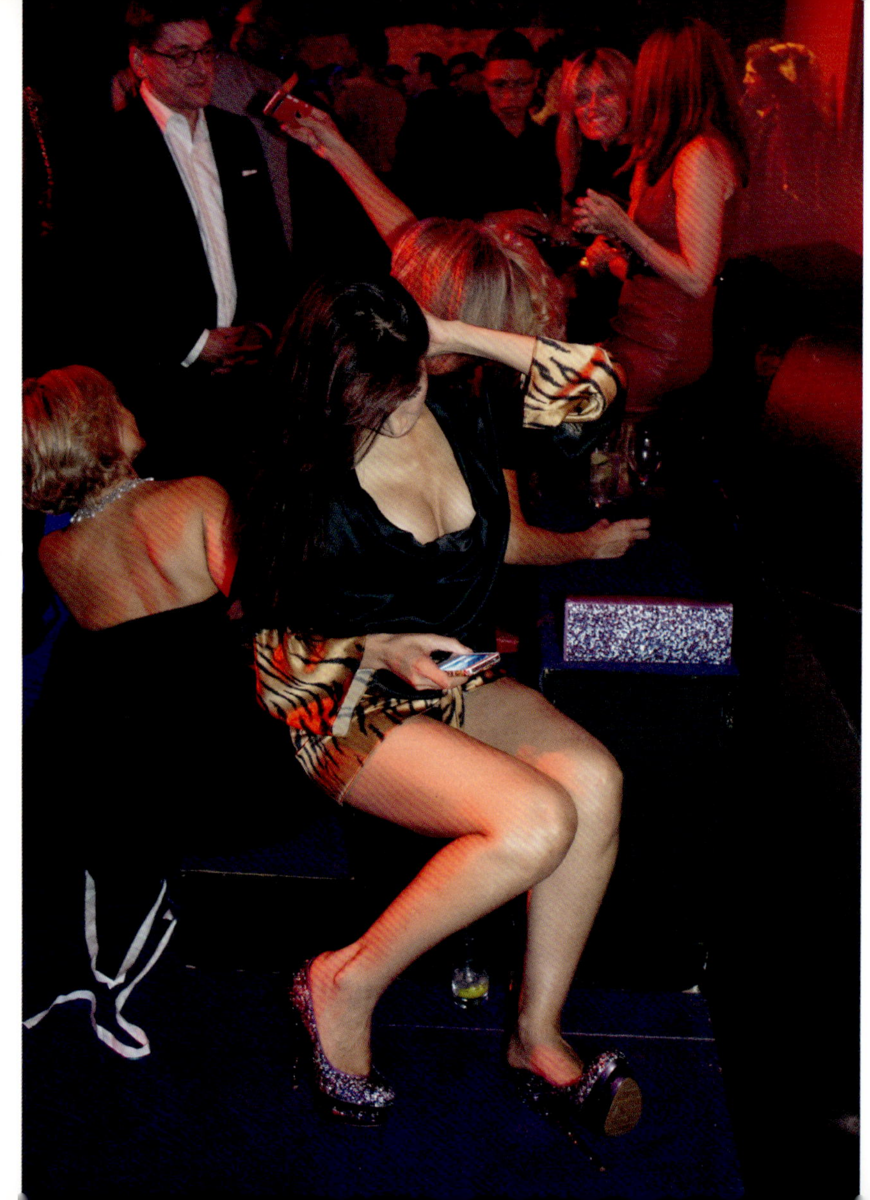

Battersea, London 2011

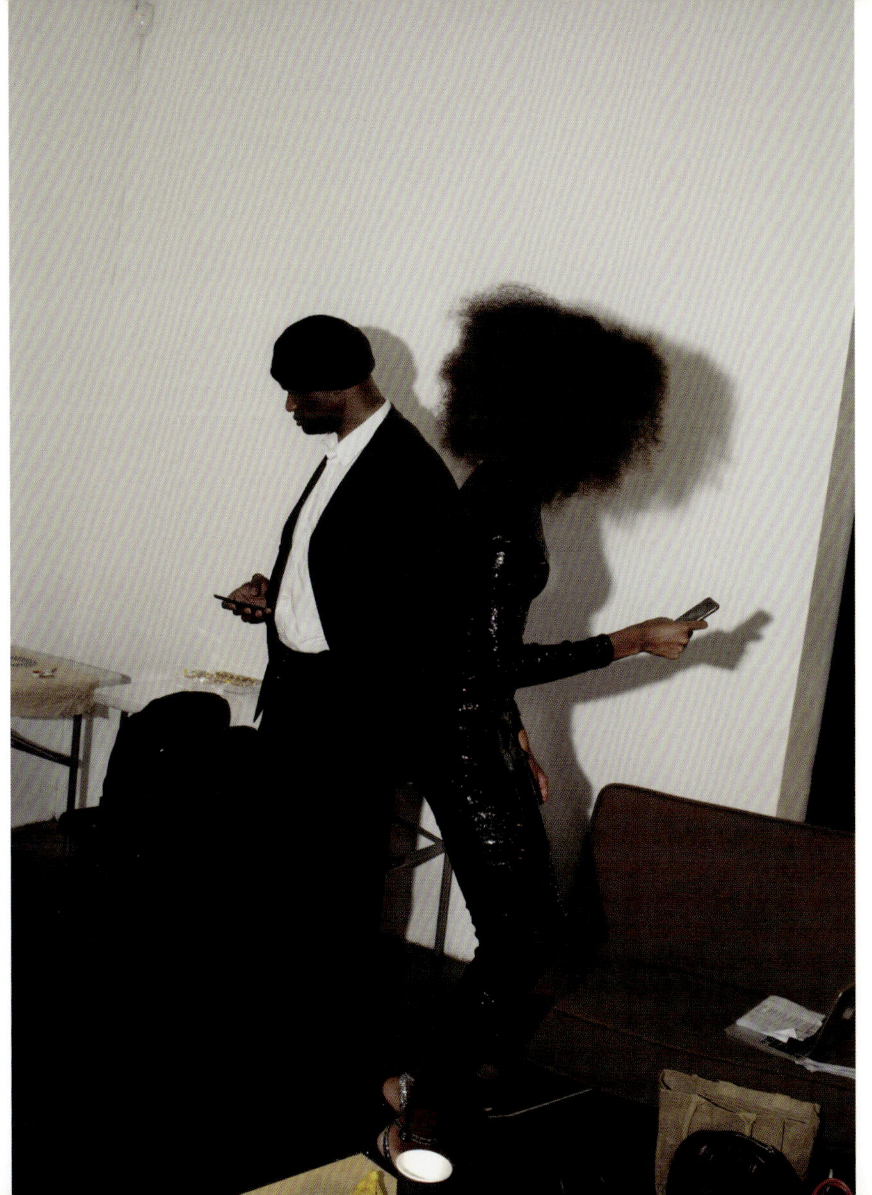

Shadwell, London 2016

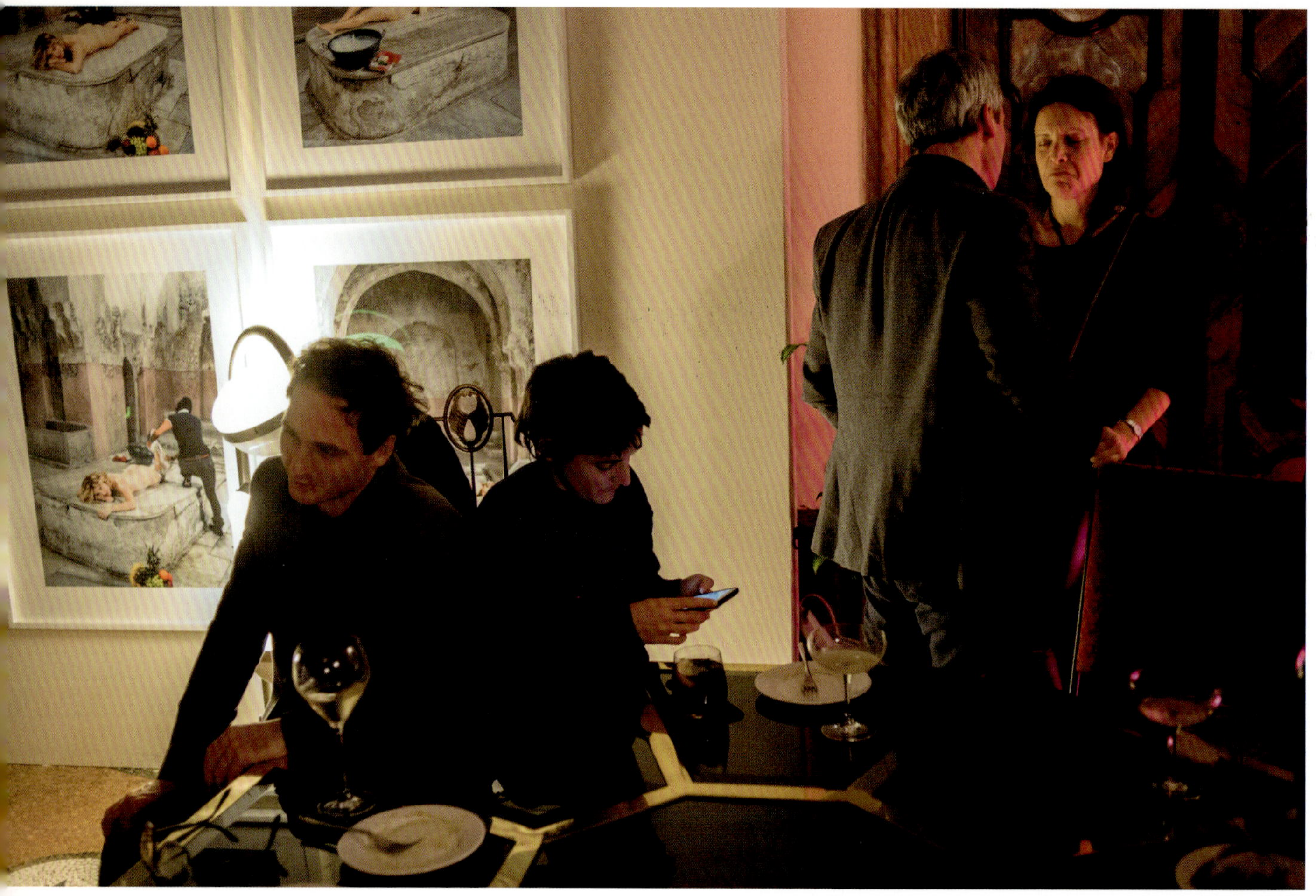

Palazzo Benzon, Venice 2019

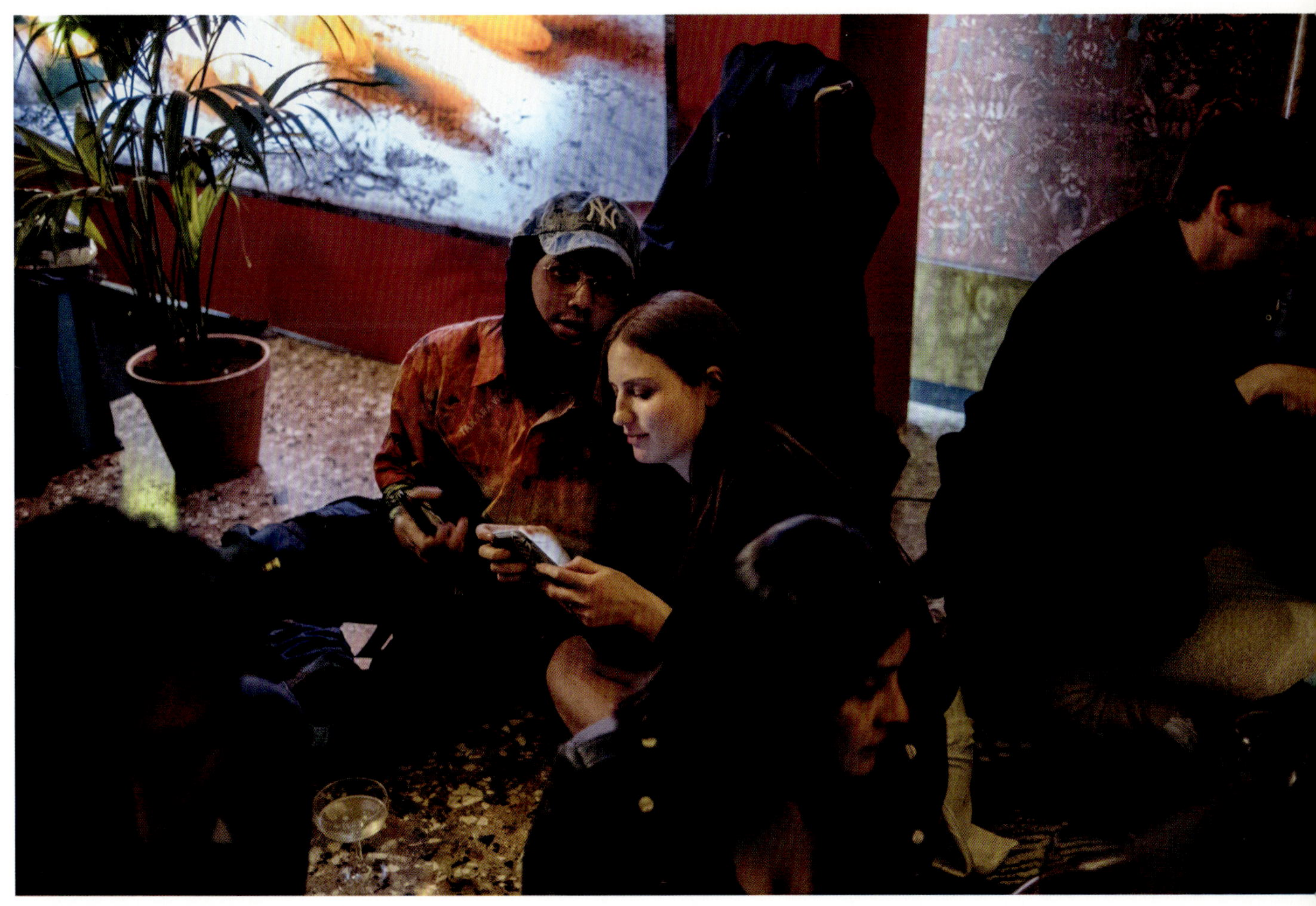

Palazzo Benzon, Venice 2019

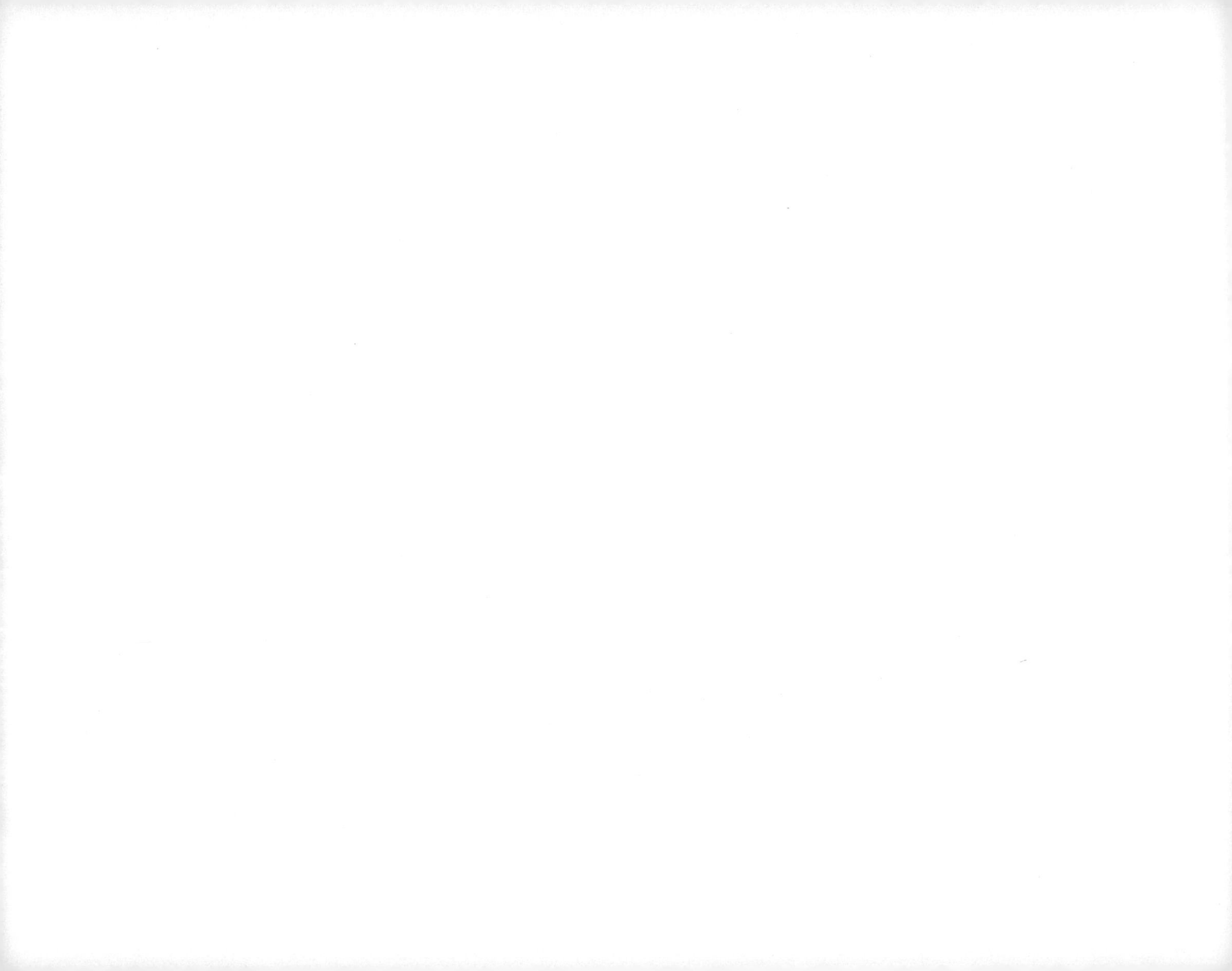

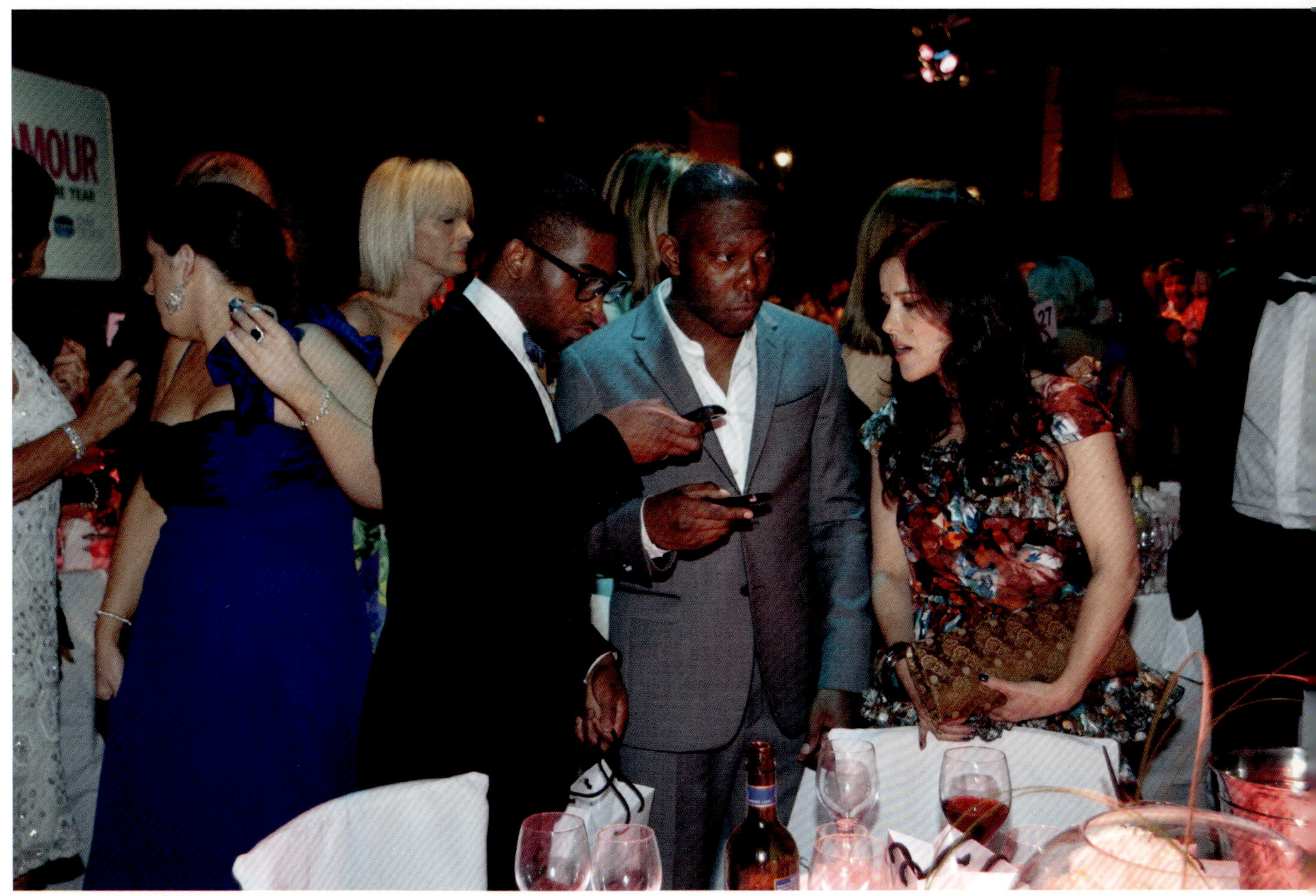

Mayfair, London 2010

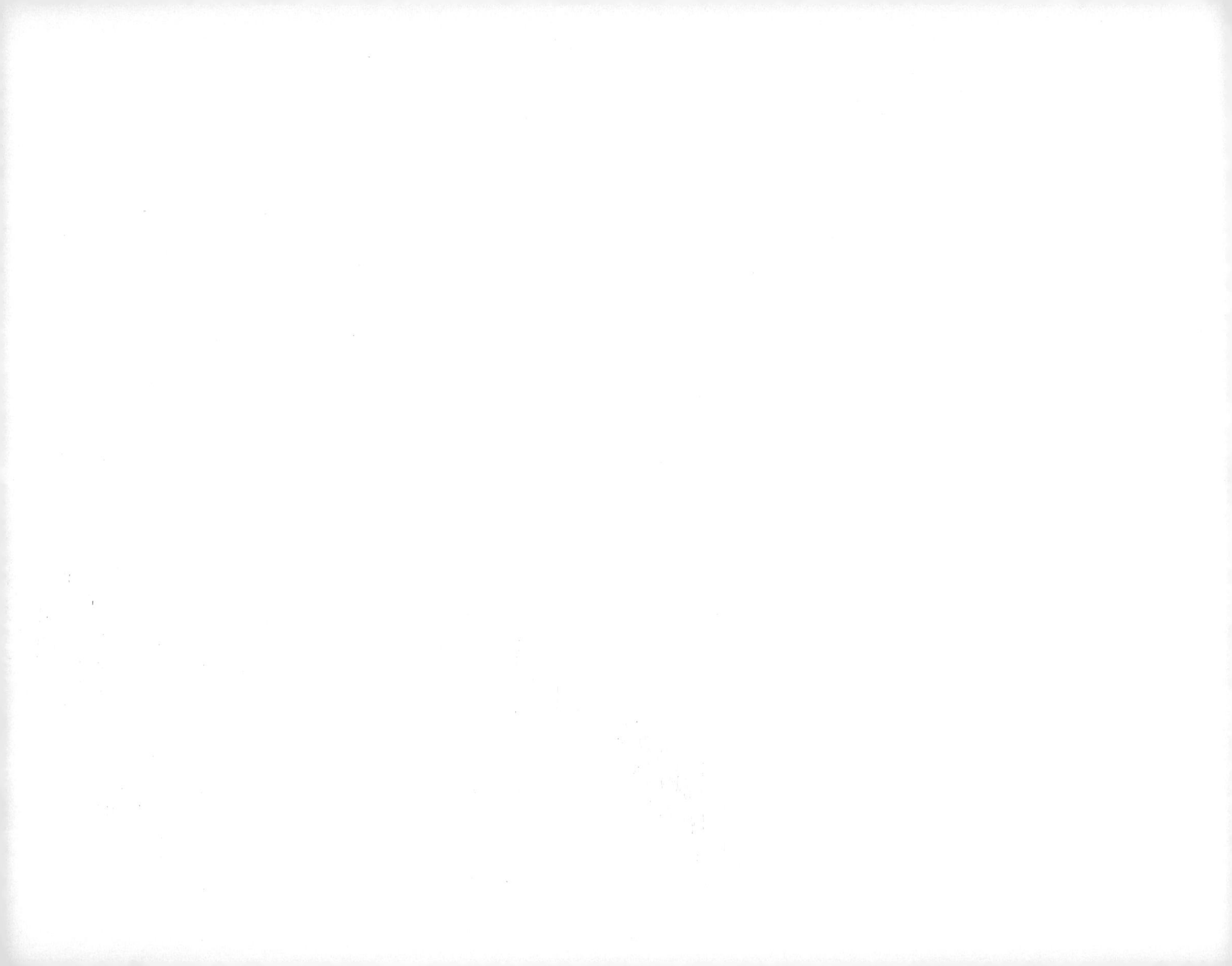

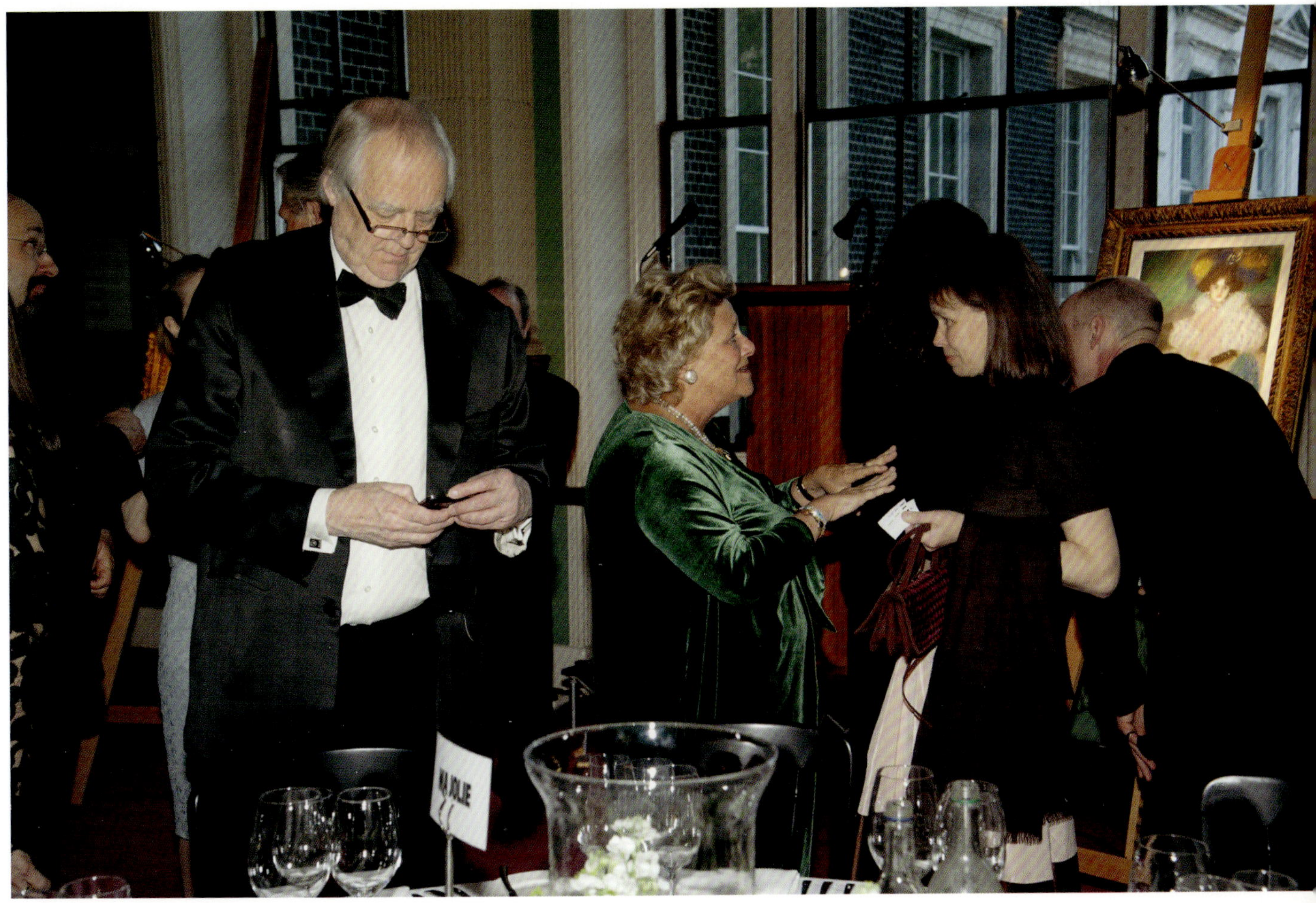

St James's, London 2013

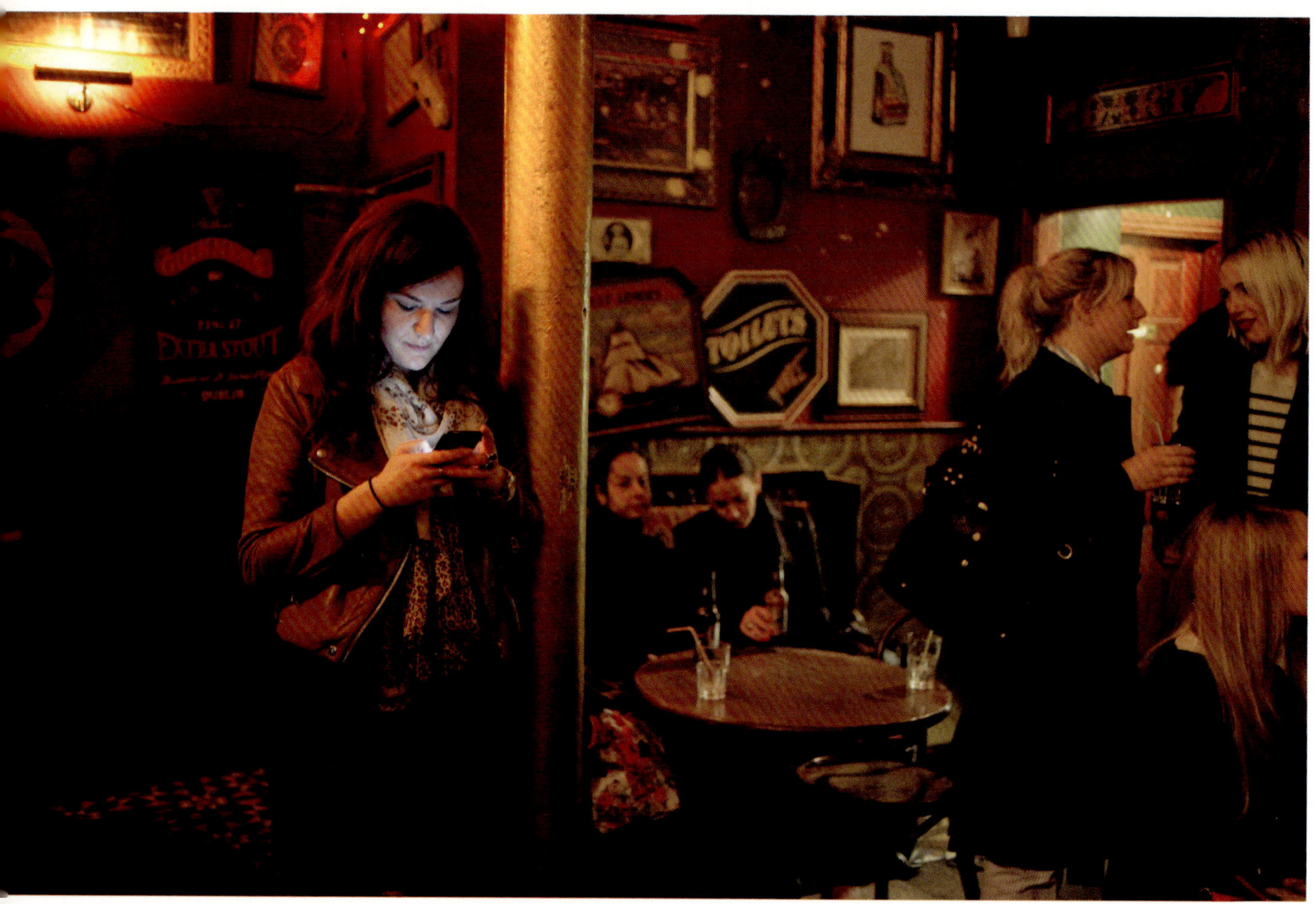

Hackney, London 2012

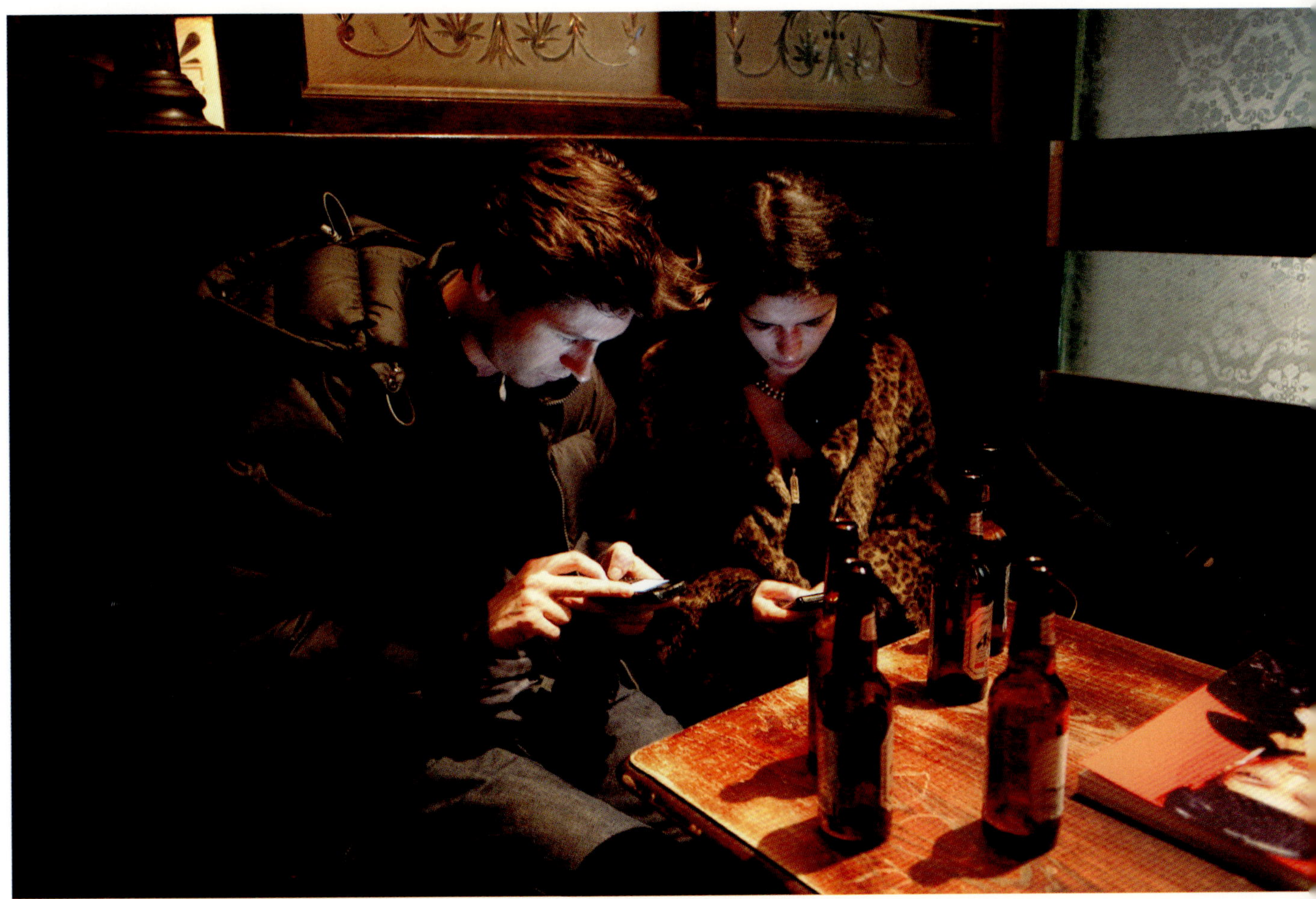

Hackney, London 2012

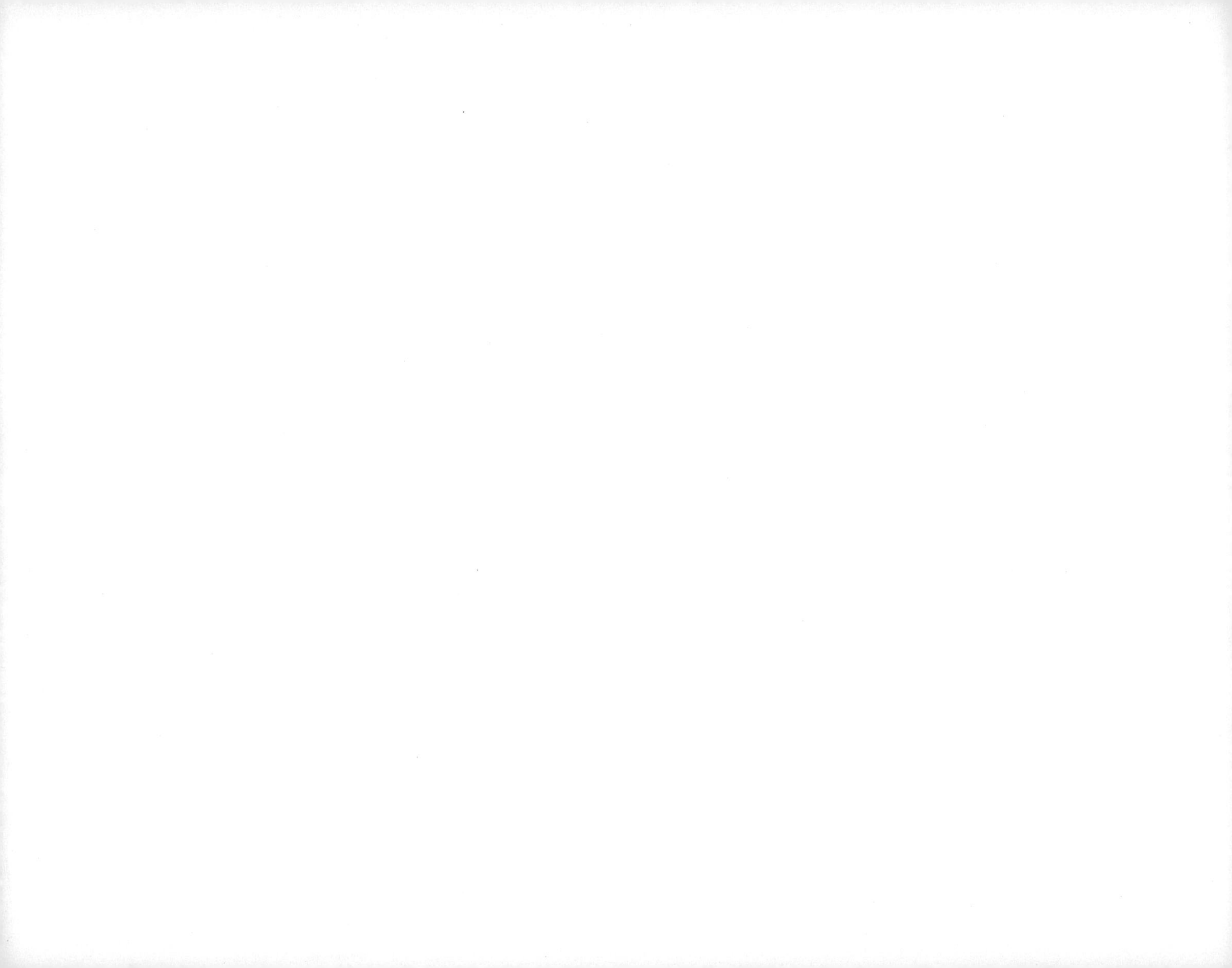

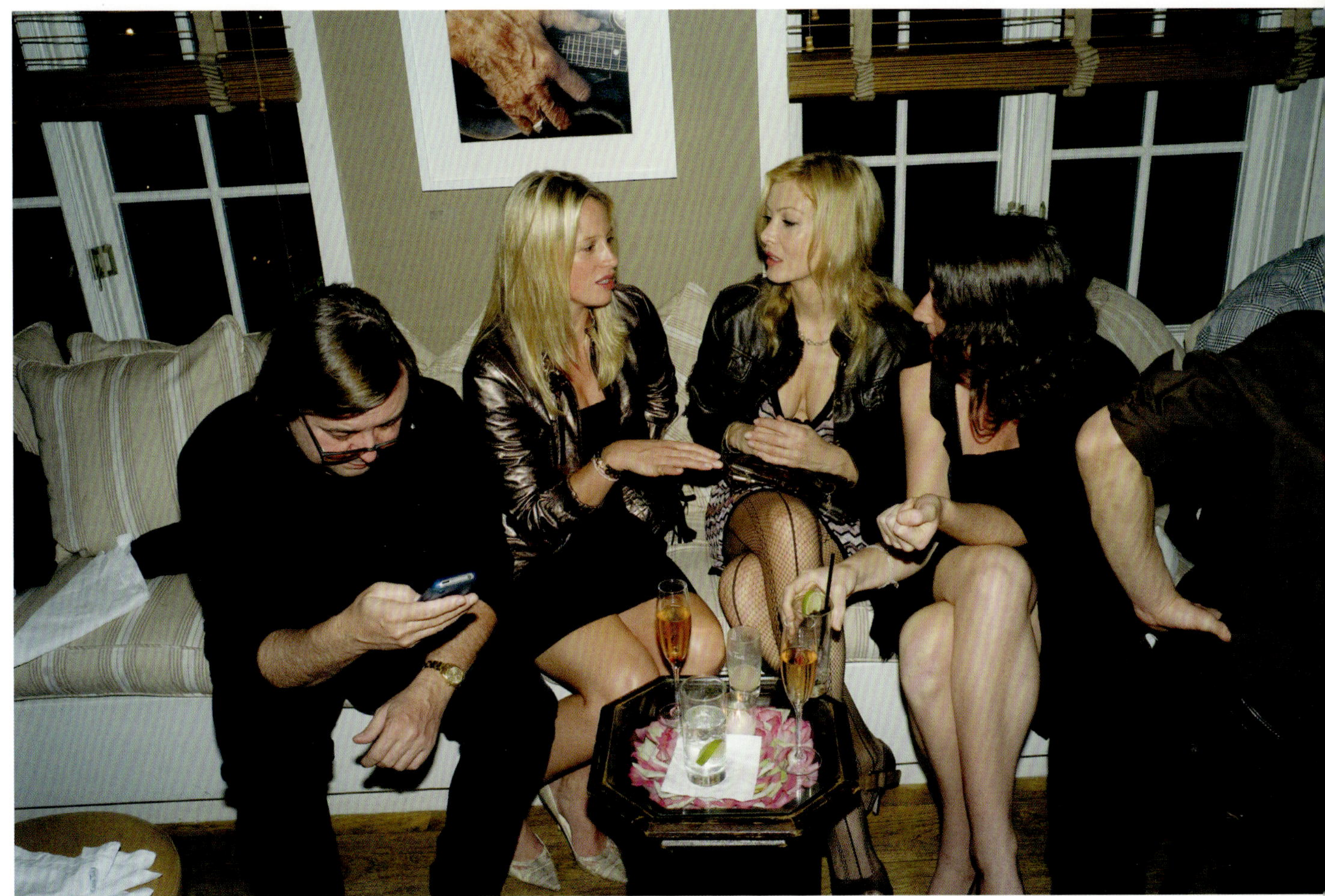

Art Basel, Miami 2008

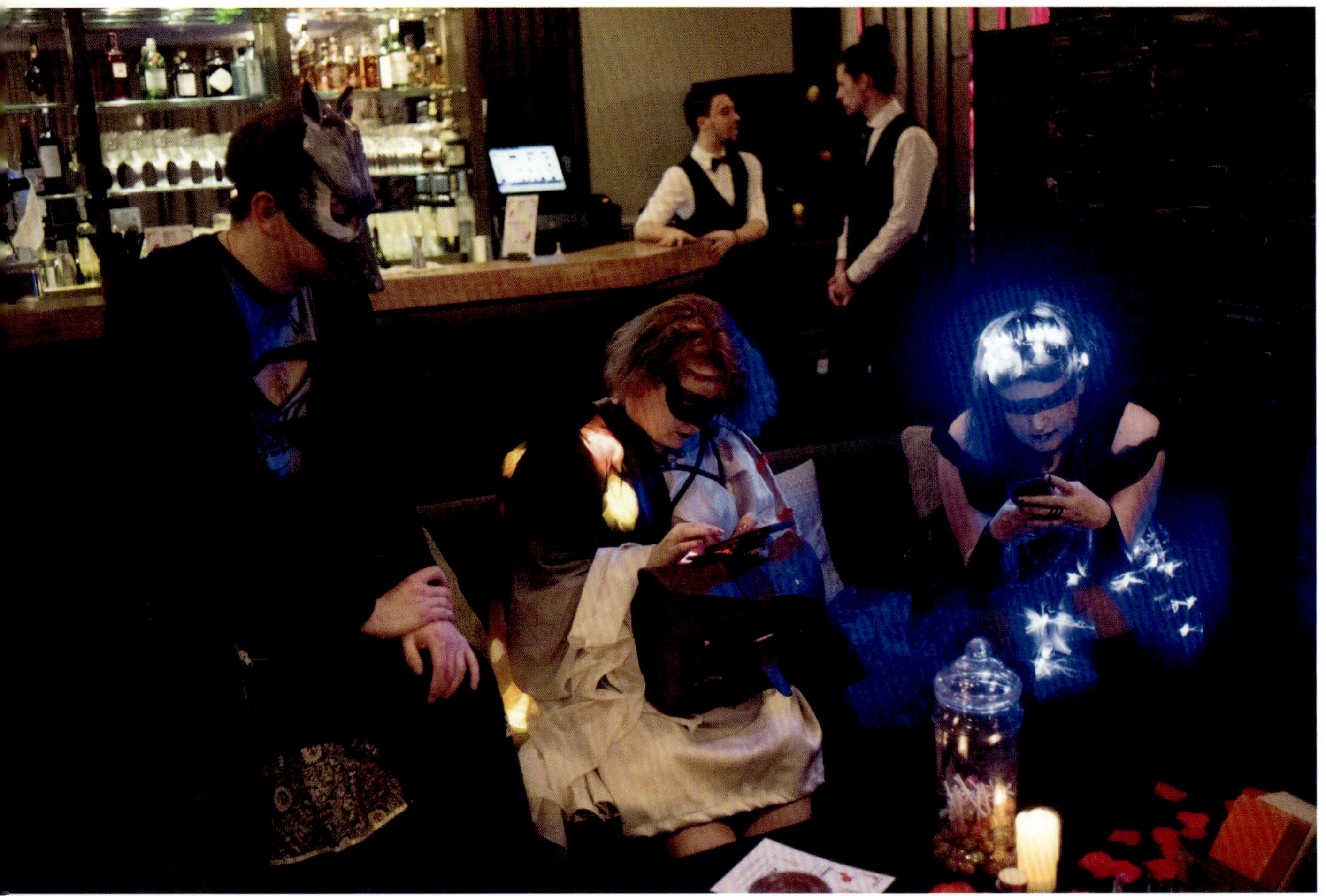

Soho, London 2019

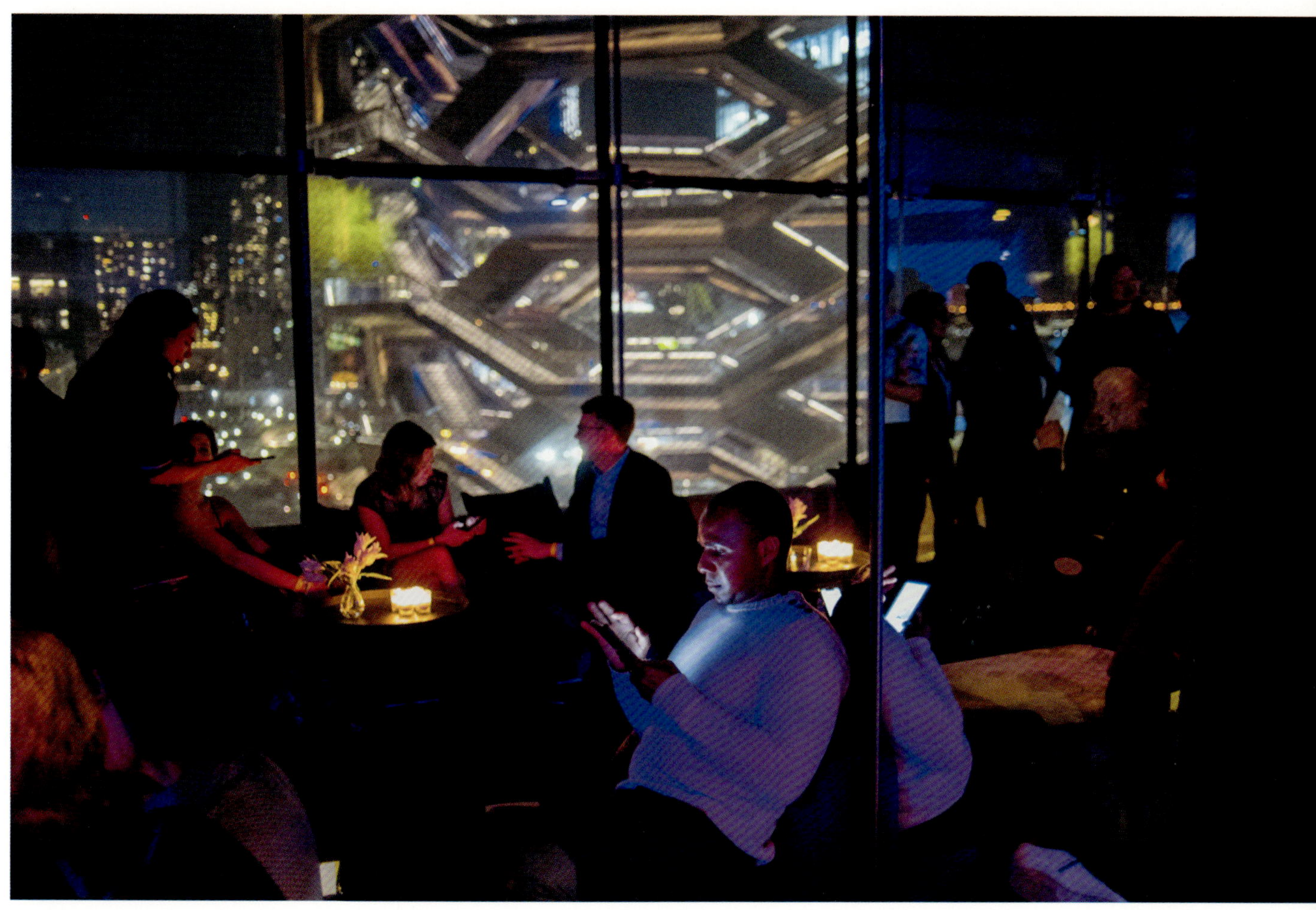

The Shed, Manhattan 2019

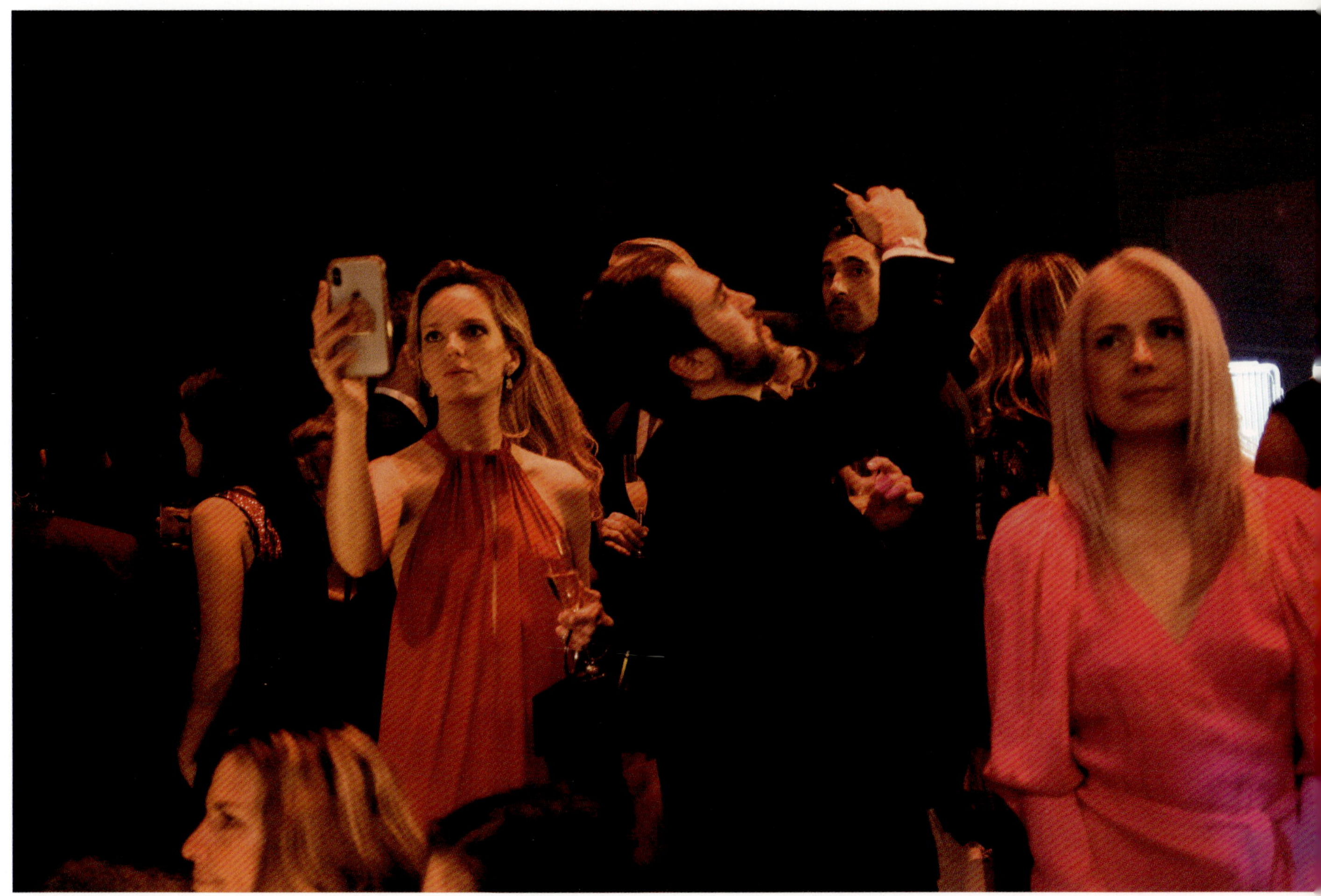

Roundhouse, London 2019

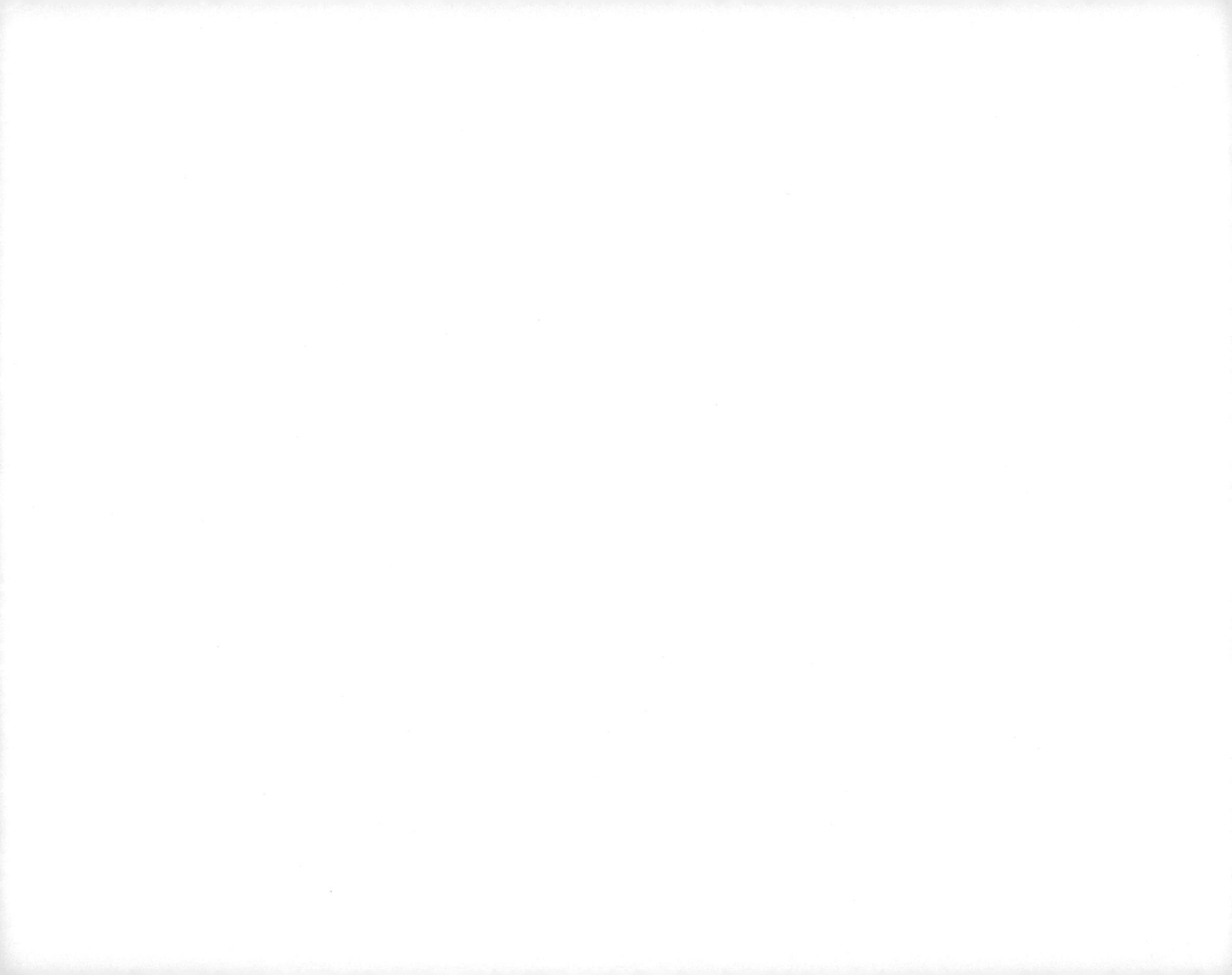

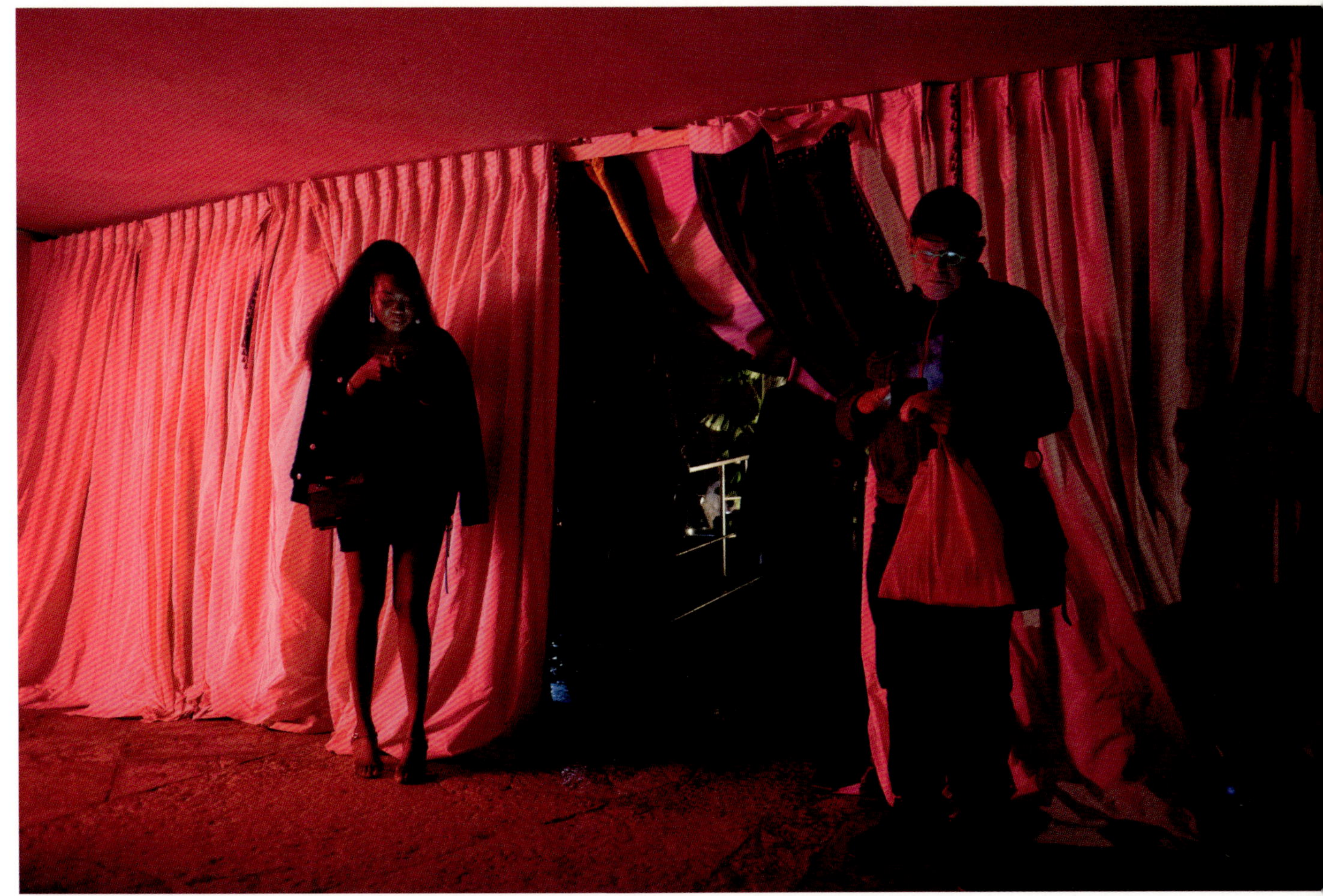

Palazzo Benzon, Venice 2019

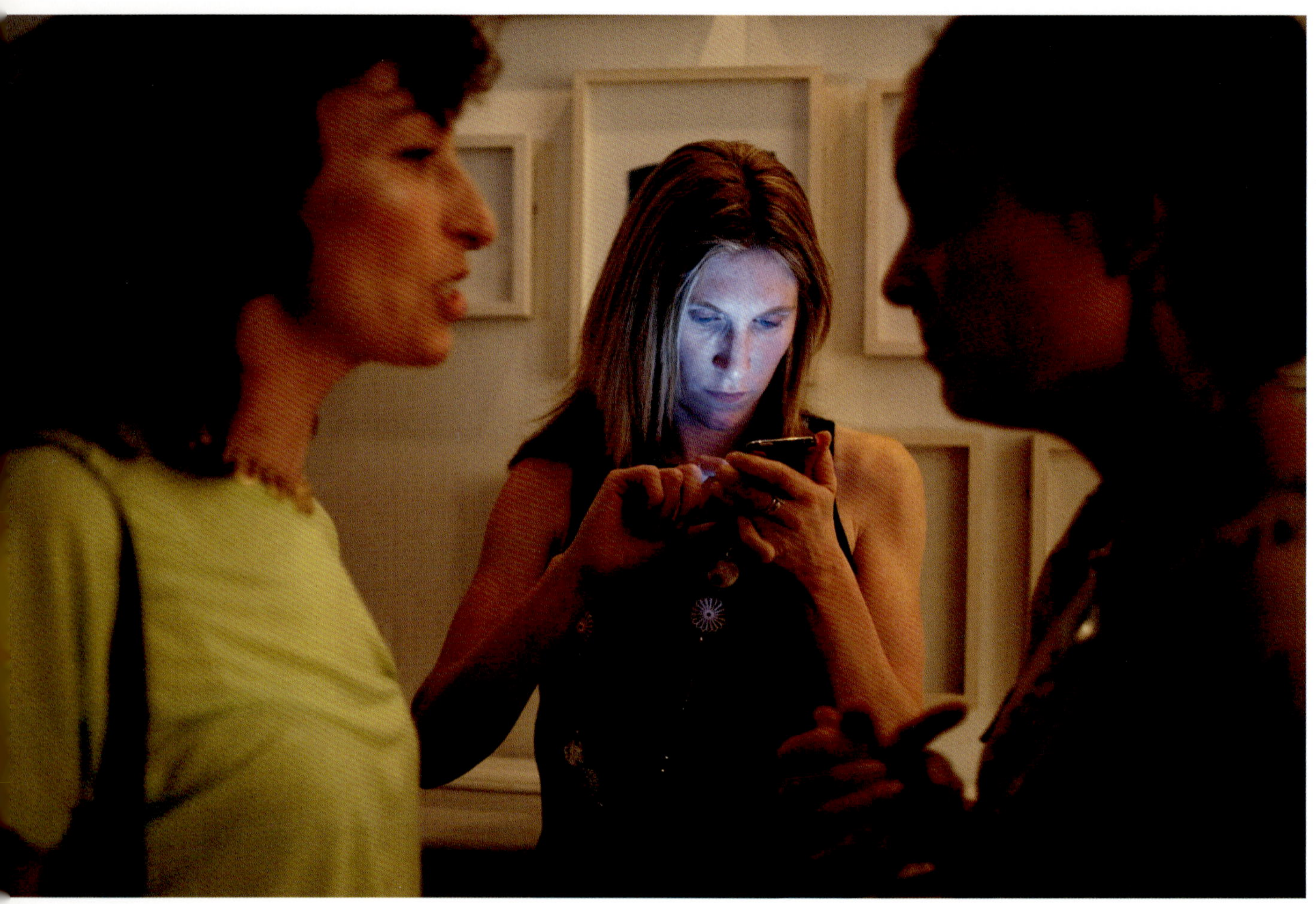

Mayfair, London 2011

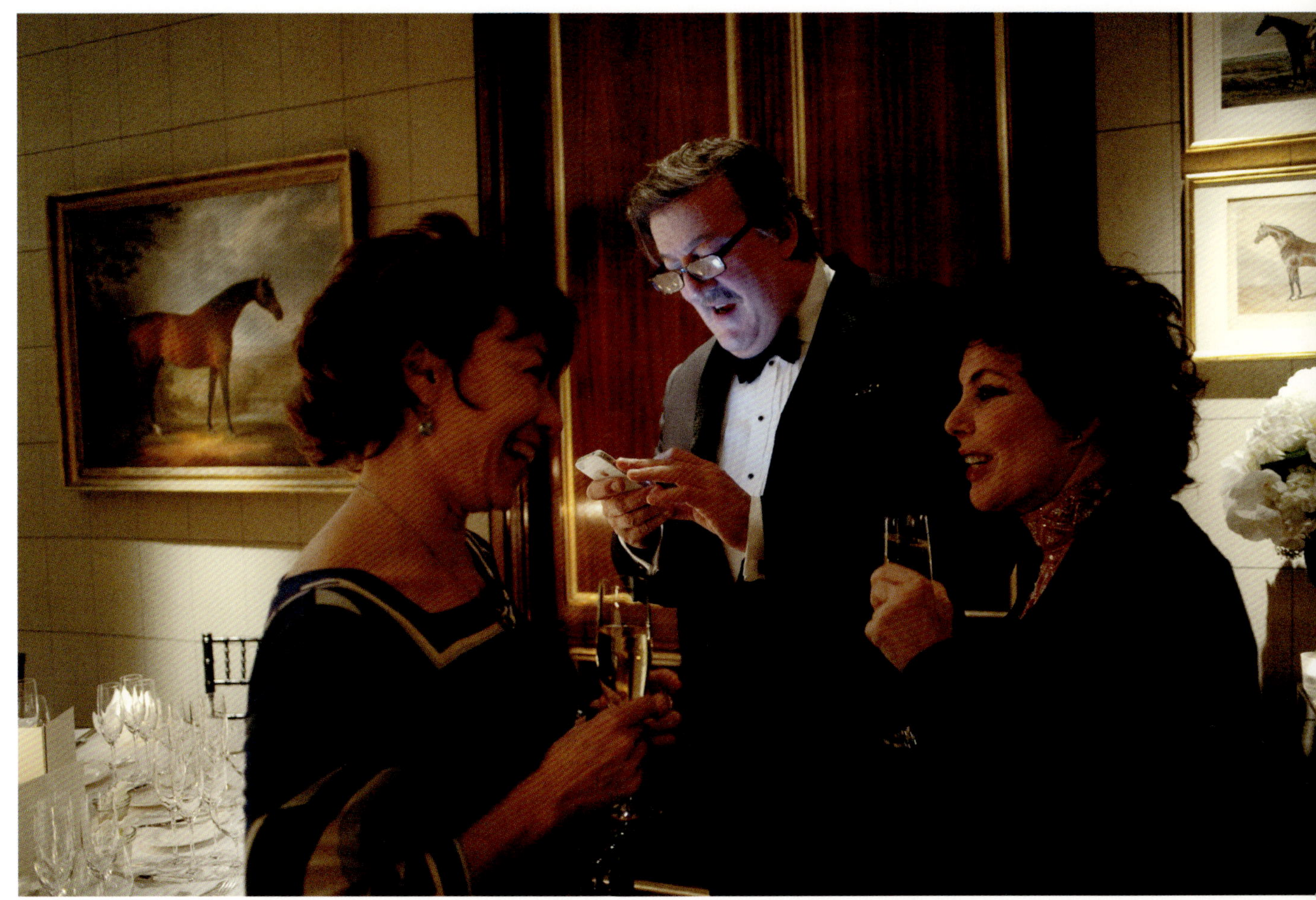

Knightsbridge, London 2011

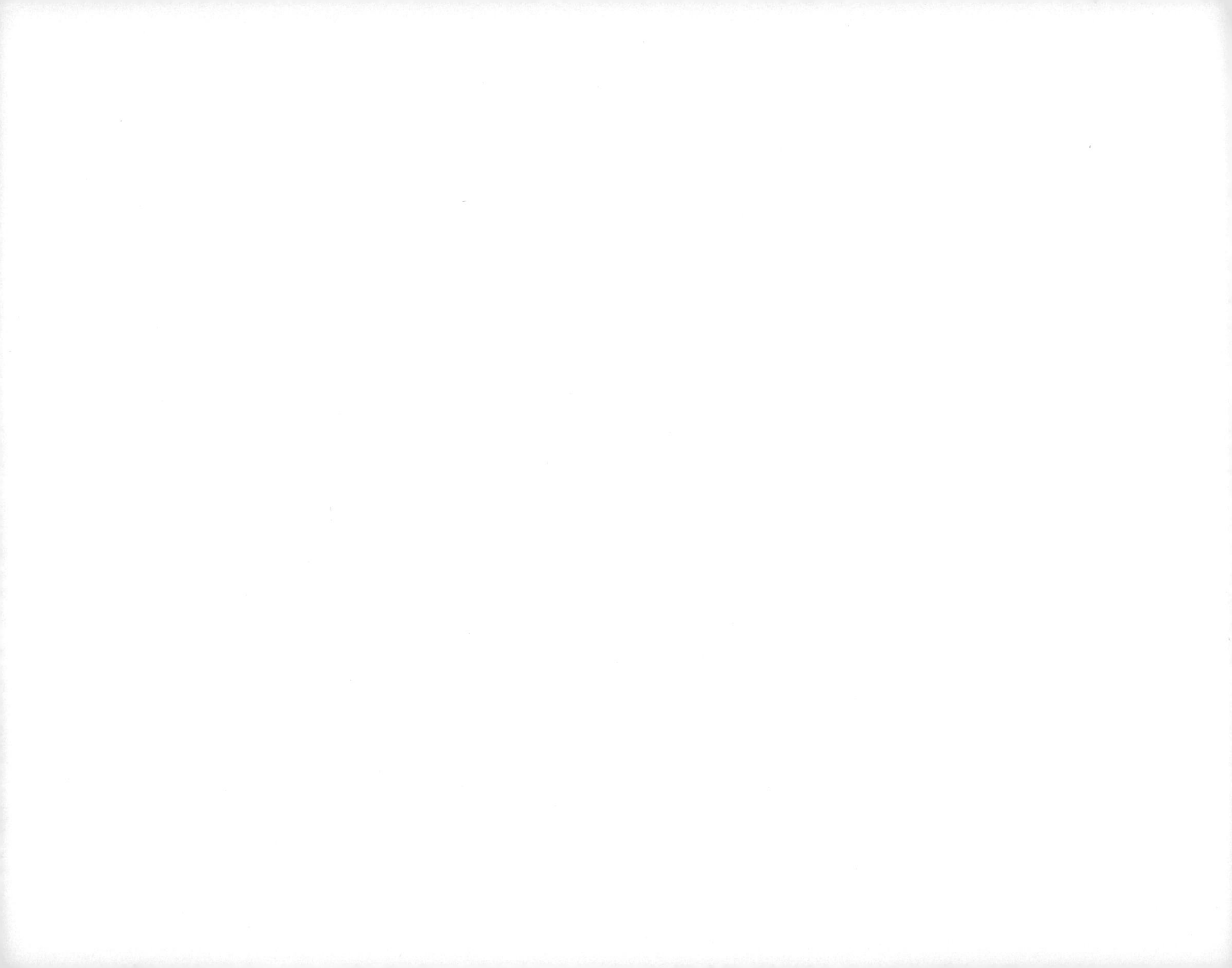

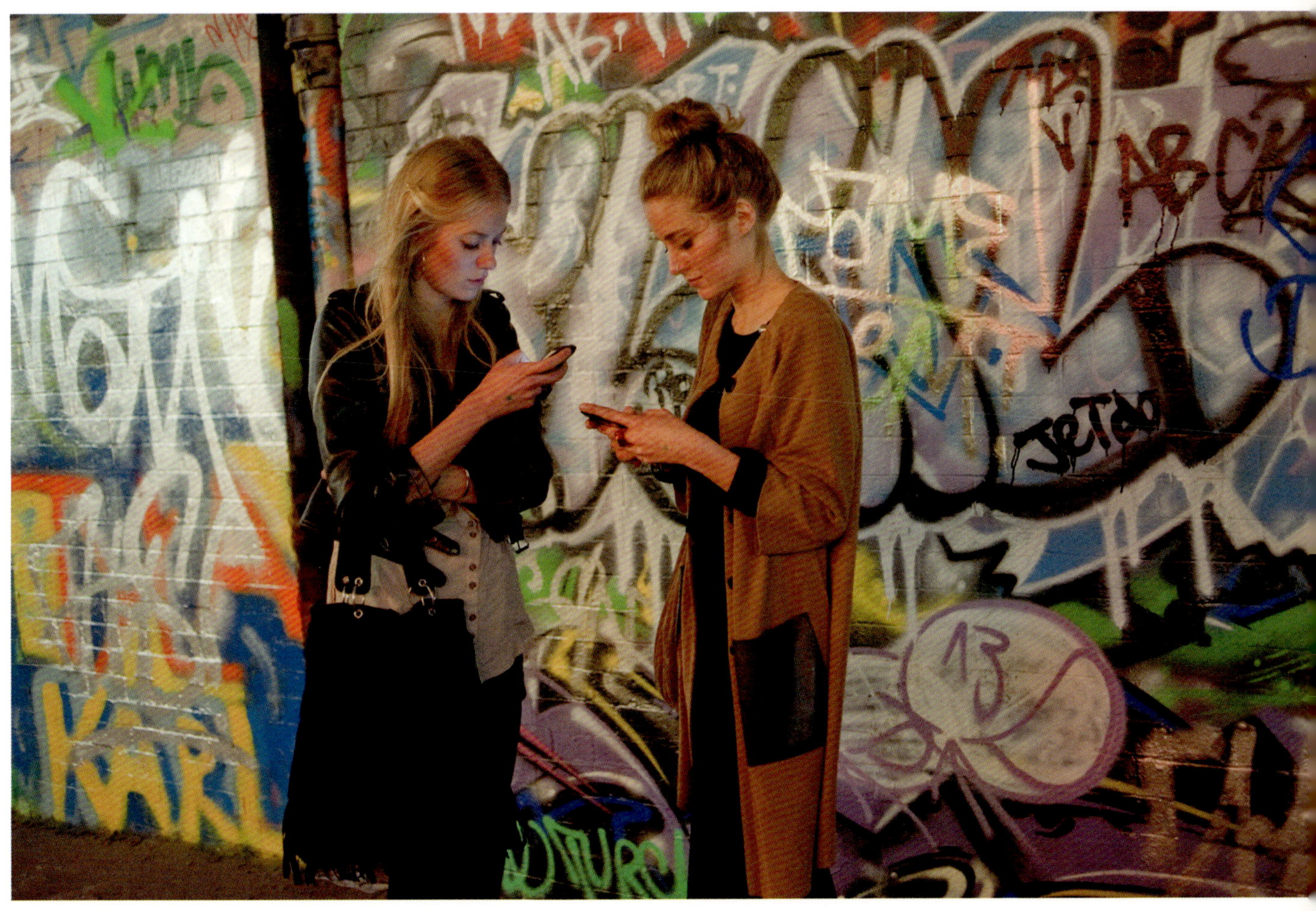

Waterloo, London 2011

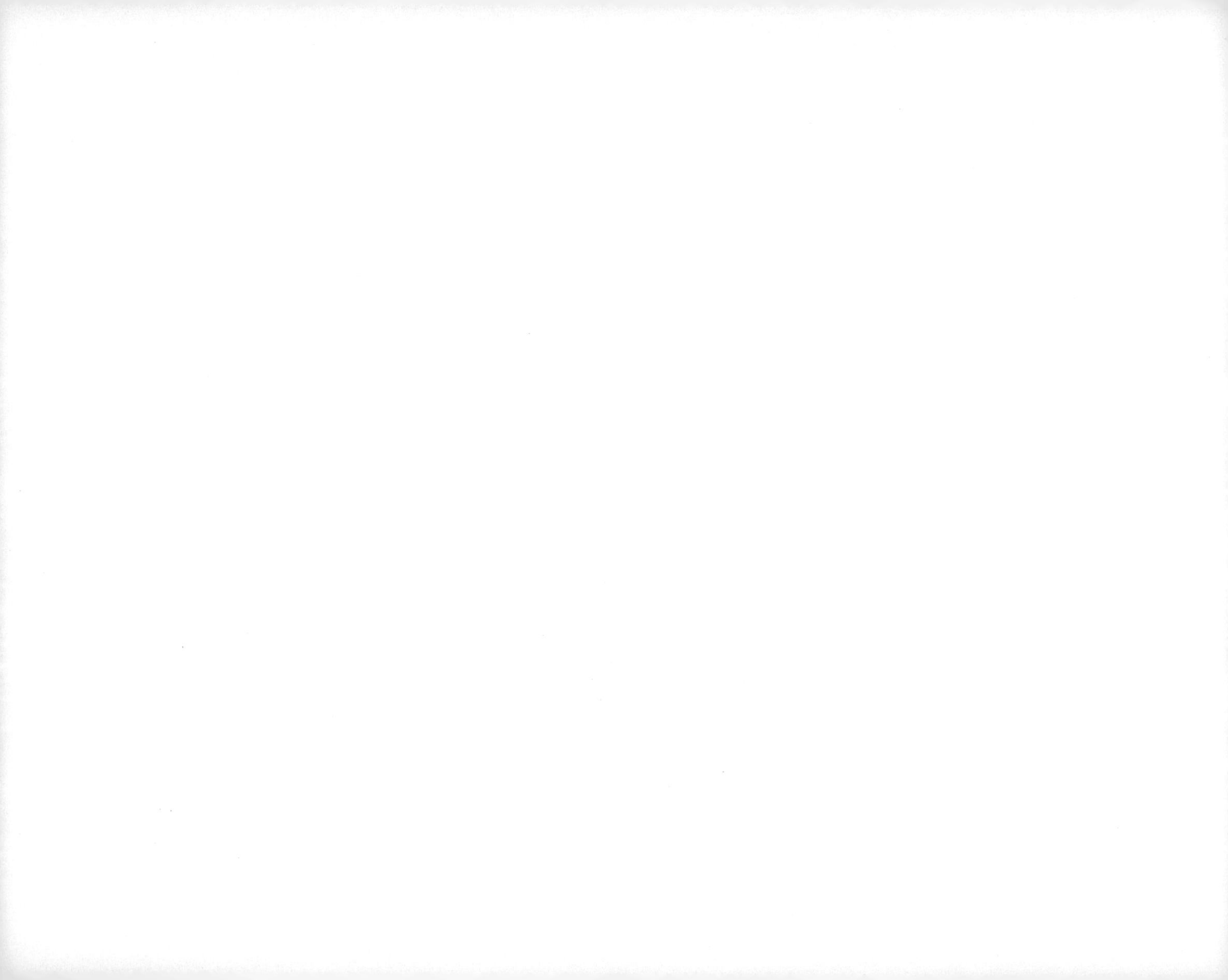

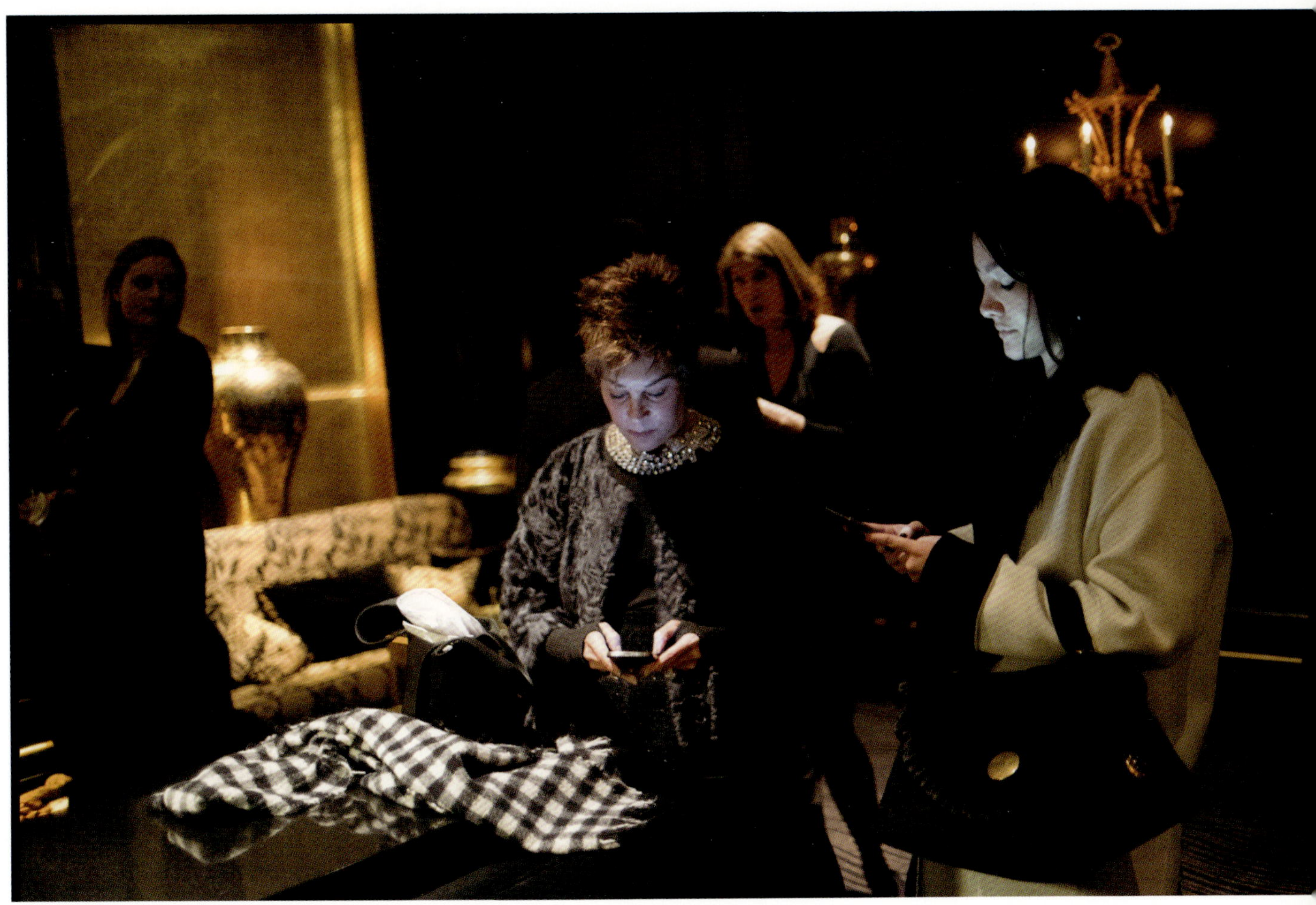

Savoy Hotel, London 2015

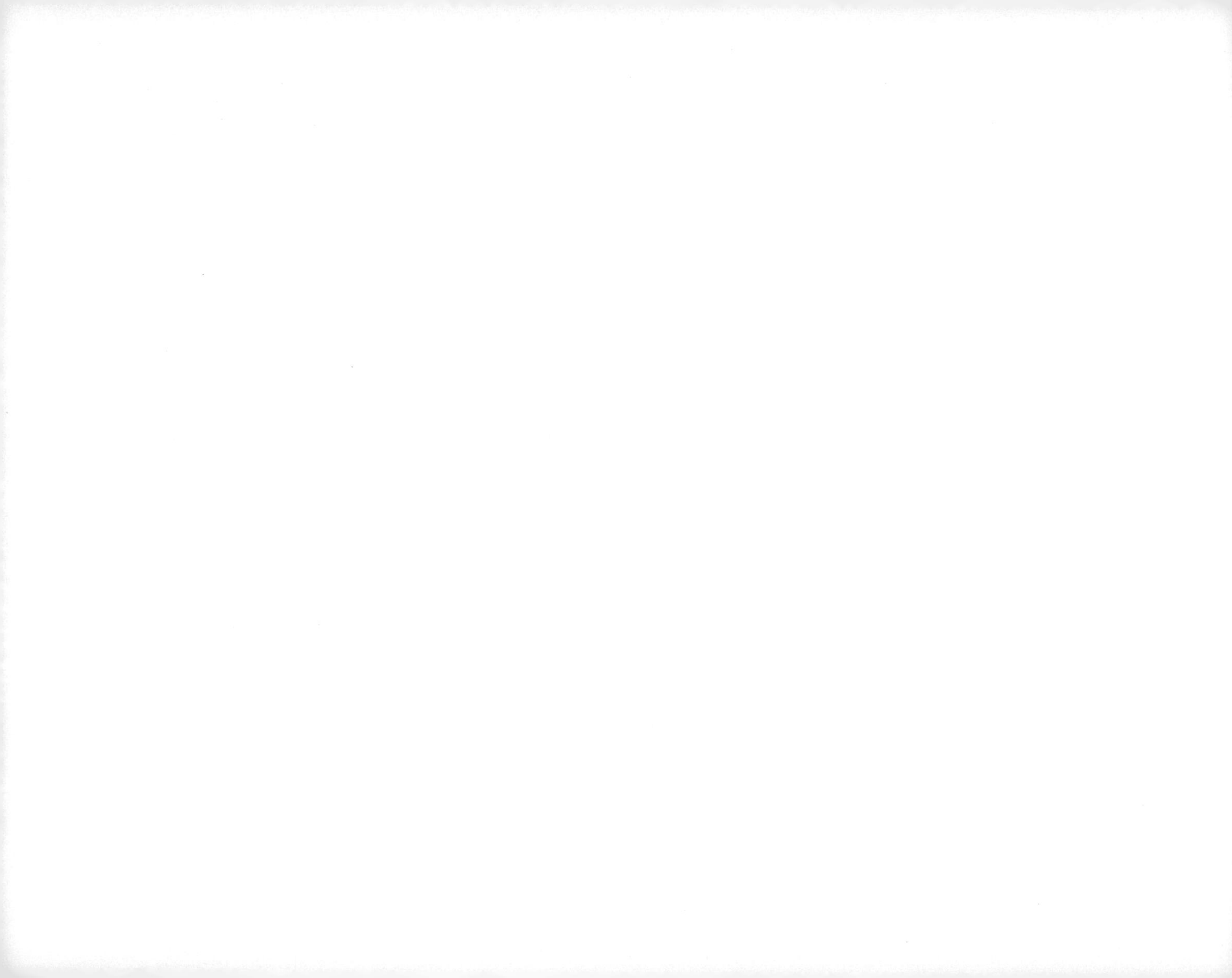

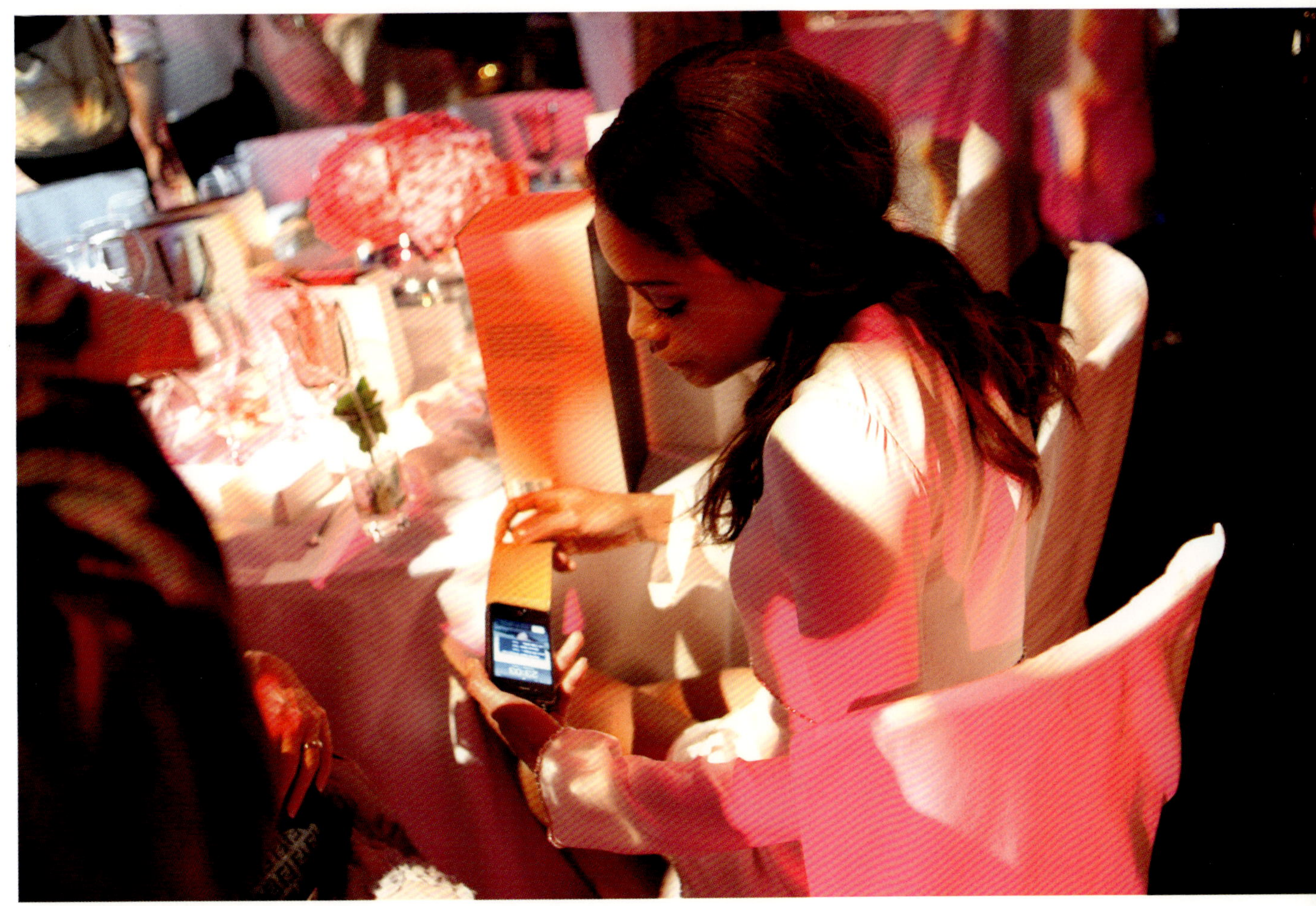

Mayfair, London 2011

Mayfair, London 2011

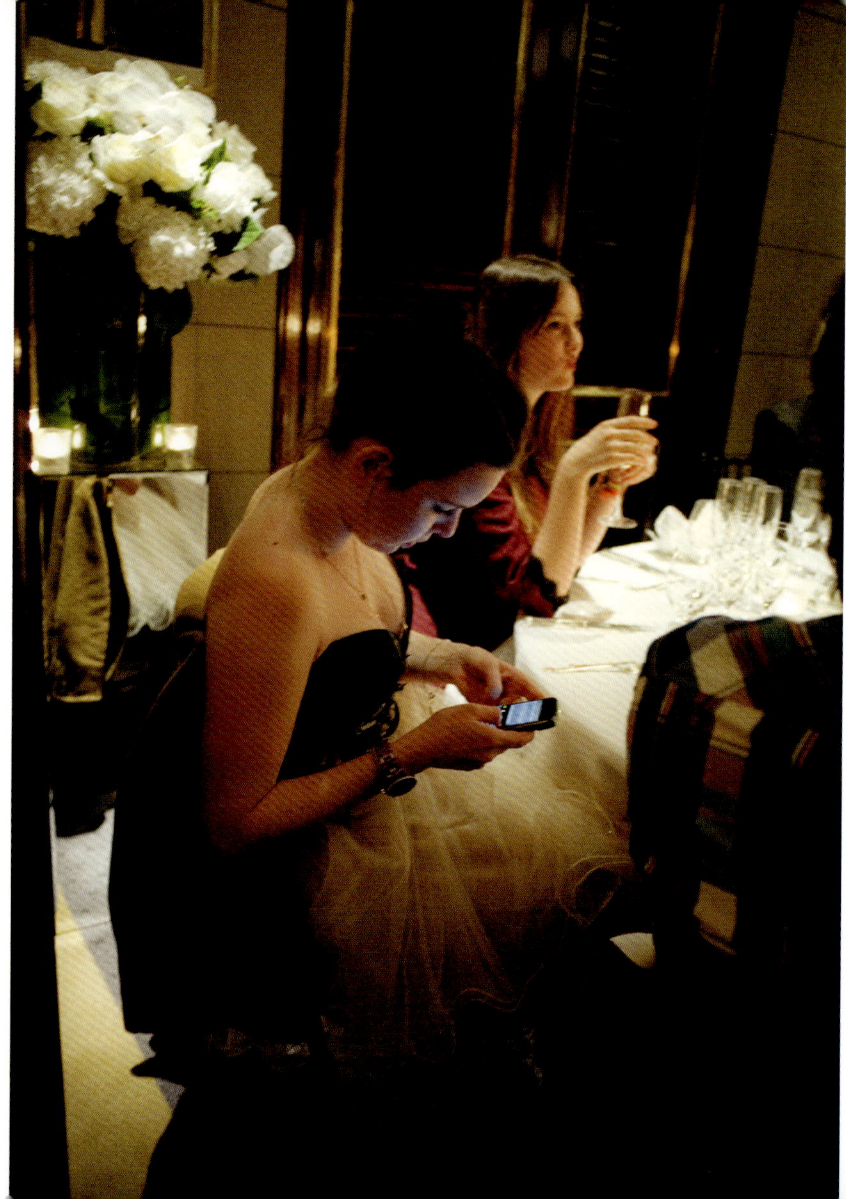

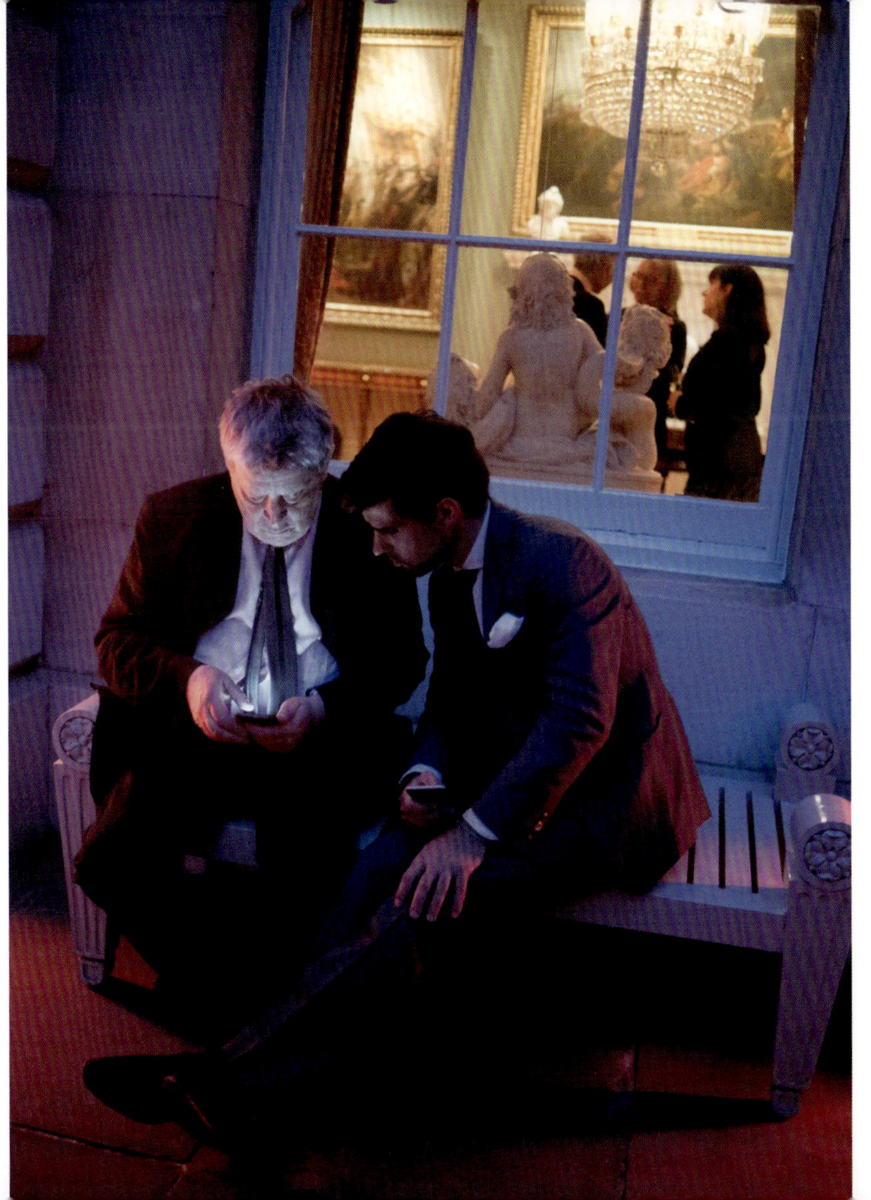

St James's, London 2017

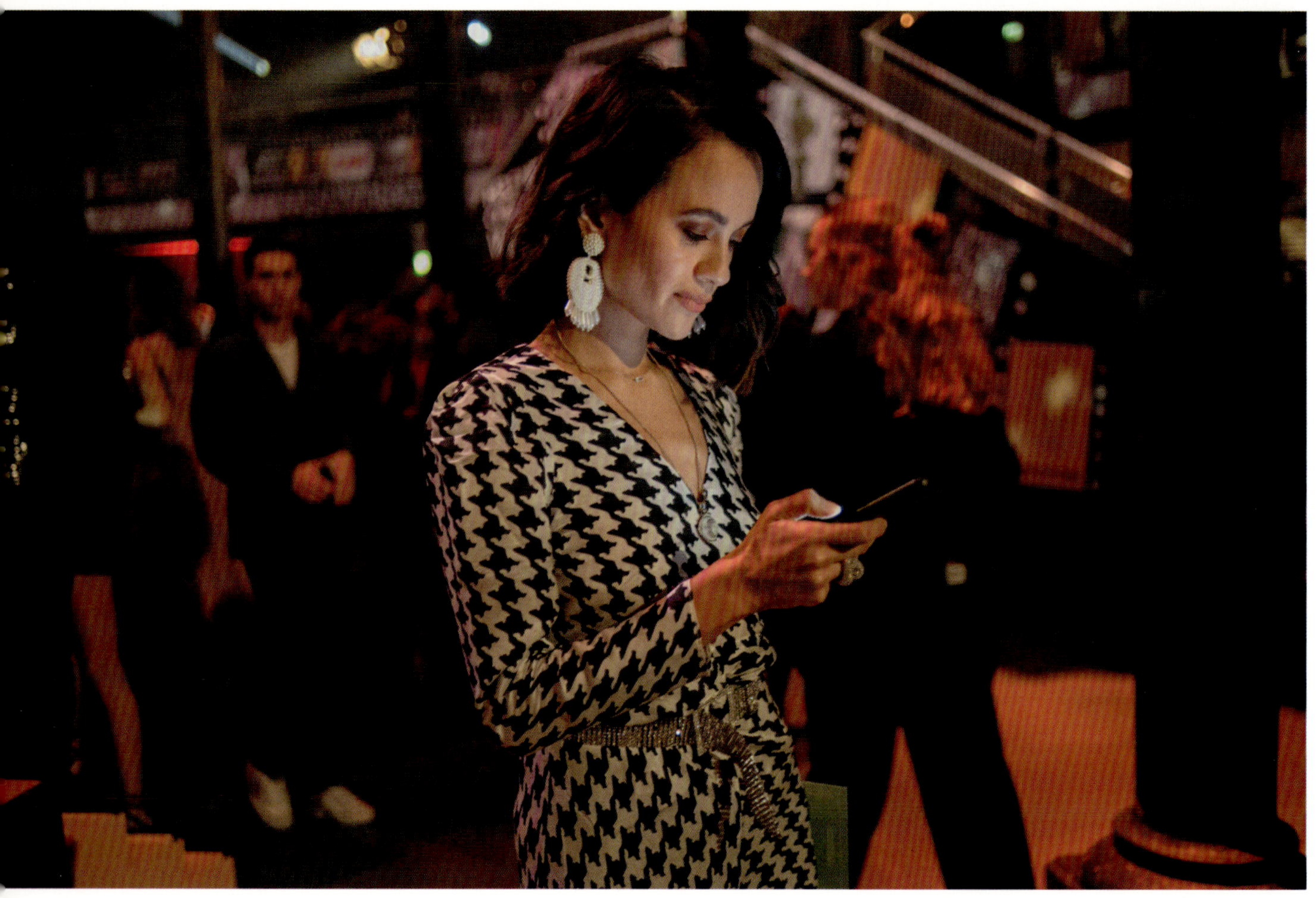

Roundhouse, London 2019

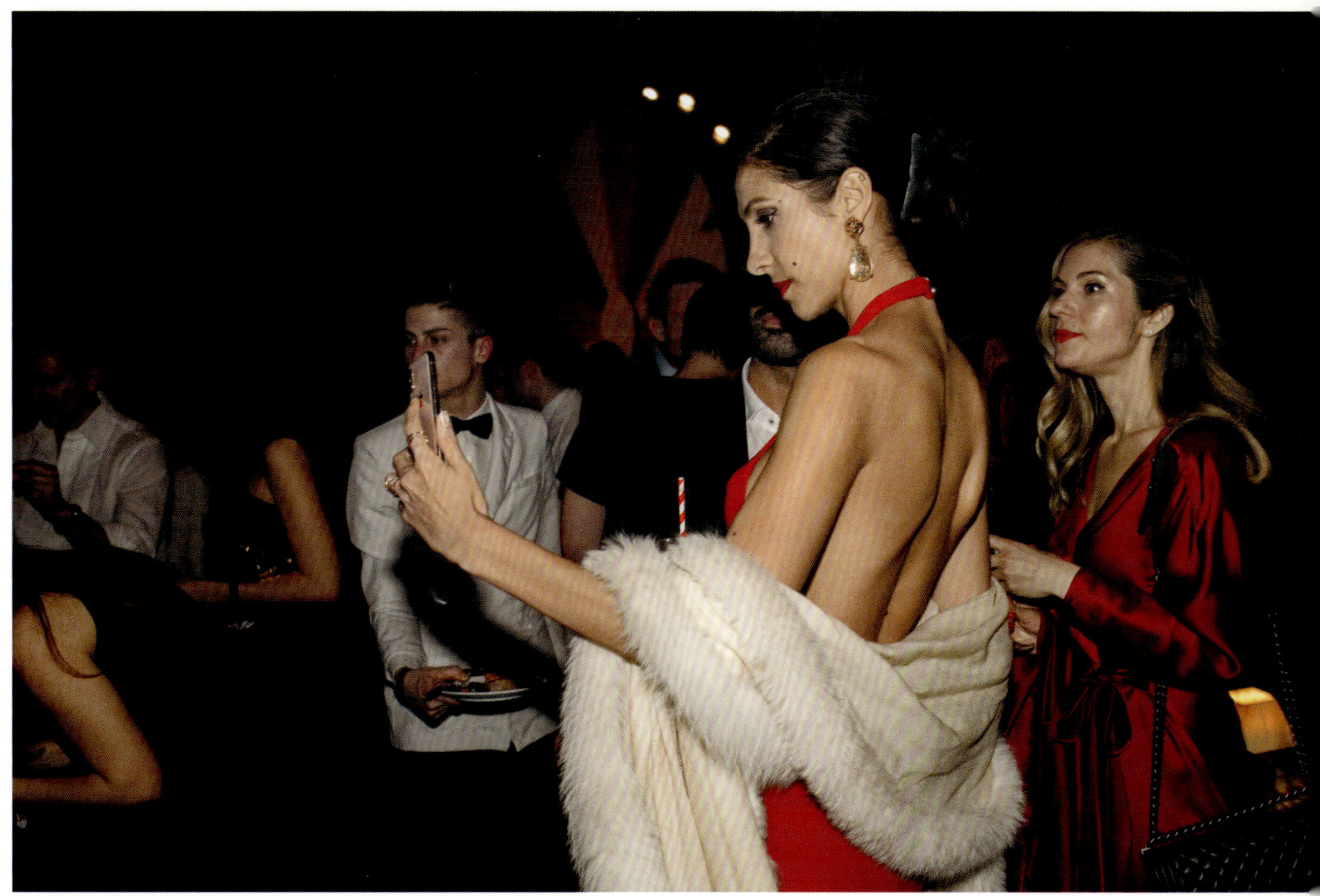

Roundhouse, London 2019

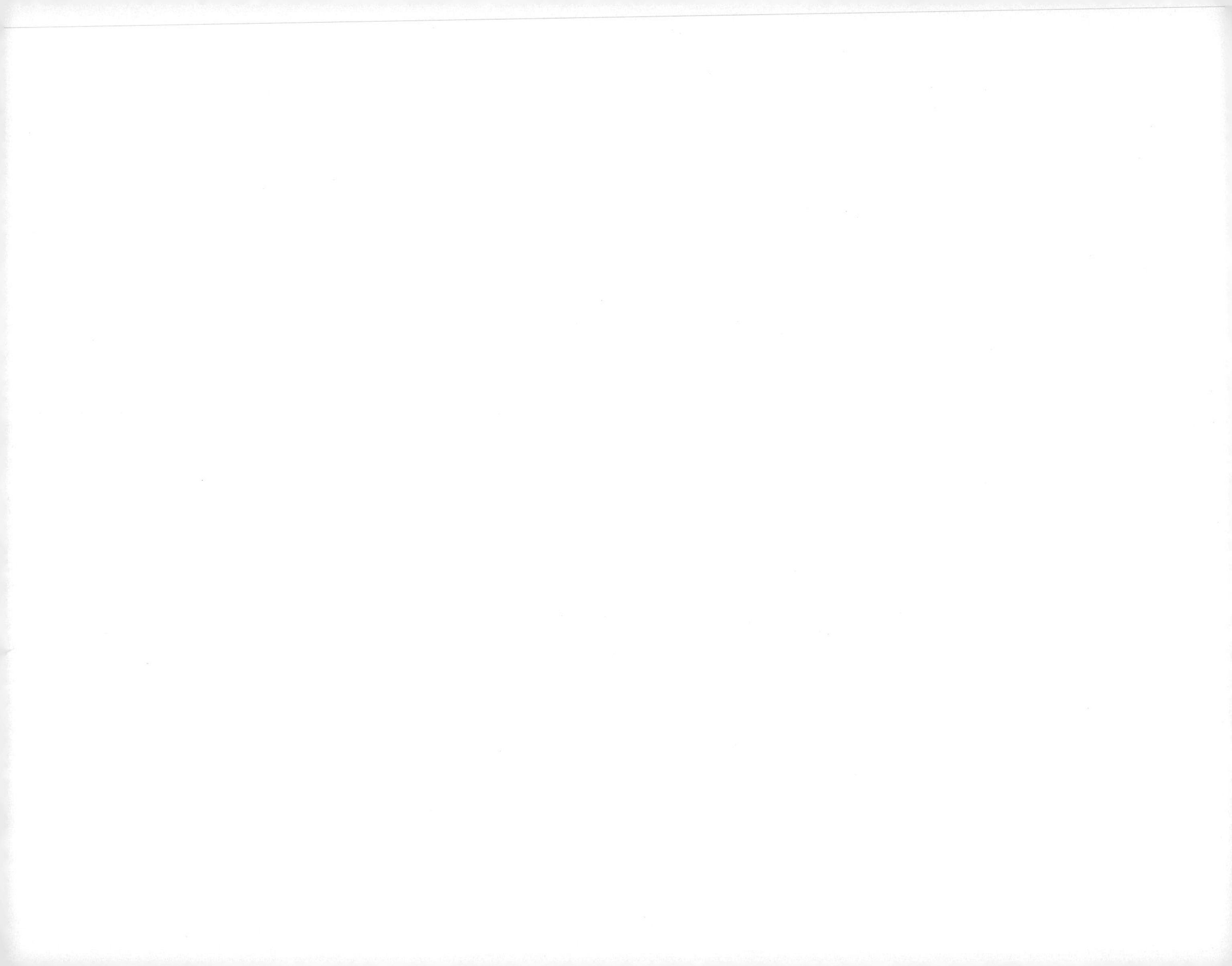

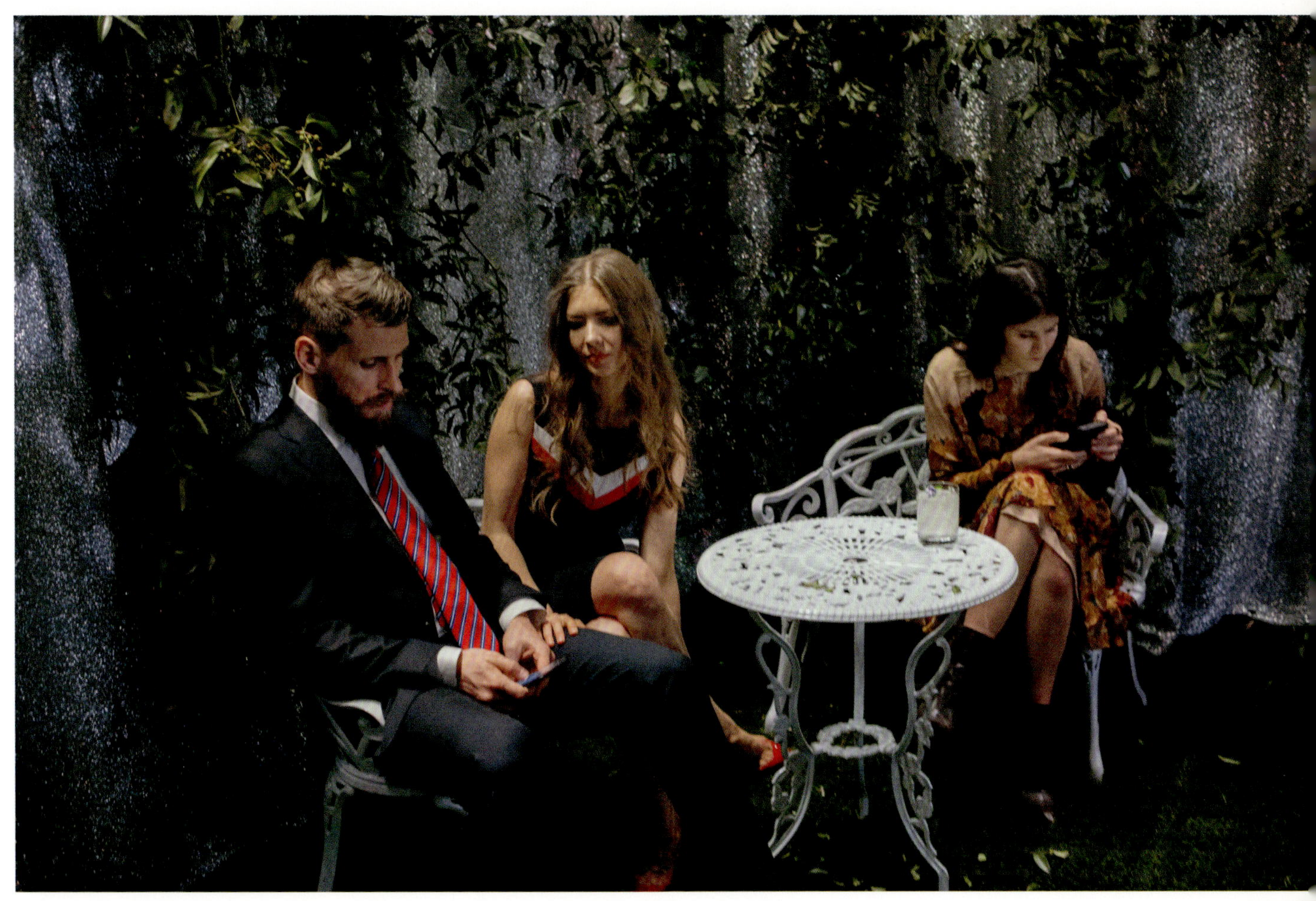

Vesey St, Manhattan 2019

Hampton Court, London 2011

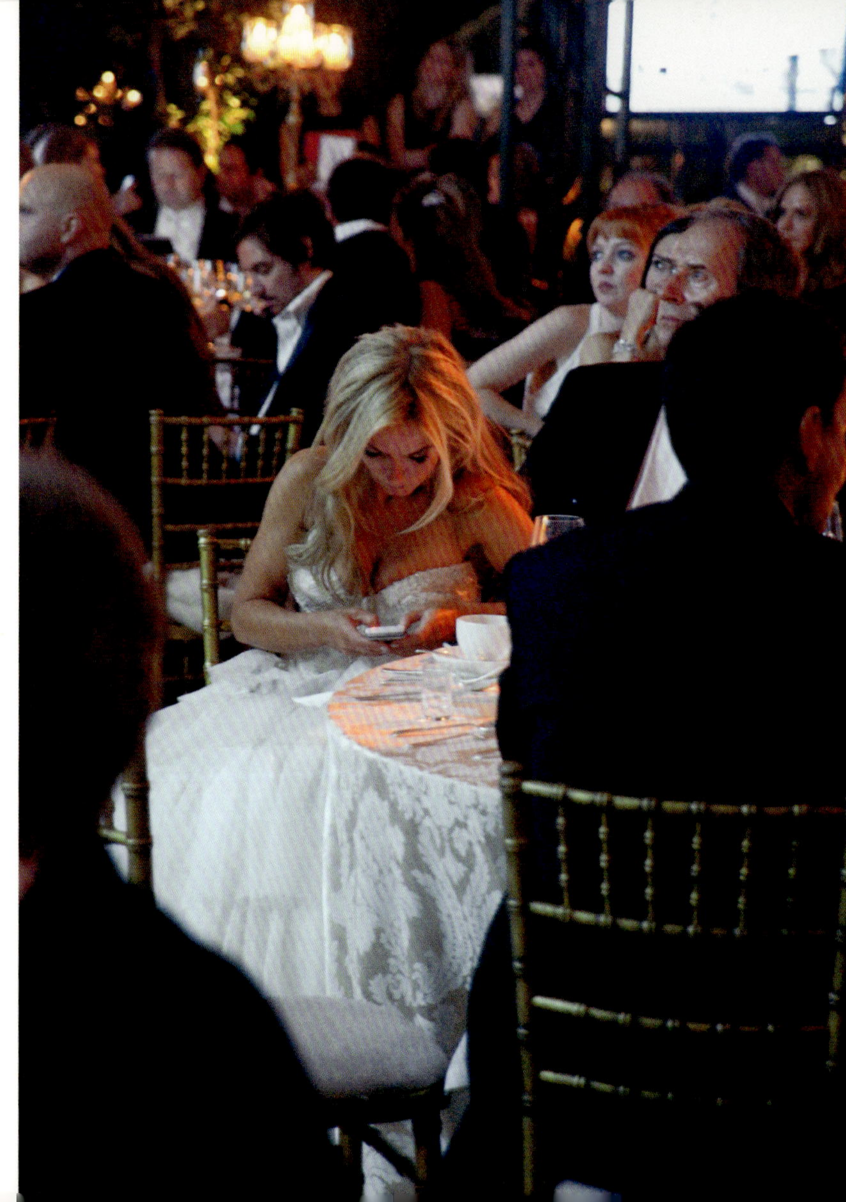

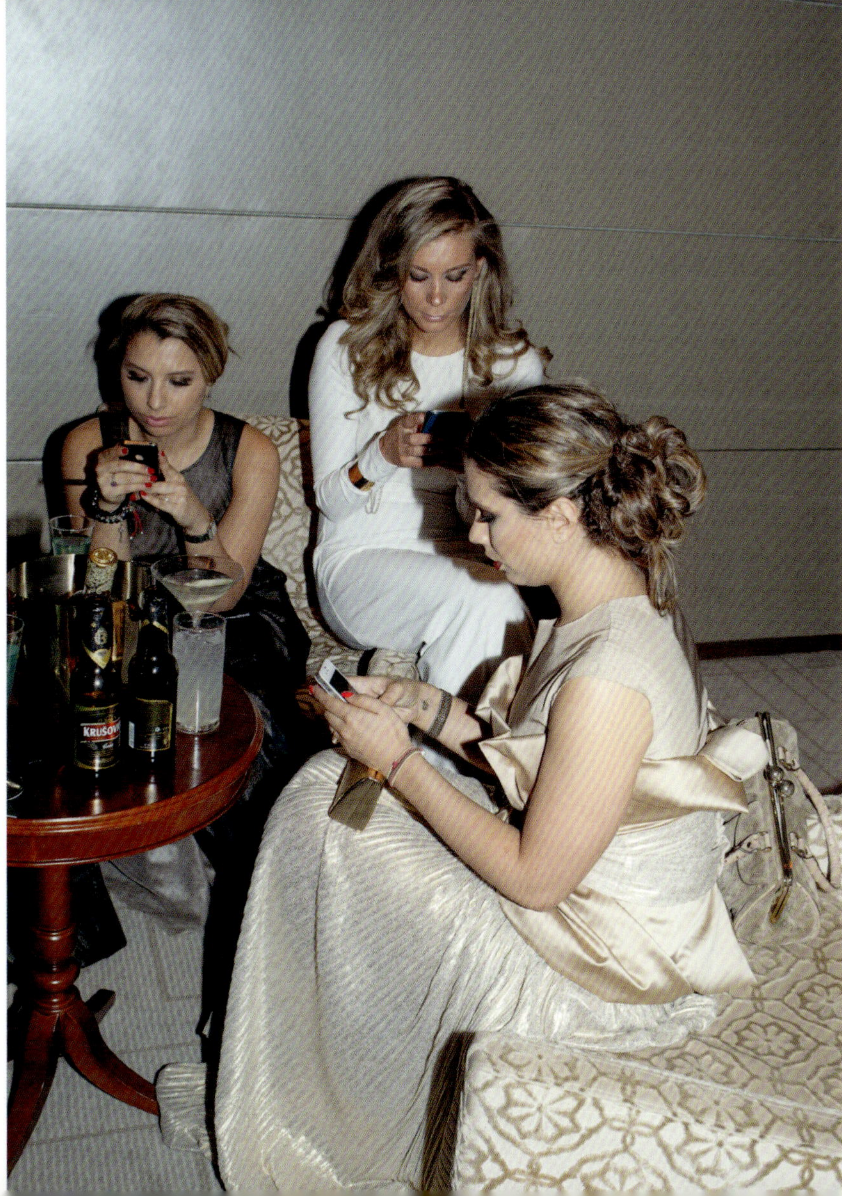

Mayfair, London 2013

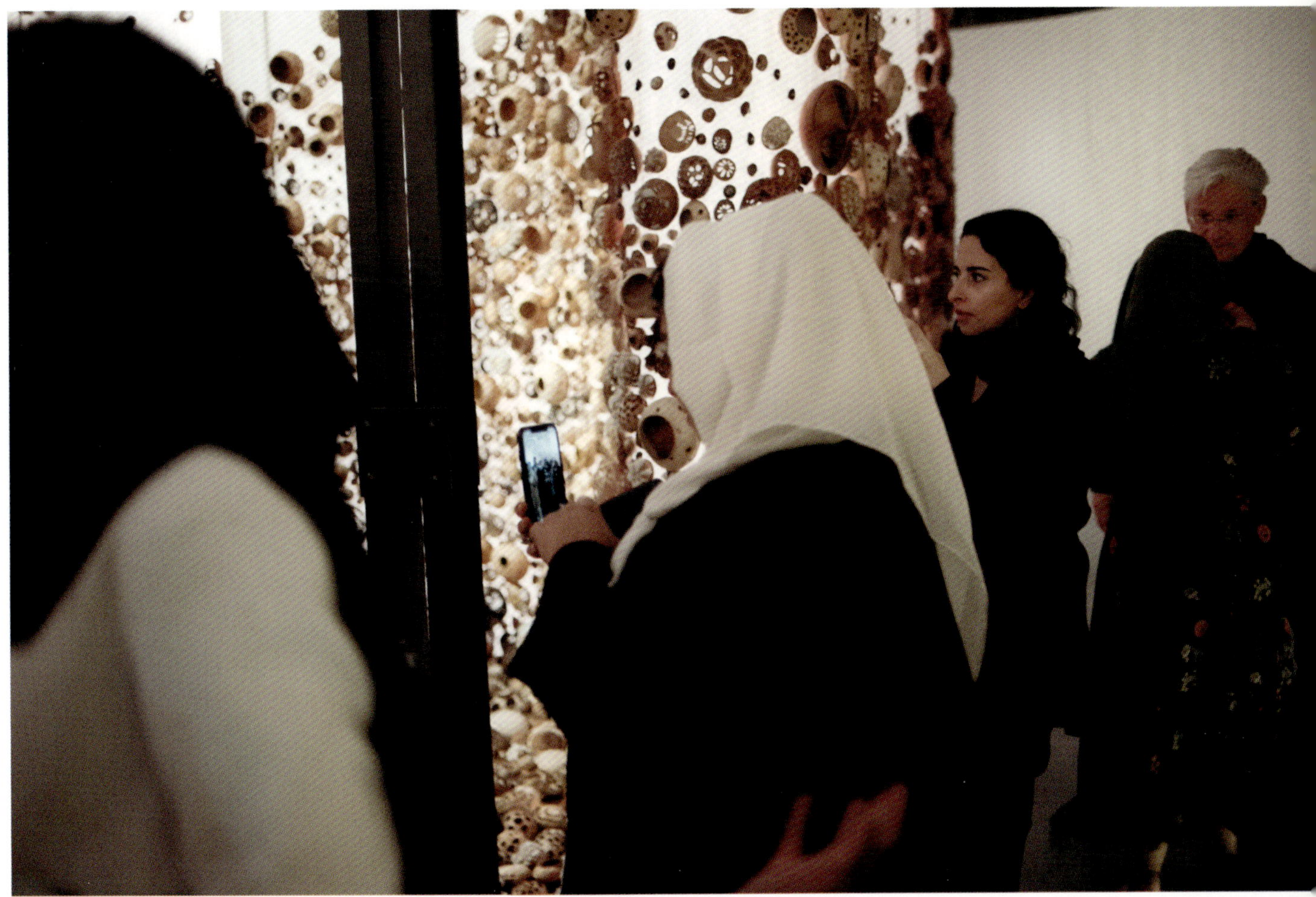

Venice 2019

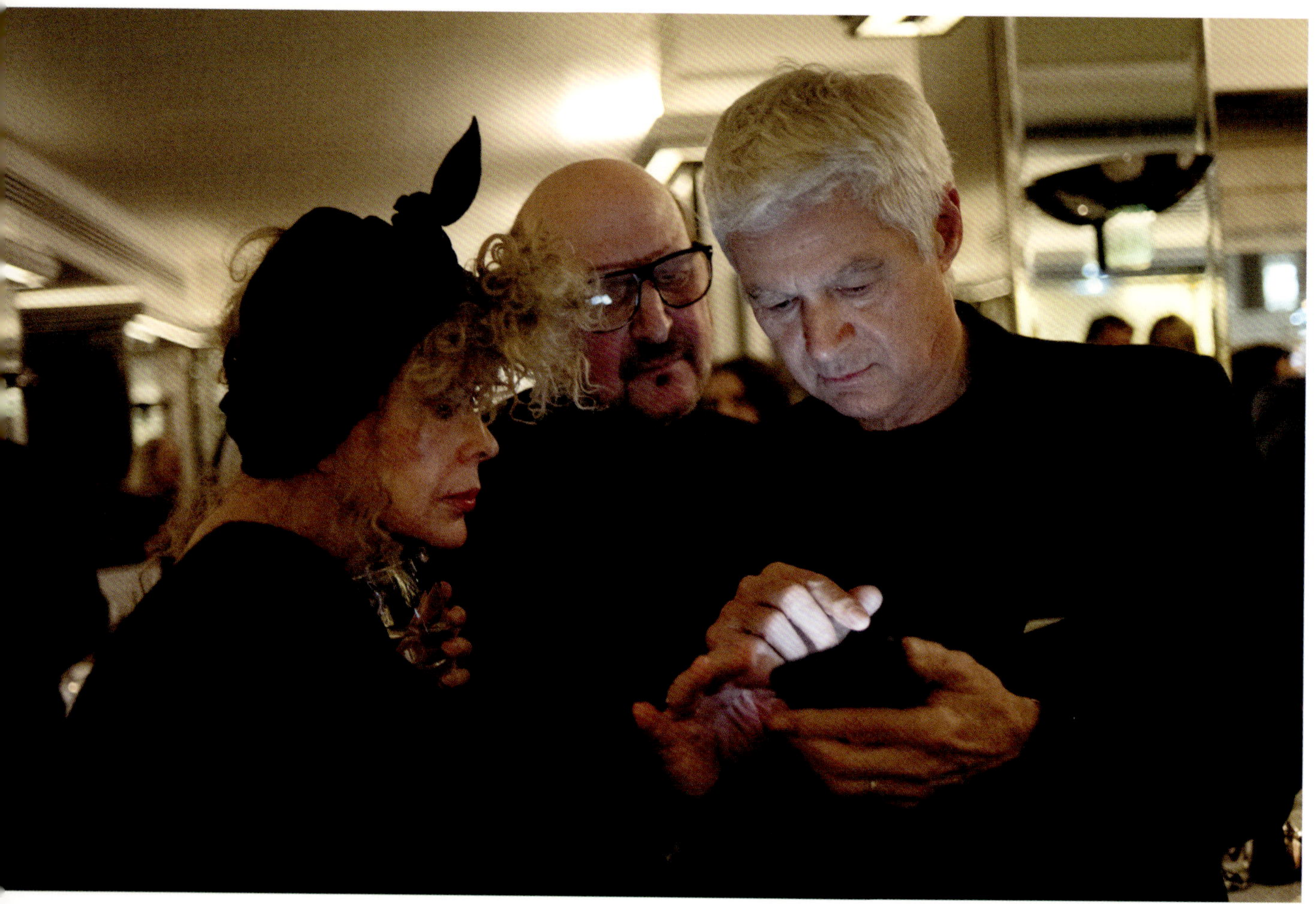

St James's, London 2019

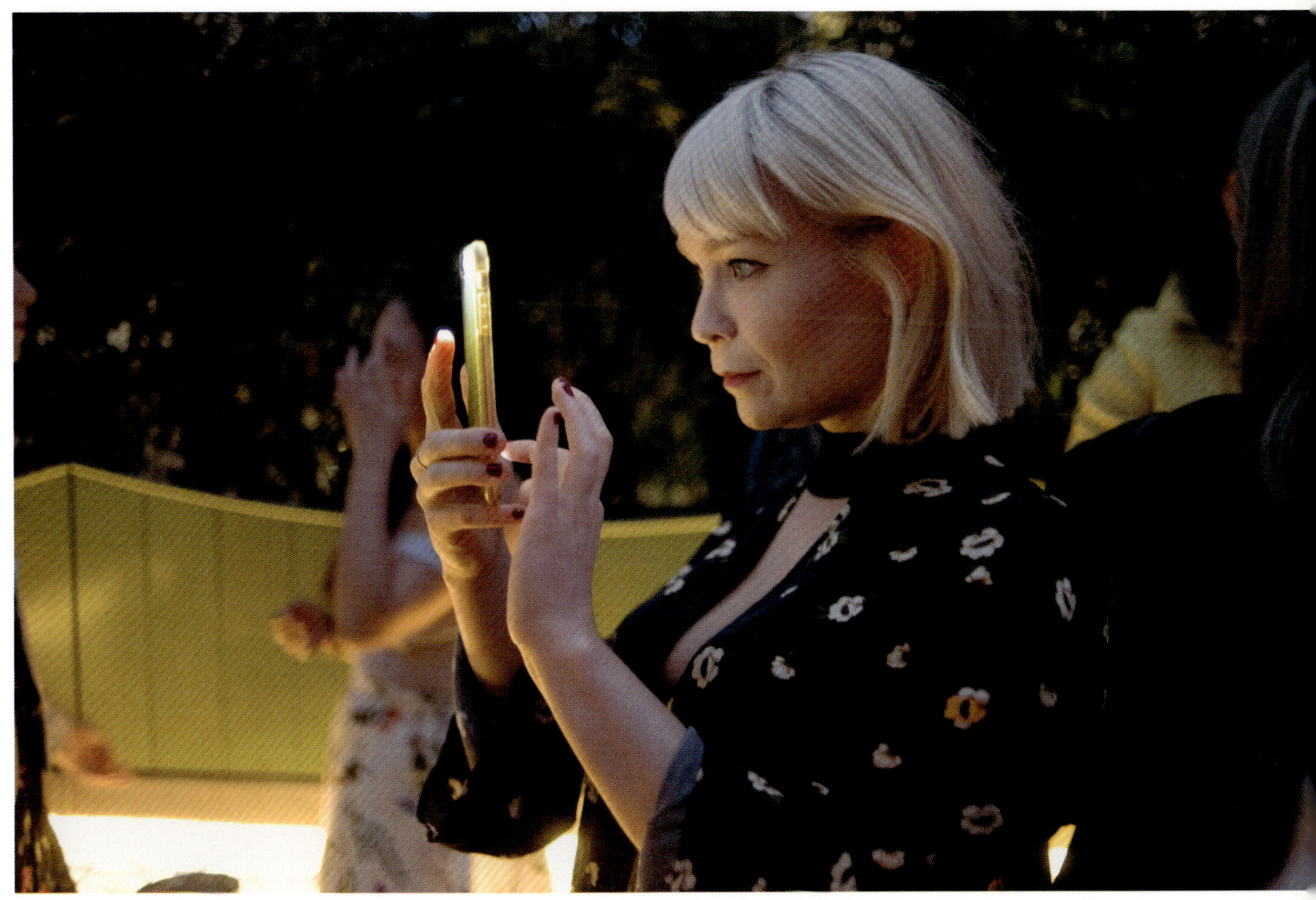

Mayfair, London 2017

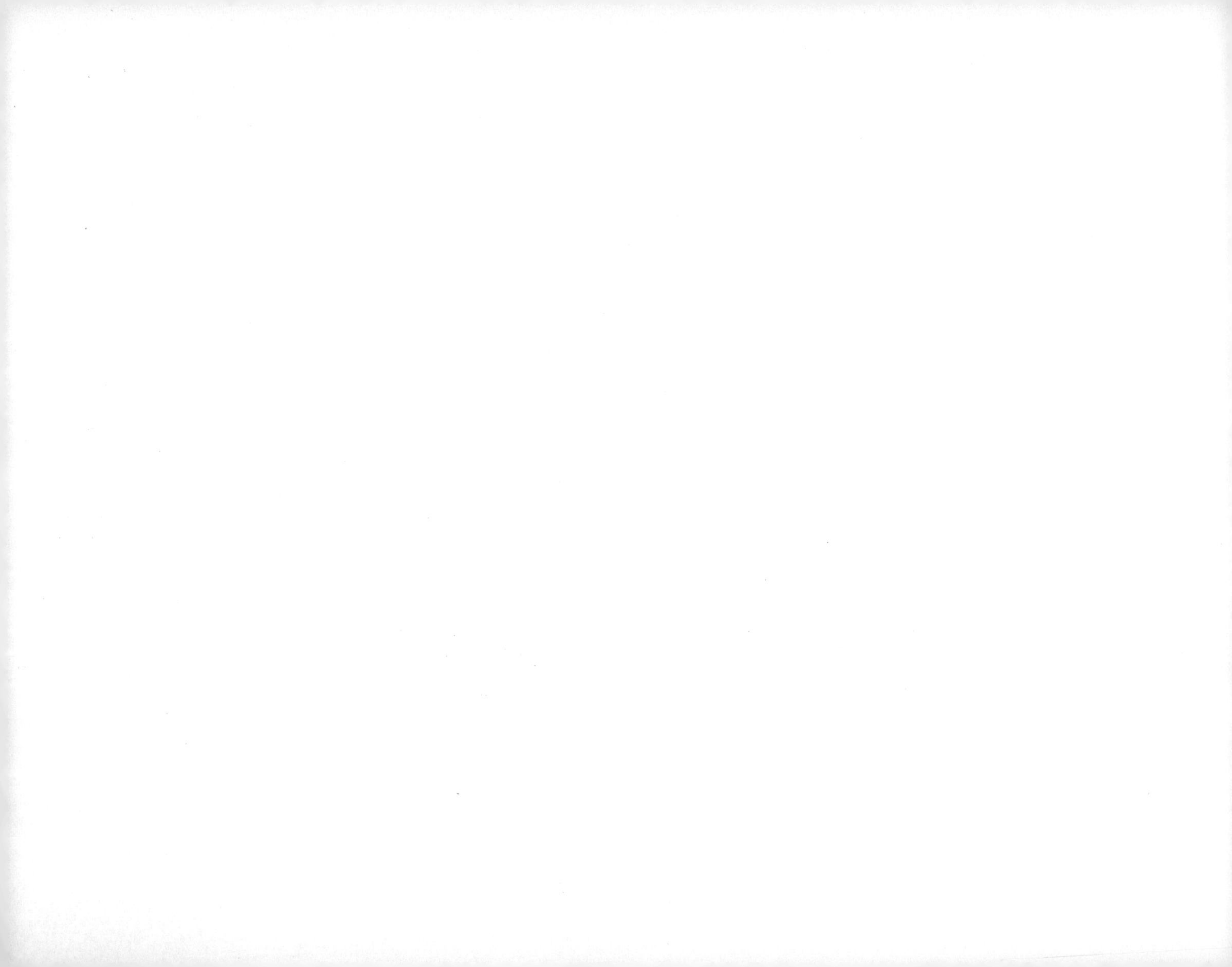

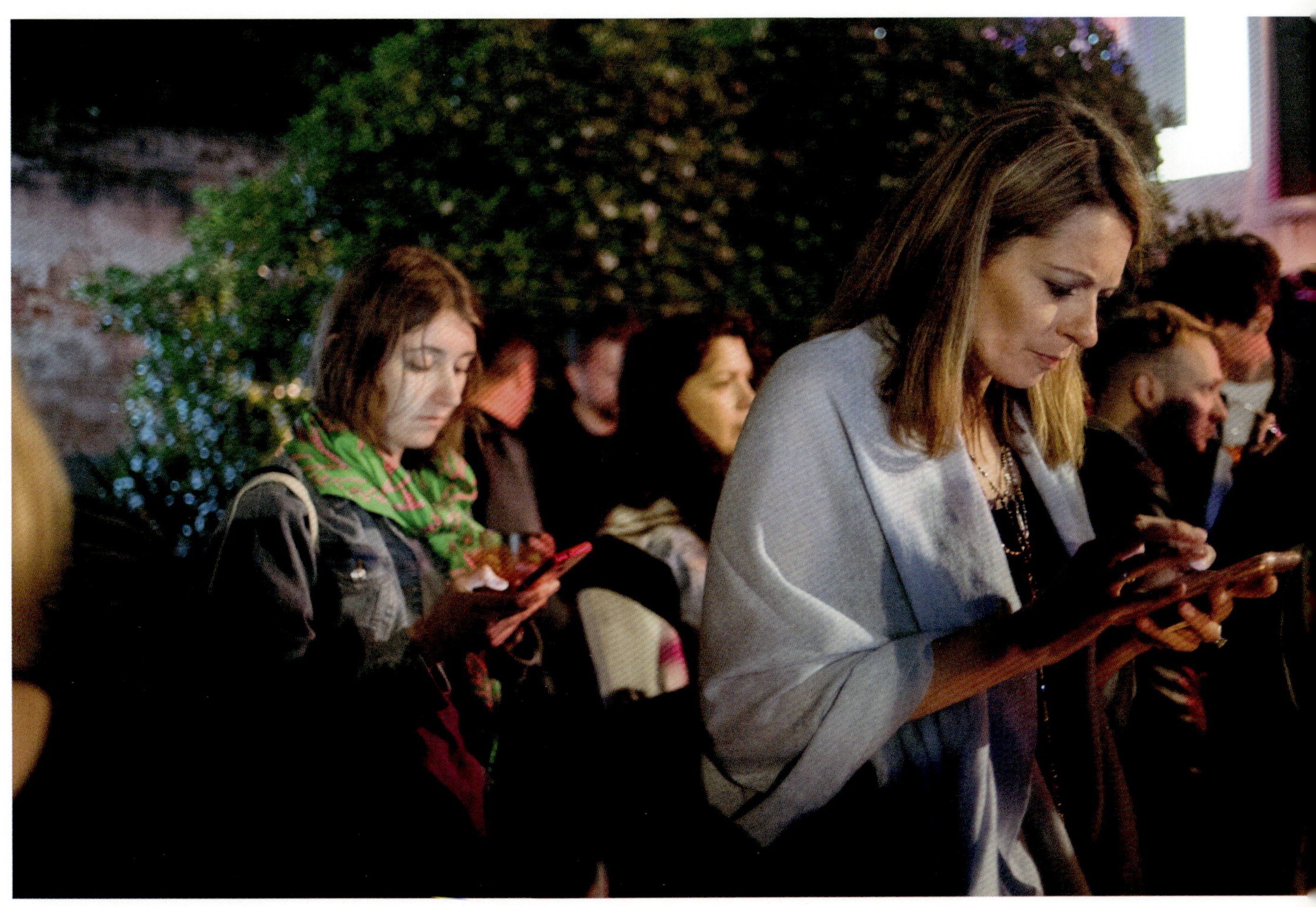

Palazzo Ca’ Tron, Venice 2019

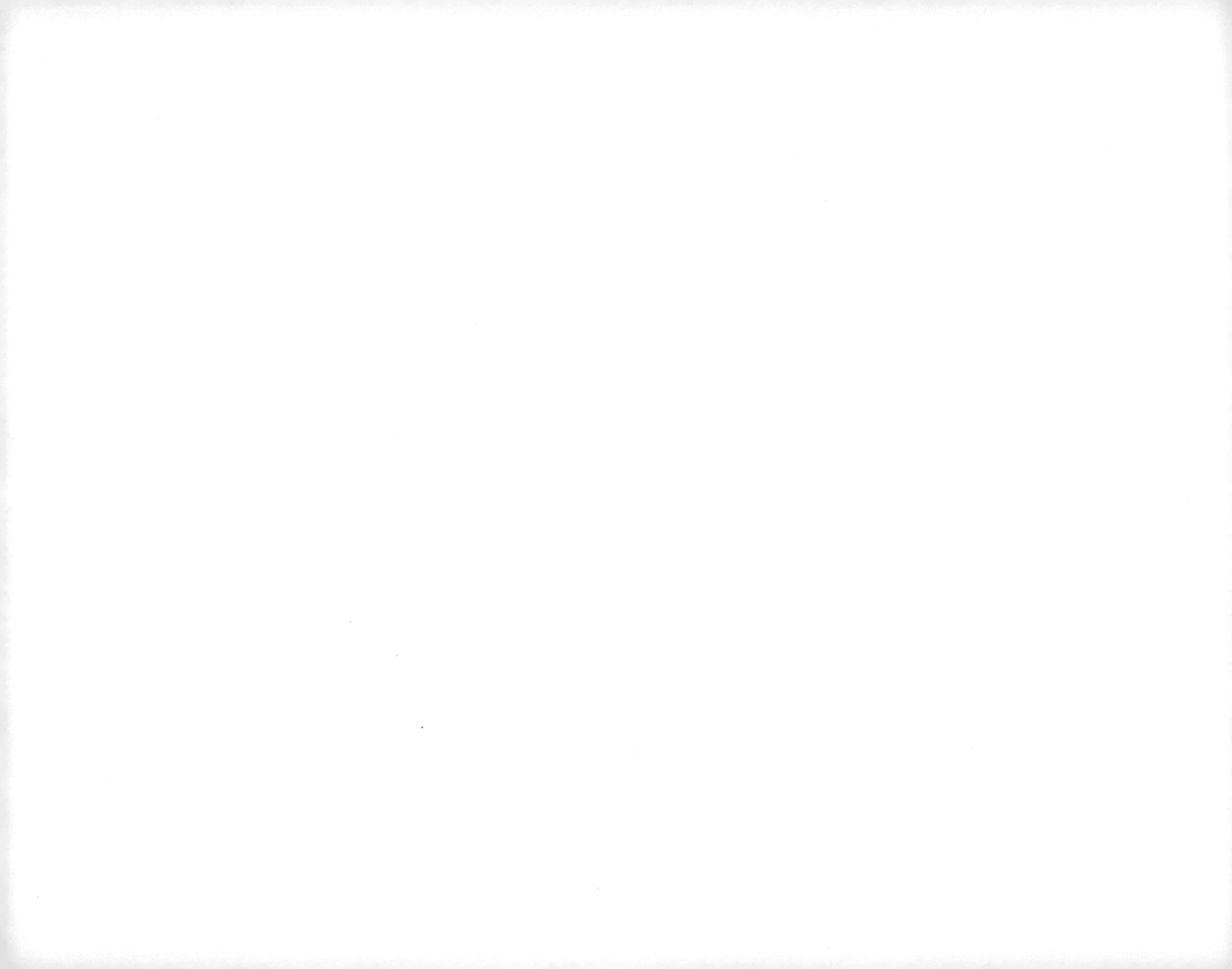

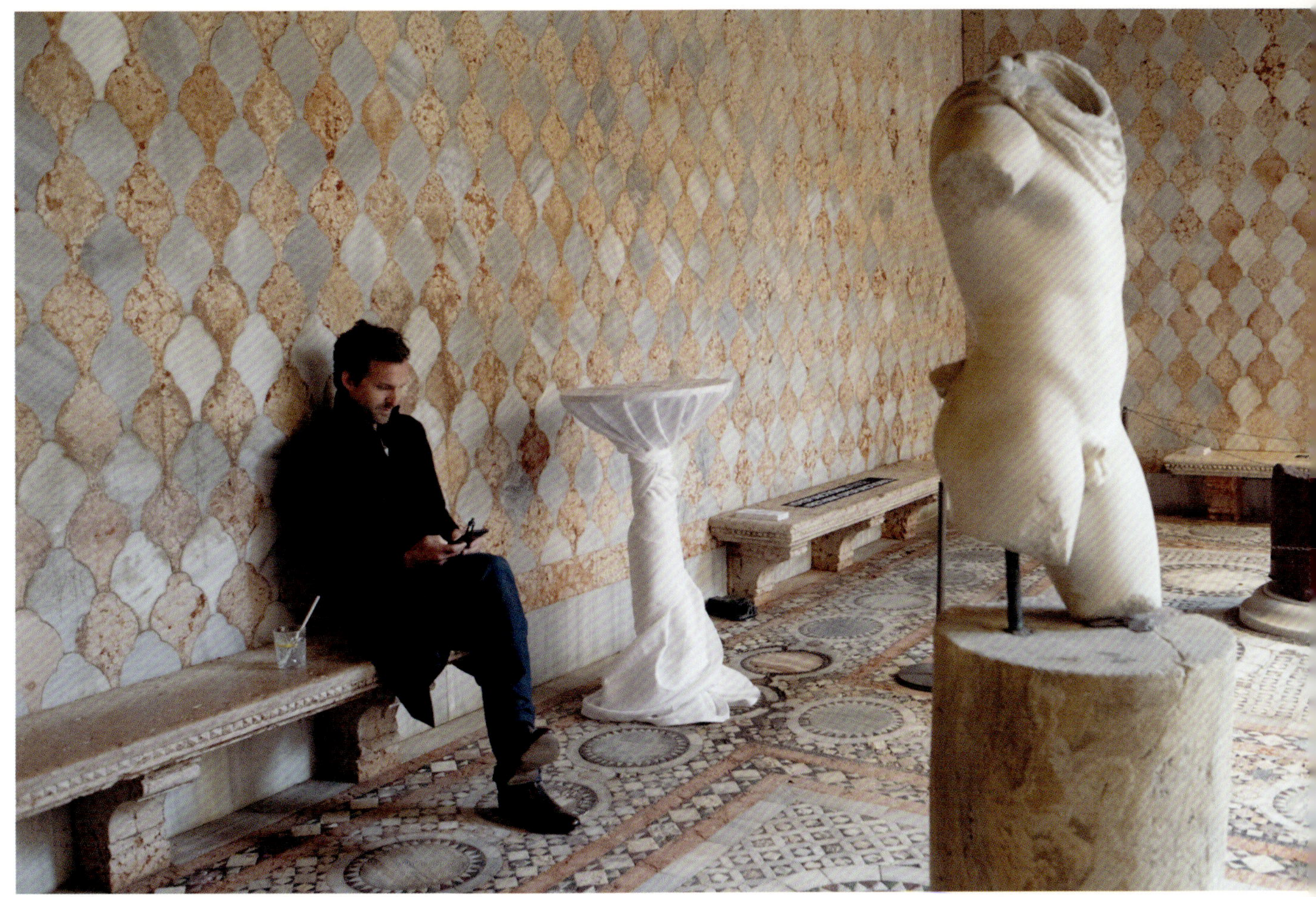

Ca’ d’Oro, Venice 2019

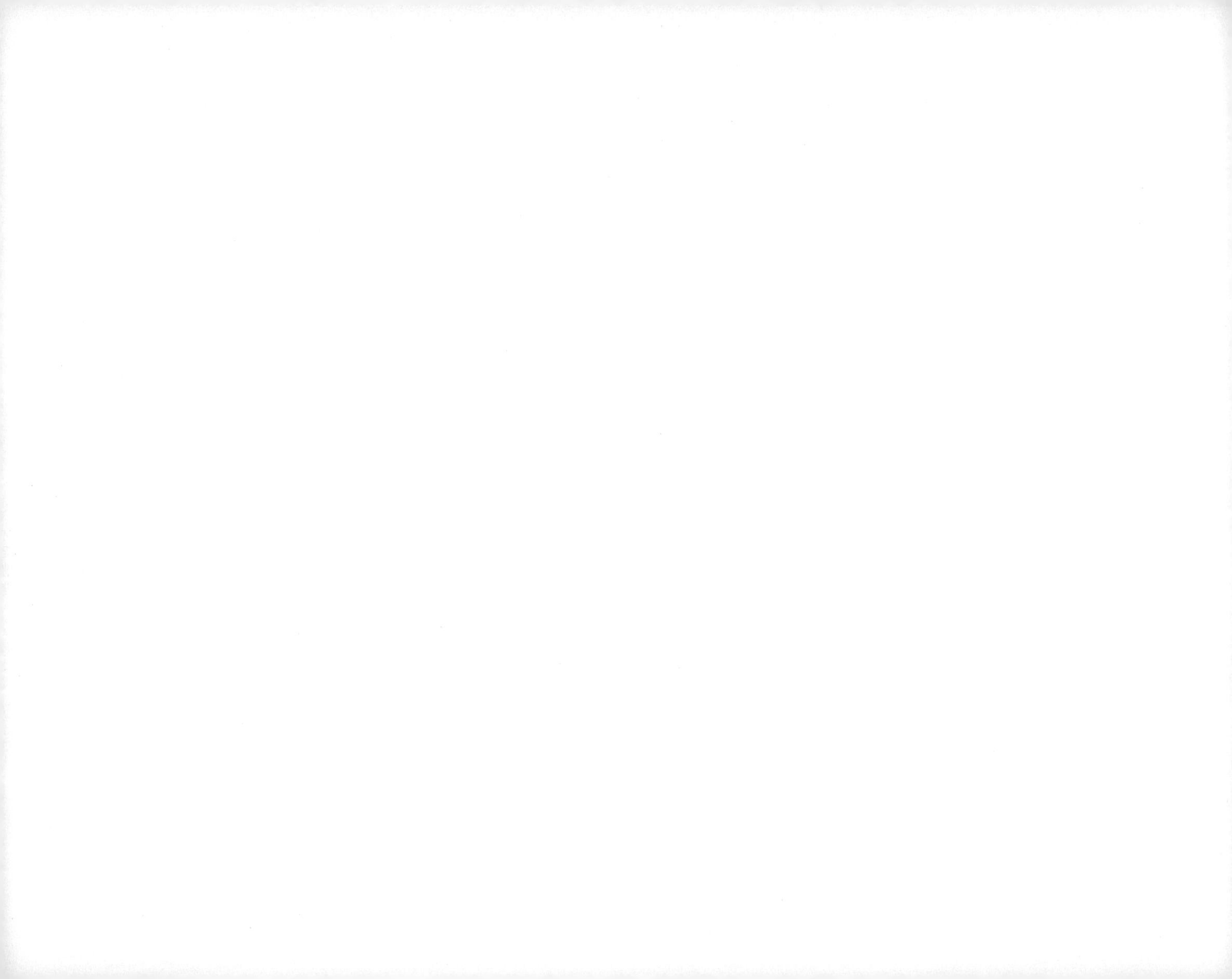

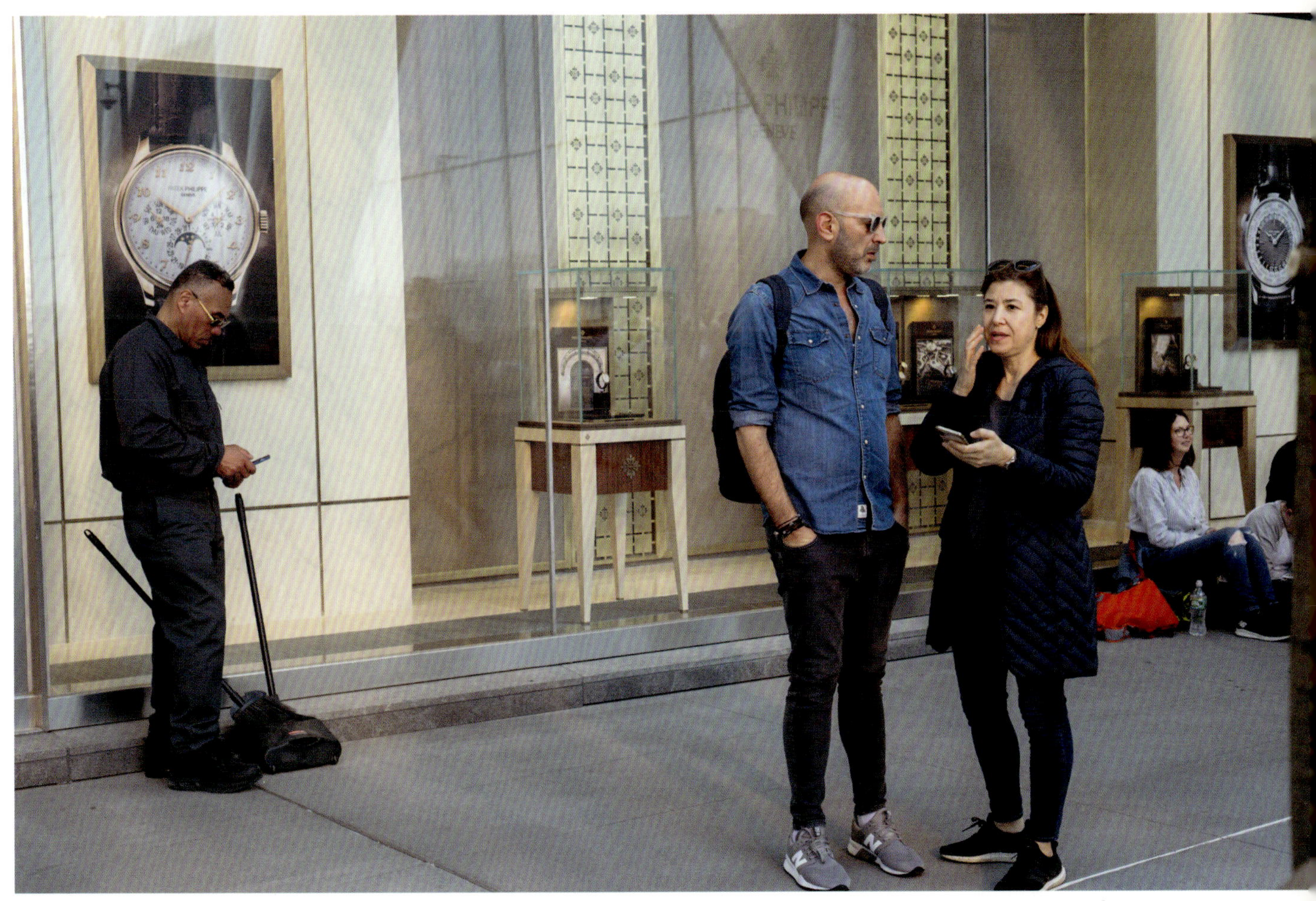

Hudson Yards, Manhattan 2019

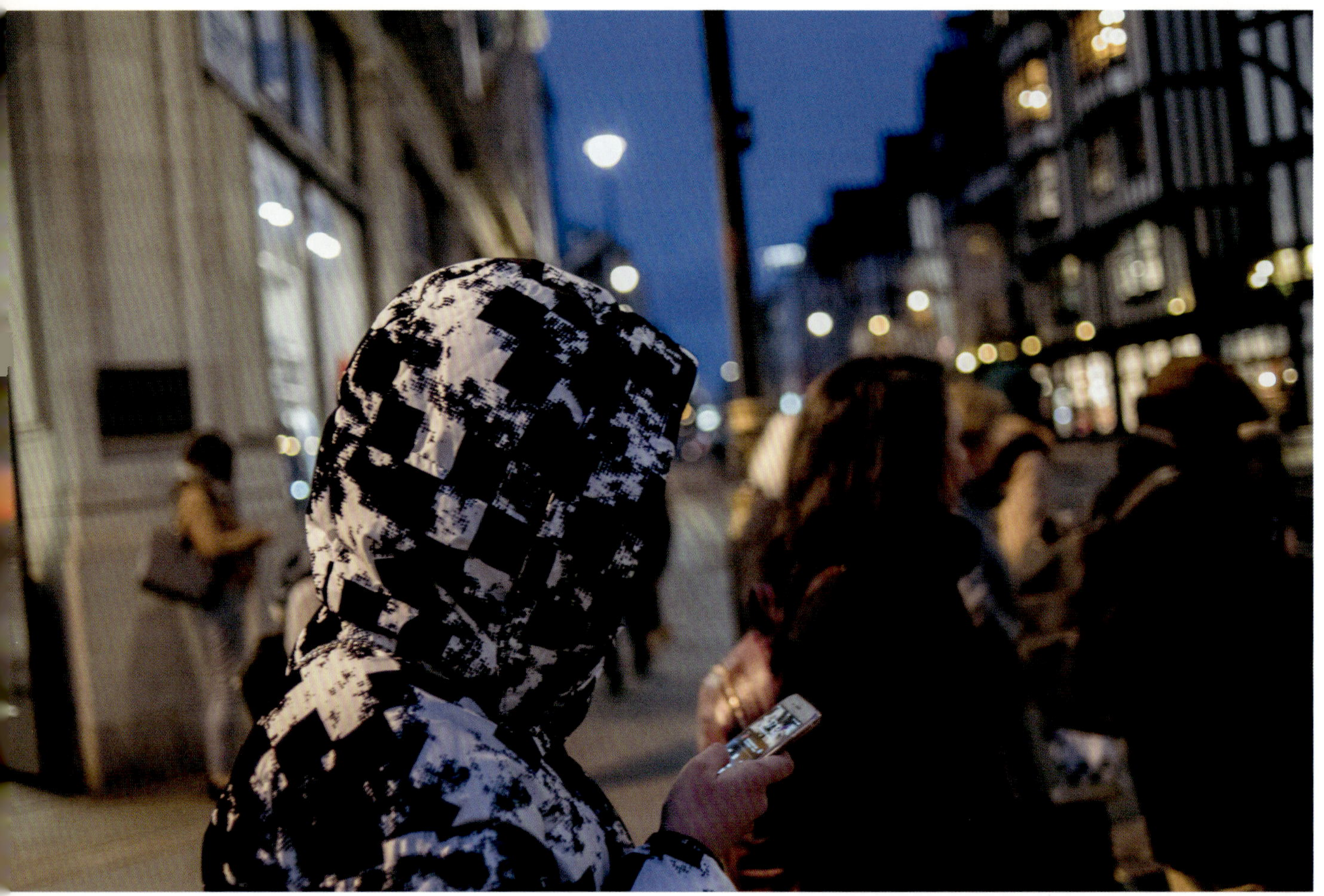

Soho, London 2019

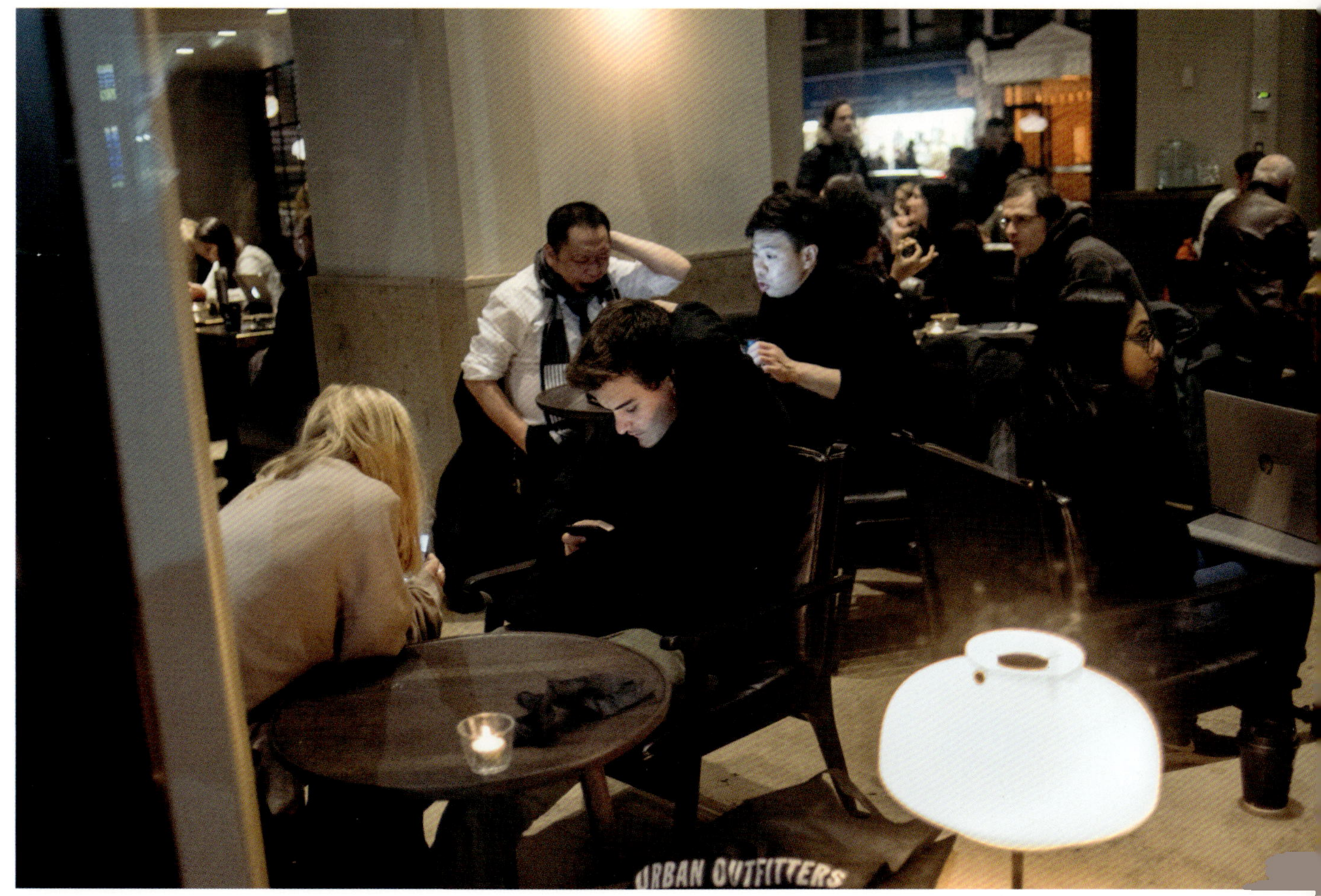

Soho, London 2019

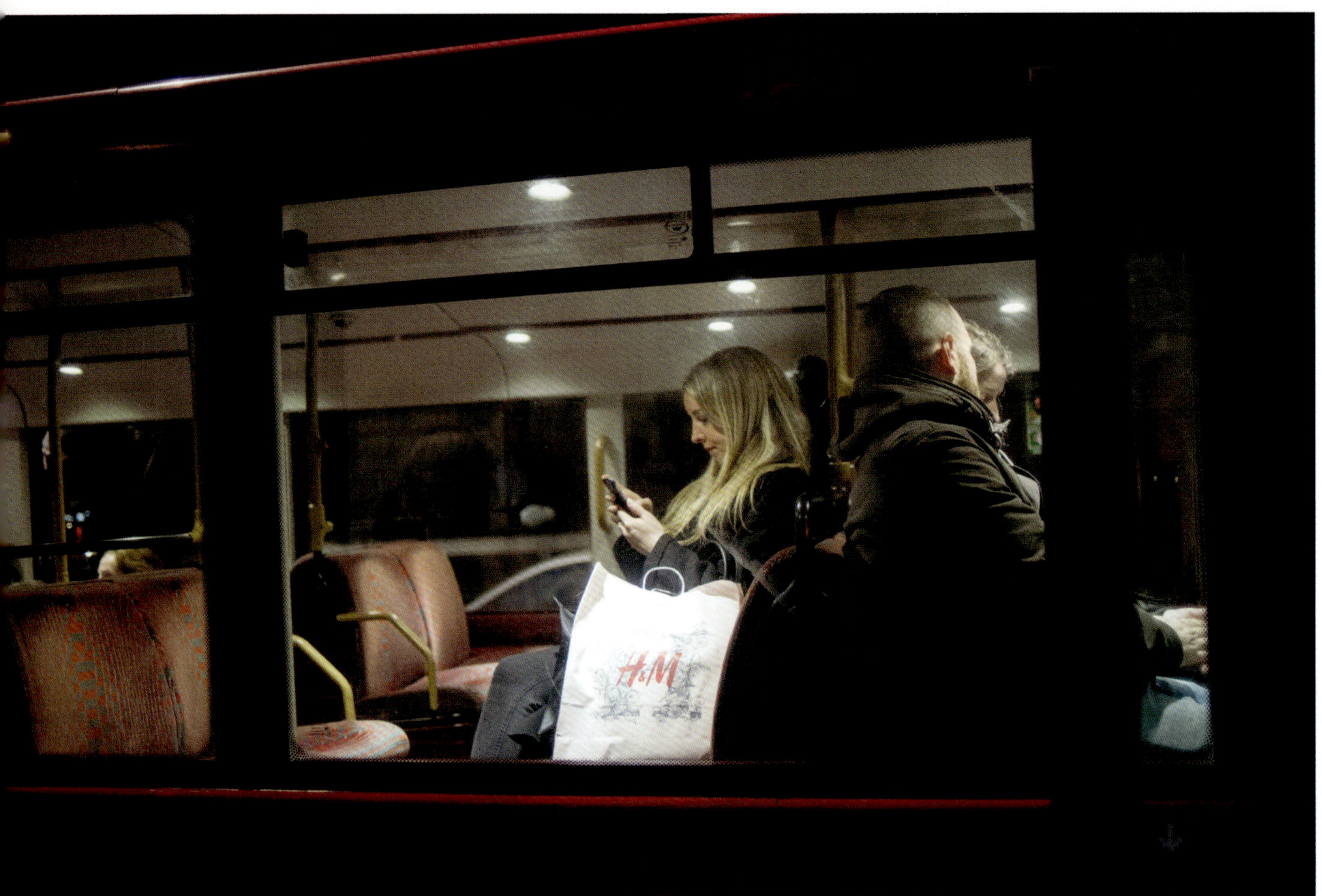

Mayfair, London 2019

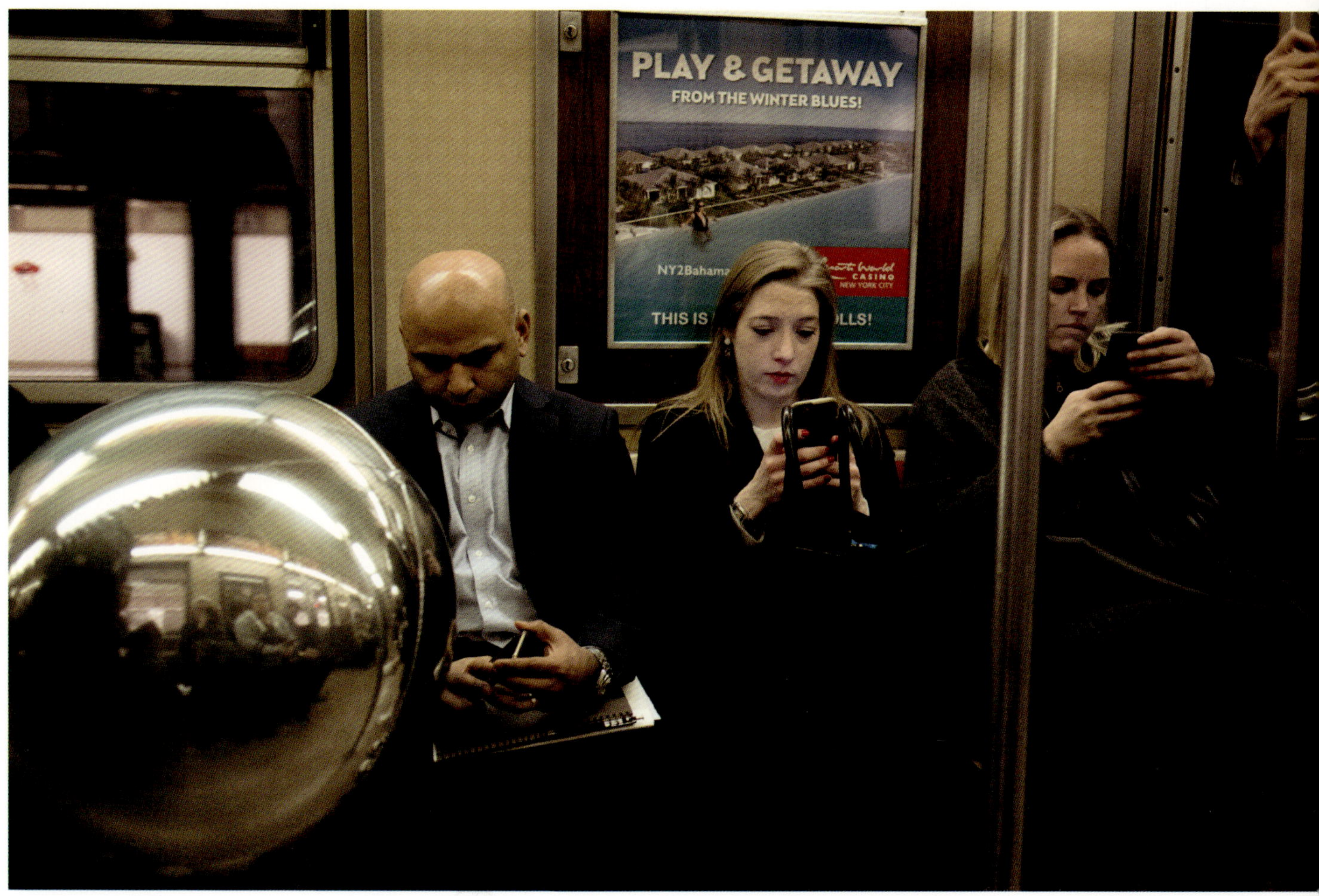

New York City Subway 2019

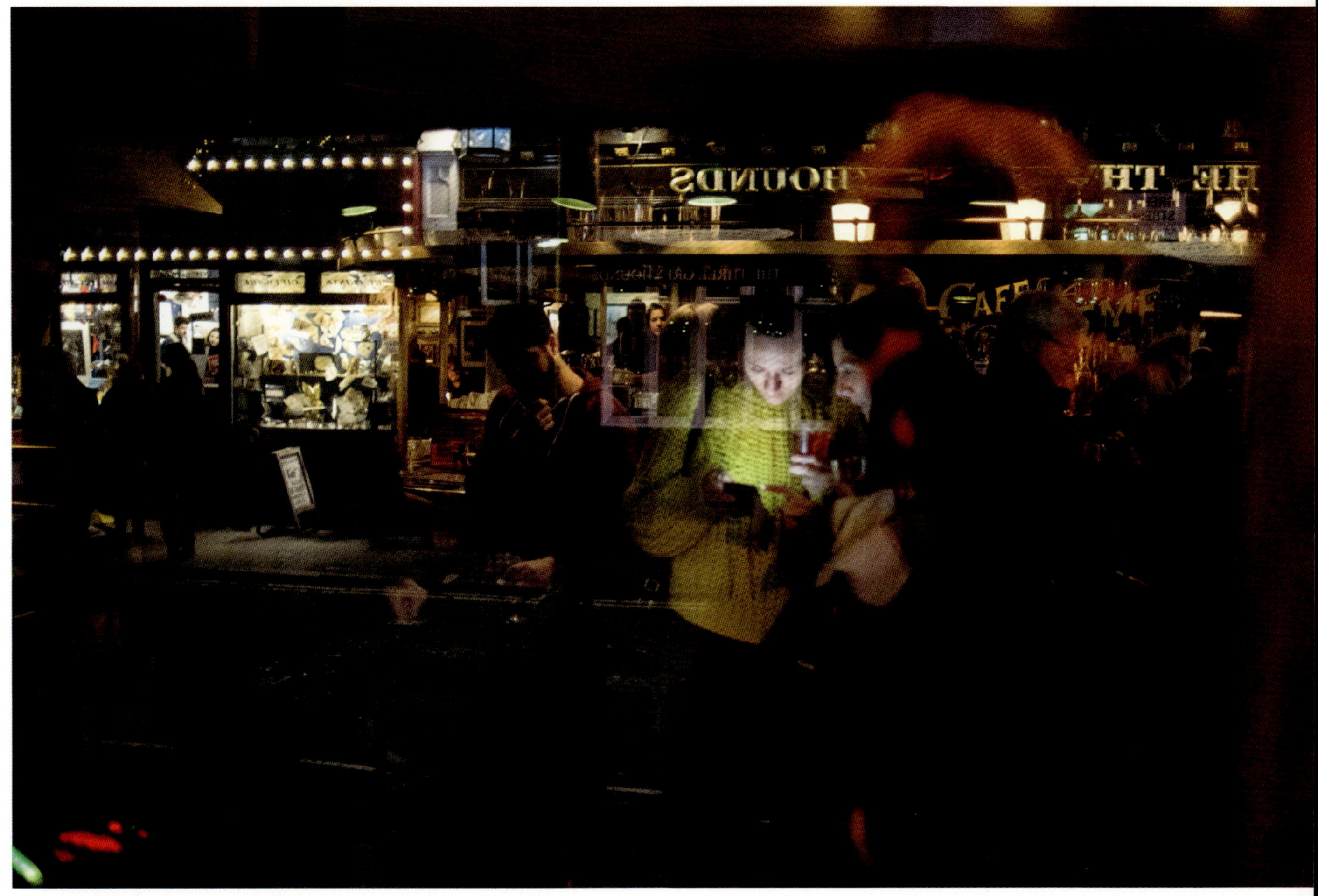

Soho, London 2019

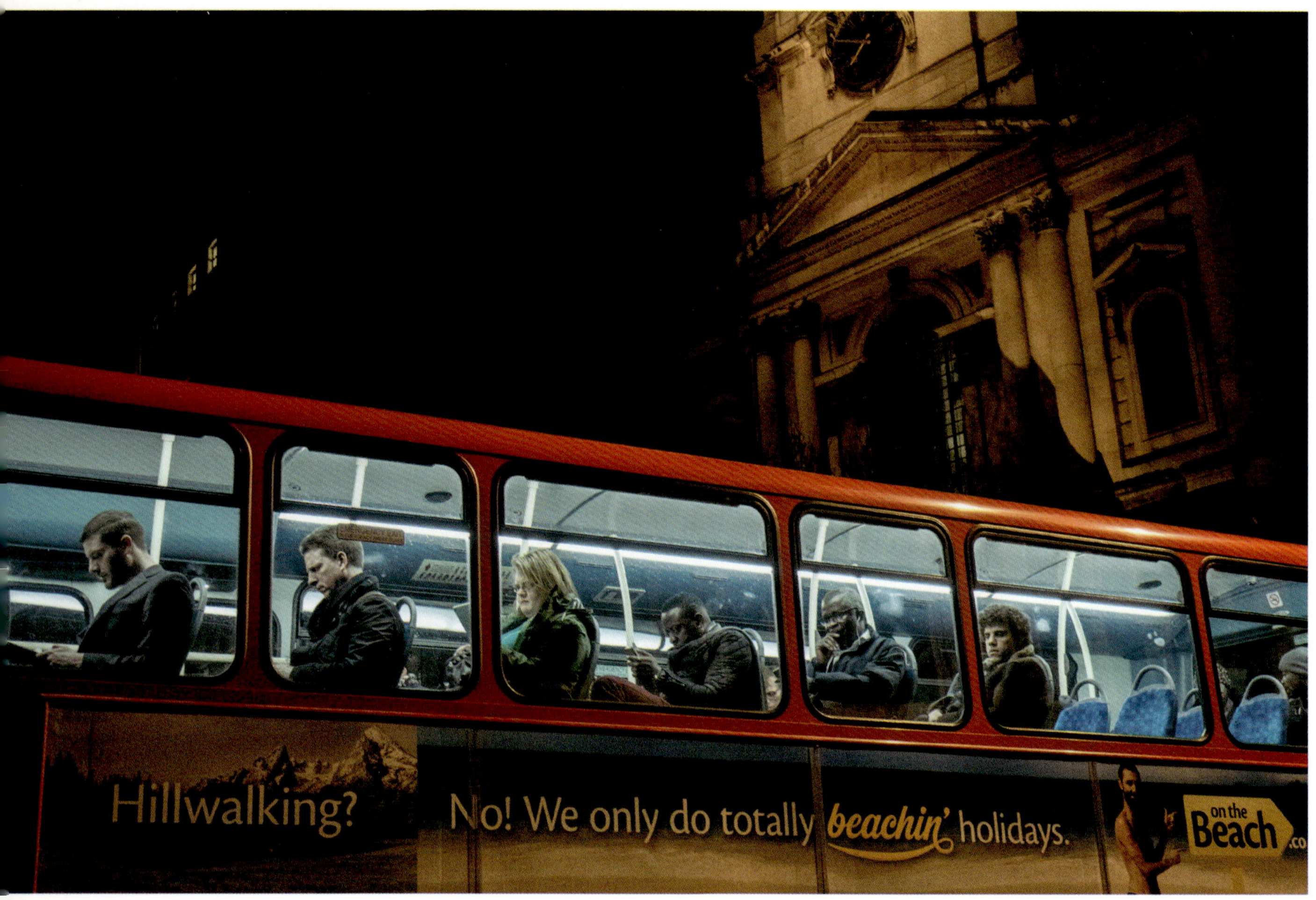

Strand, London 2016

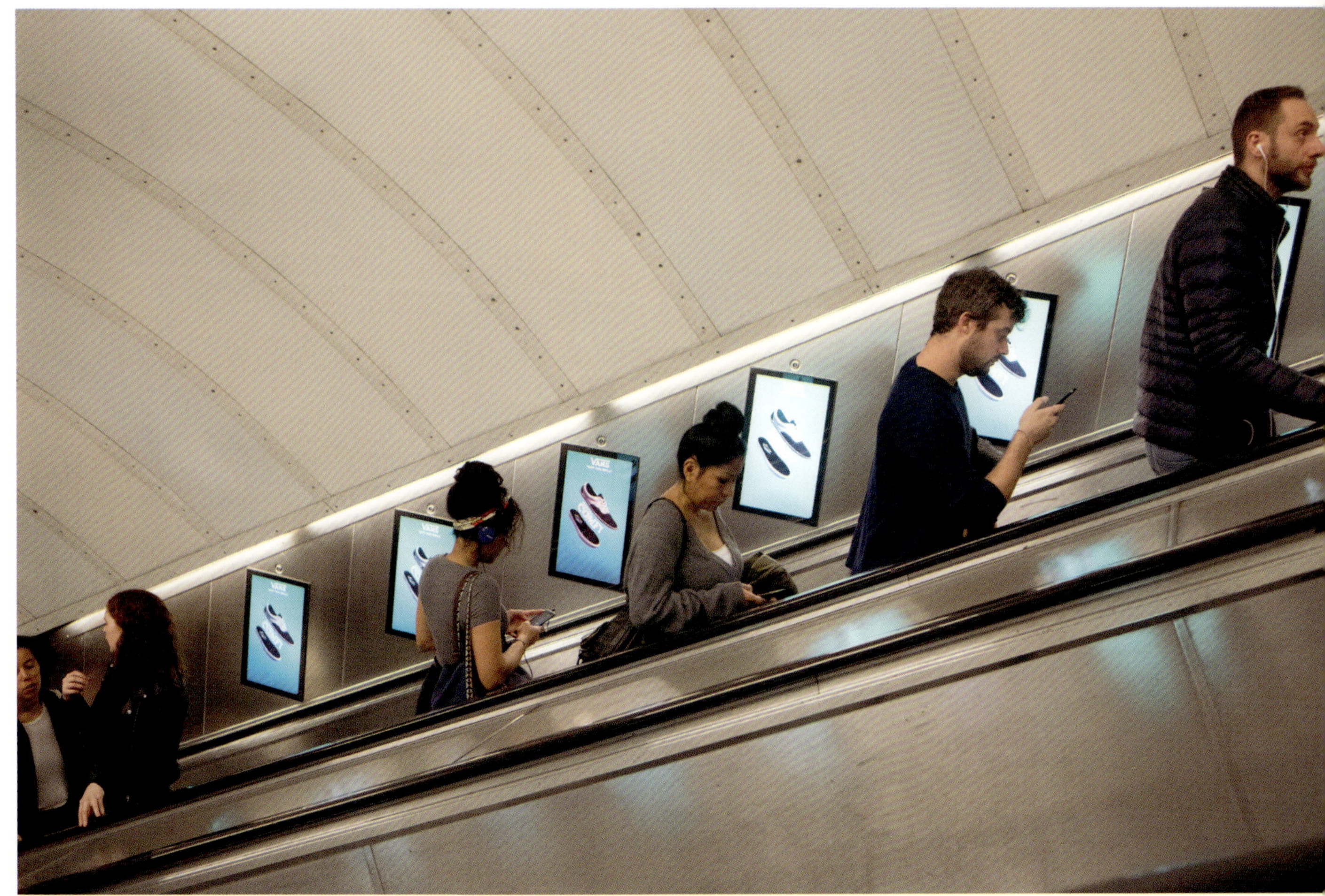

London Underground 2019

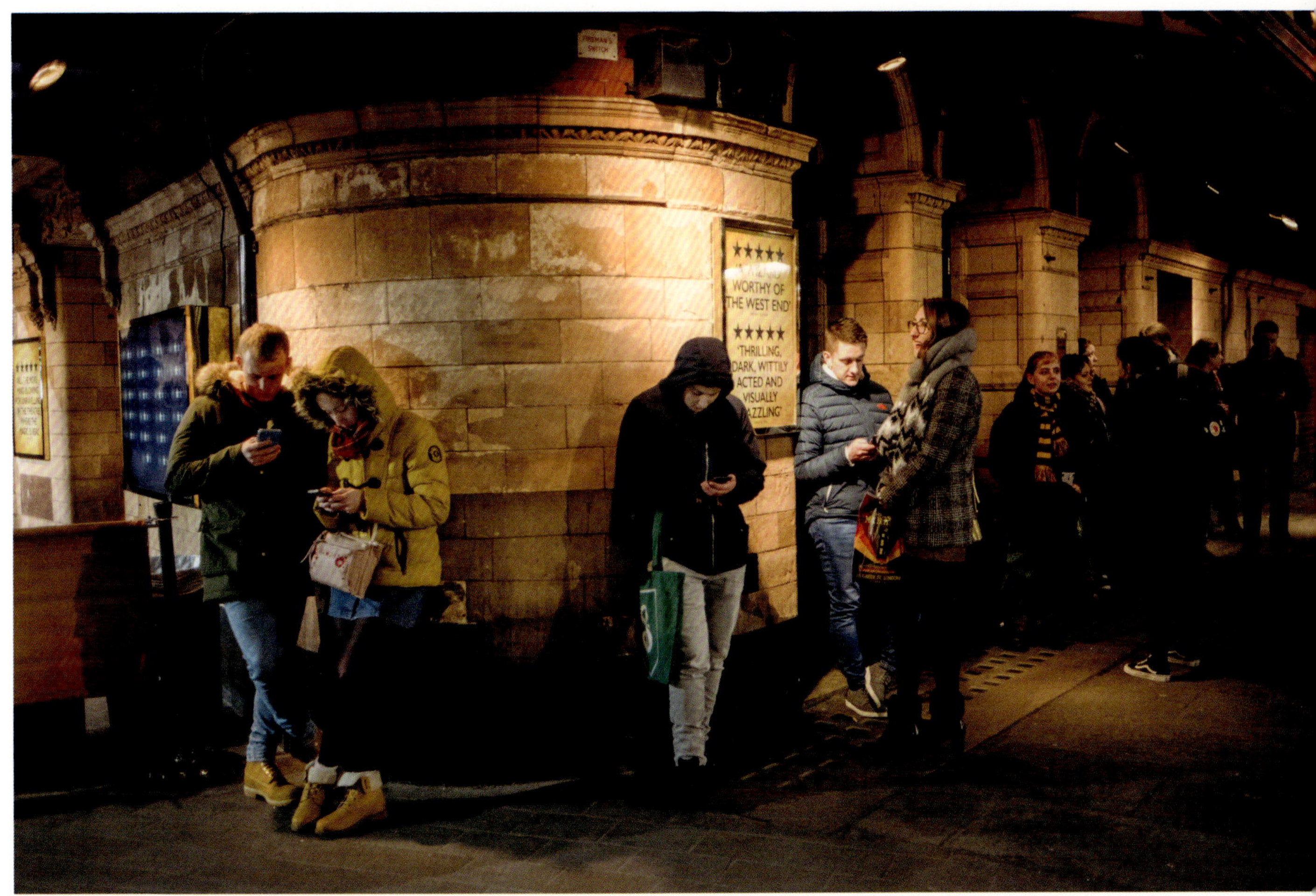

Soho, London 2019

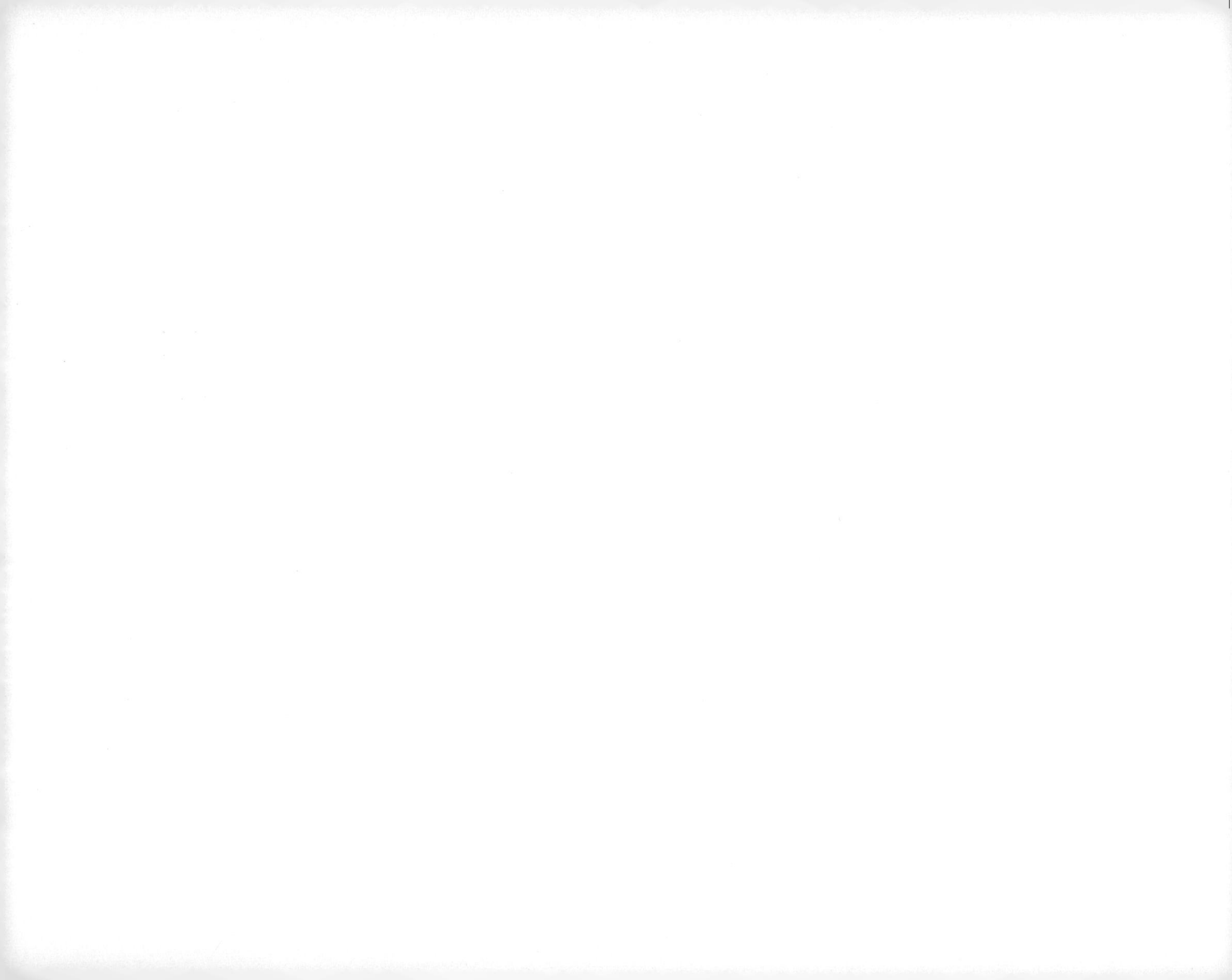

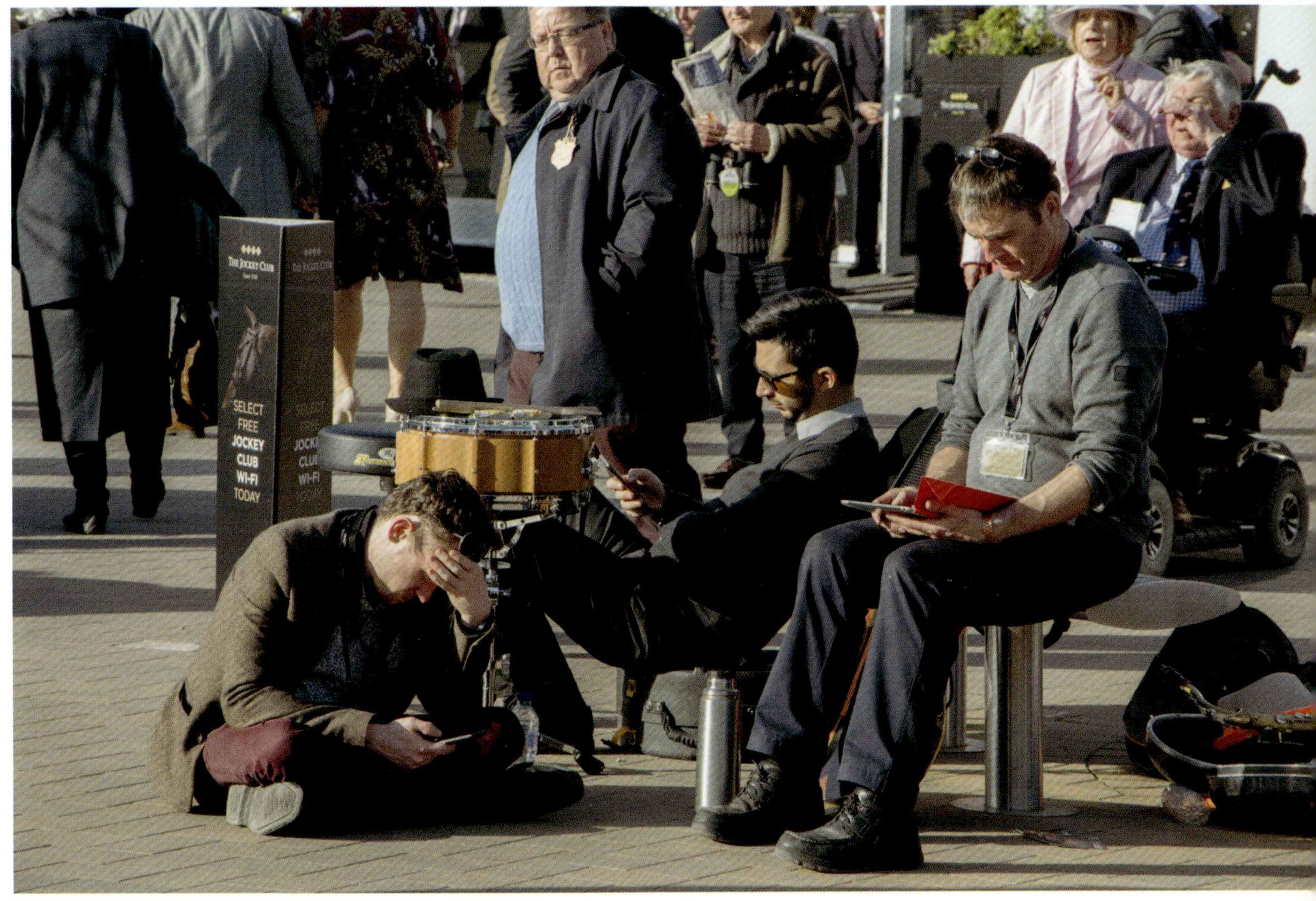

Cheltenham 2017

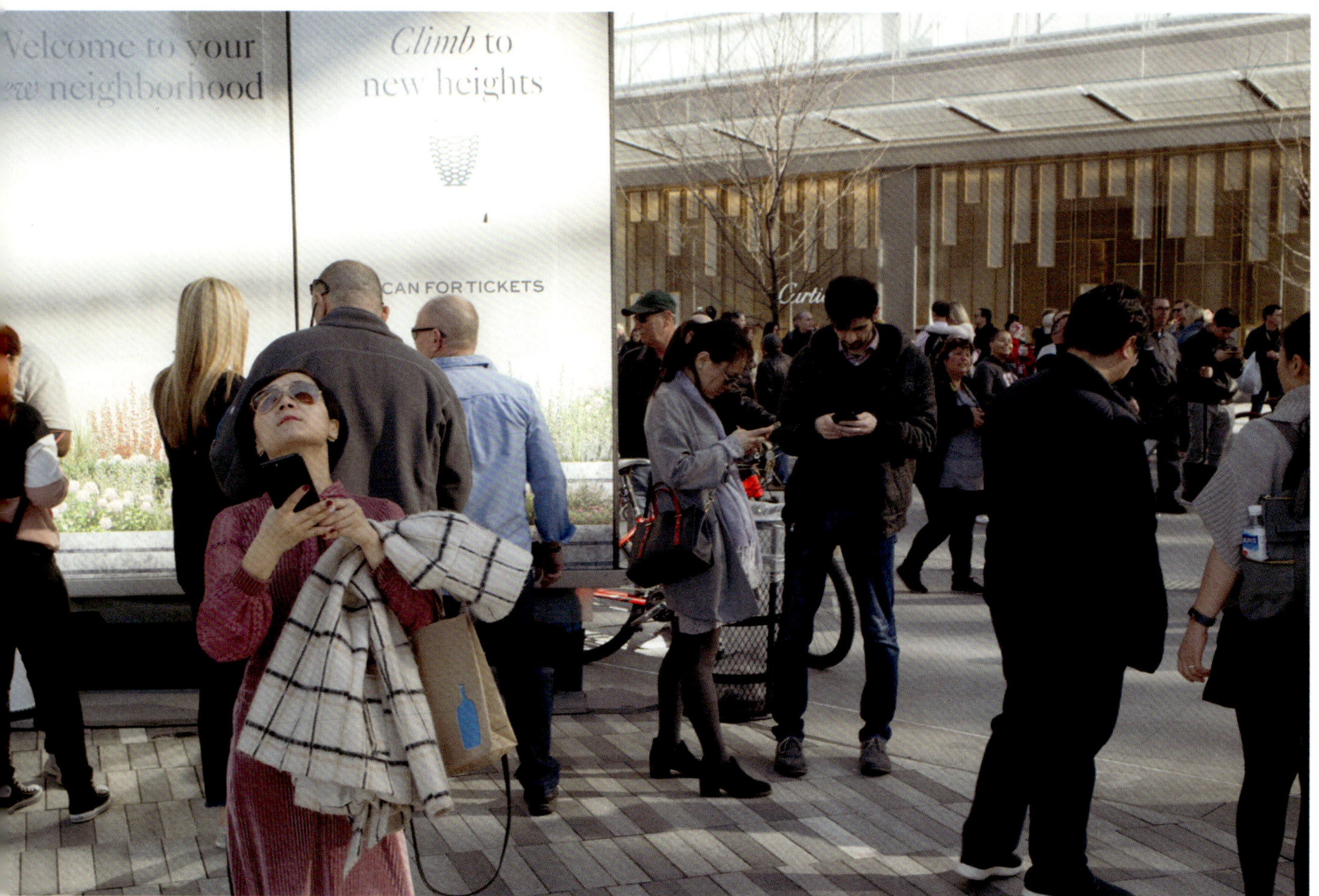

Hudson Yards, Manhattan 2019

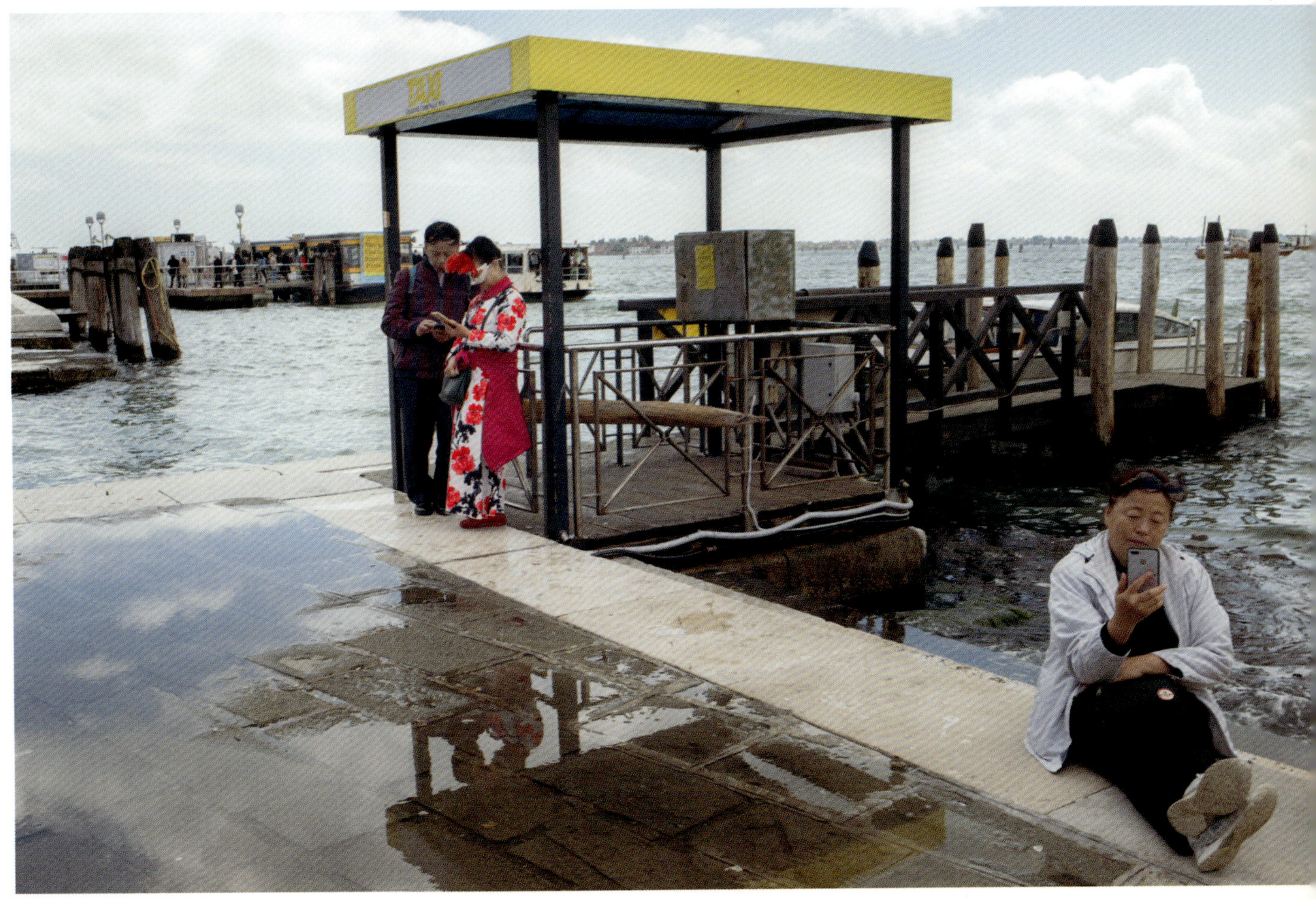

Piazza San Marco, Venice 2019

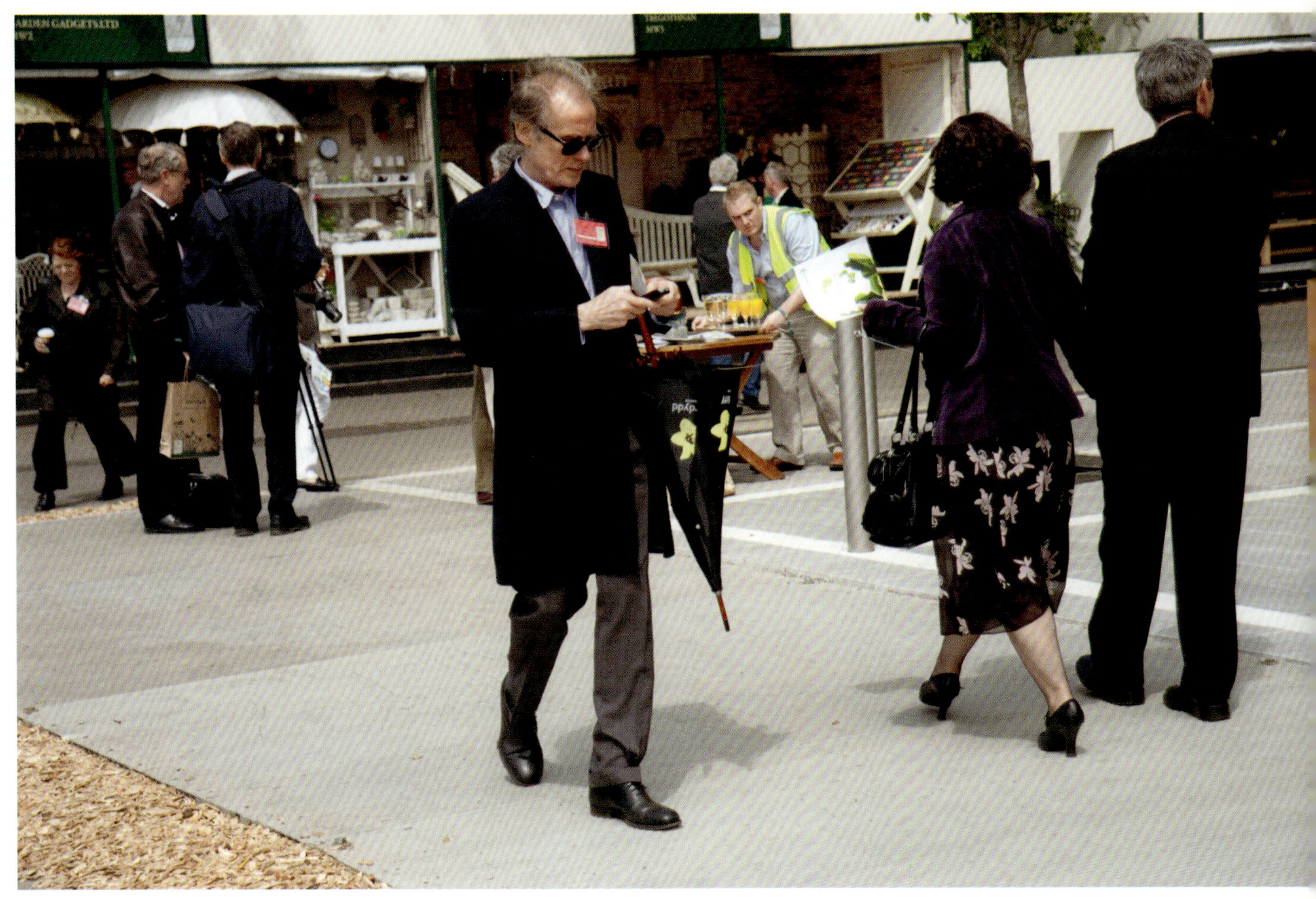

Chelsea, London 2009

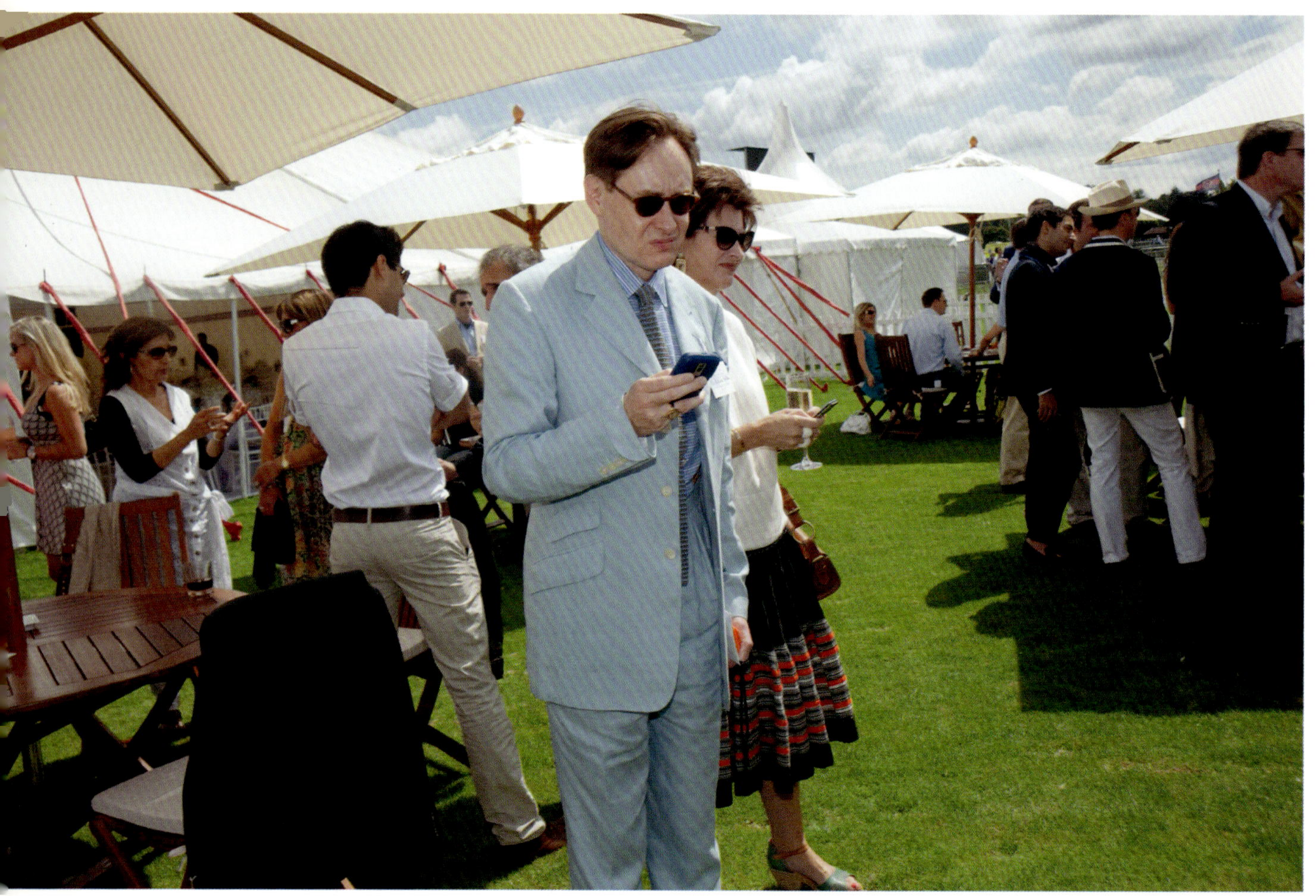

Windsor Great Park 2010

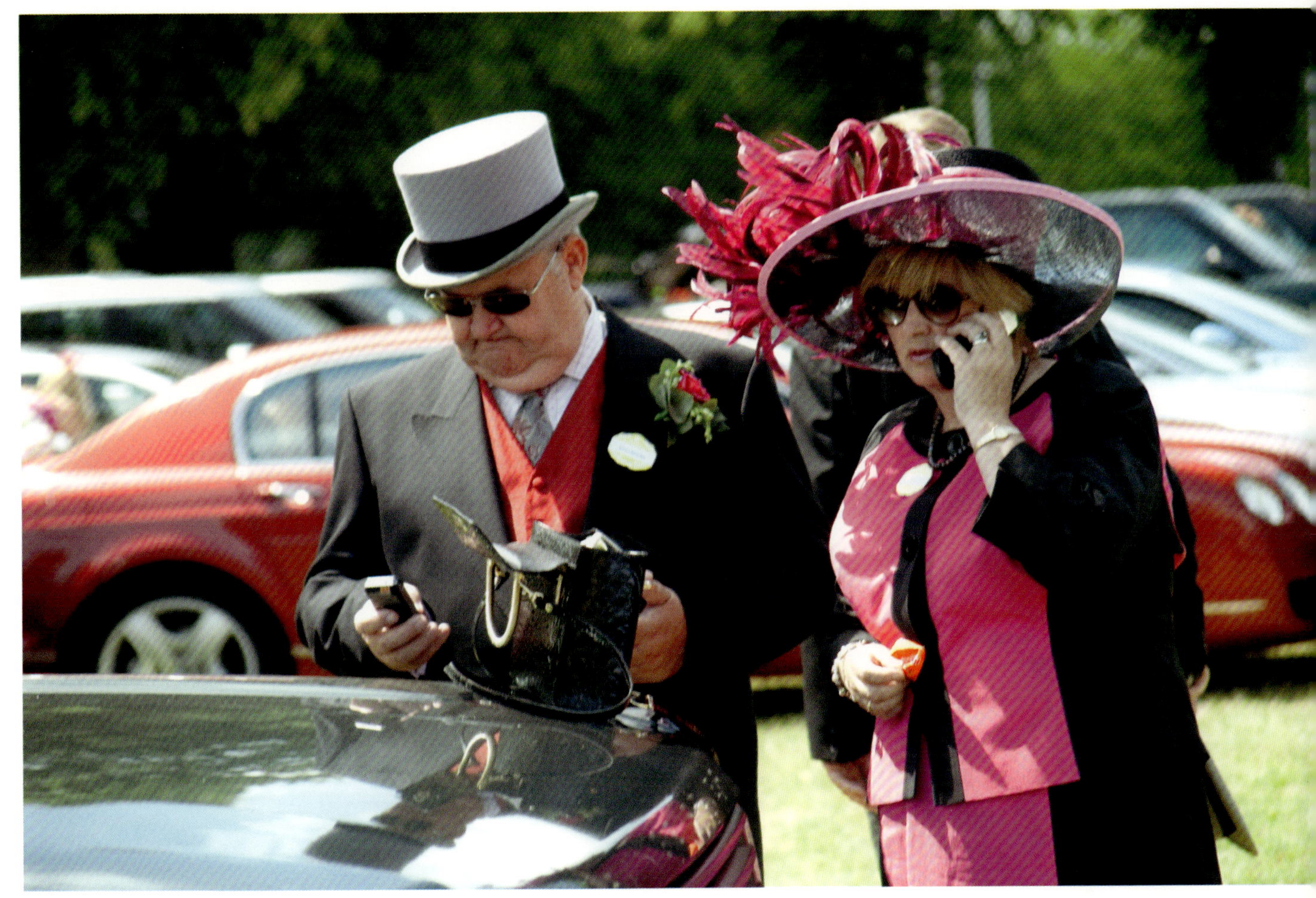

Royal Ascot 2011

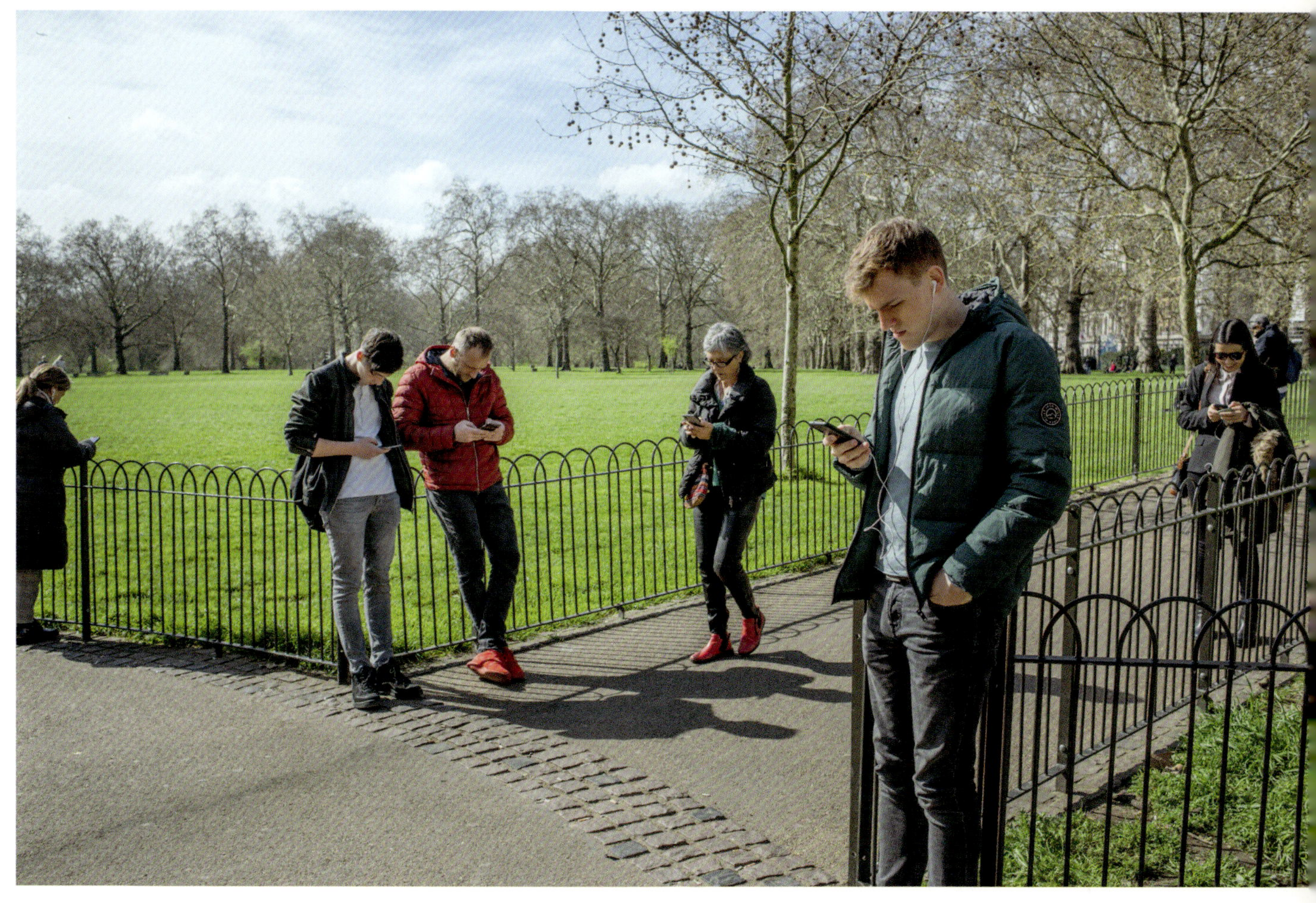

Green Park, London 2019

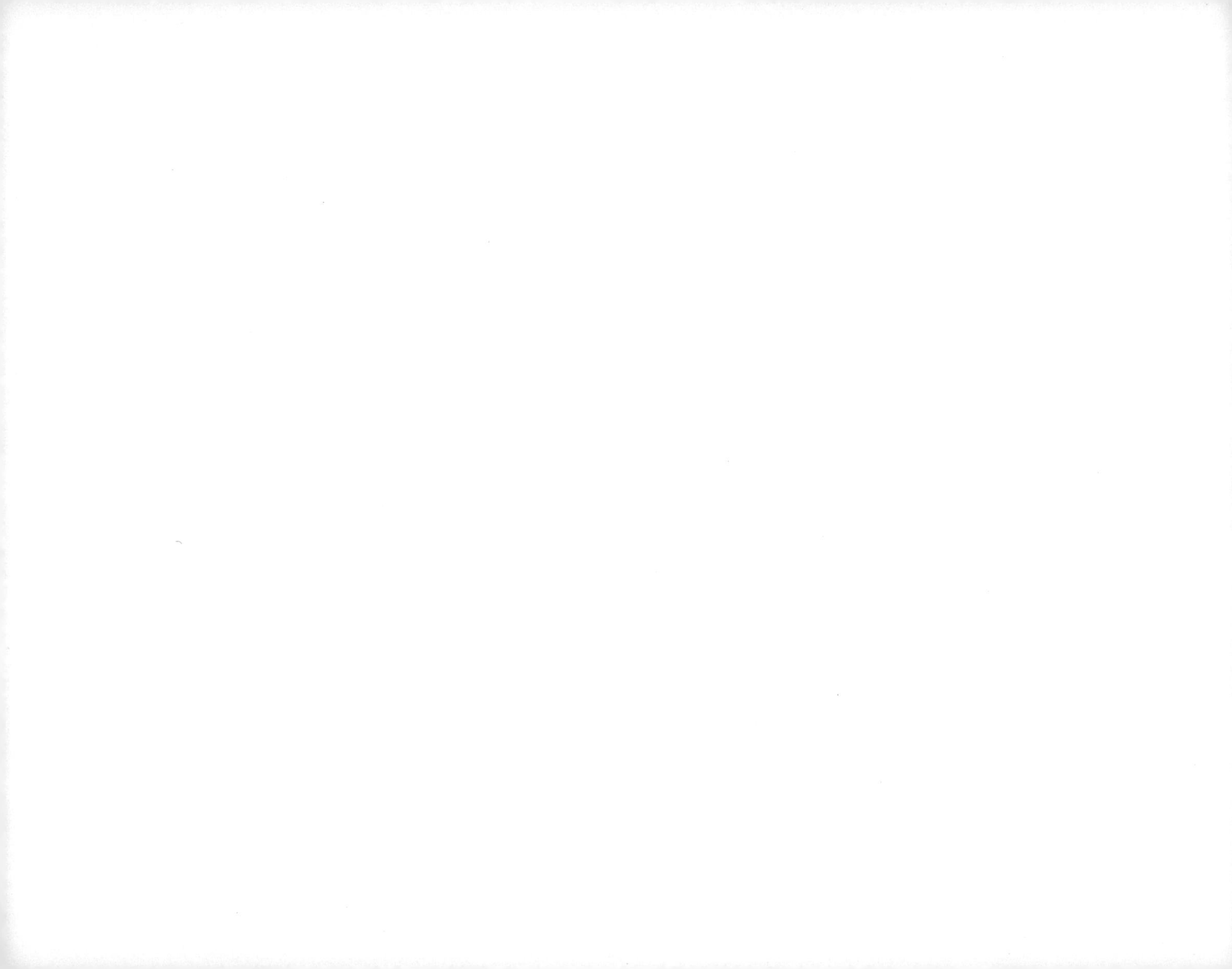

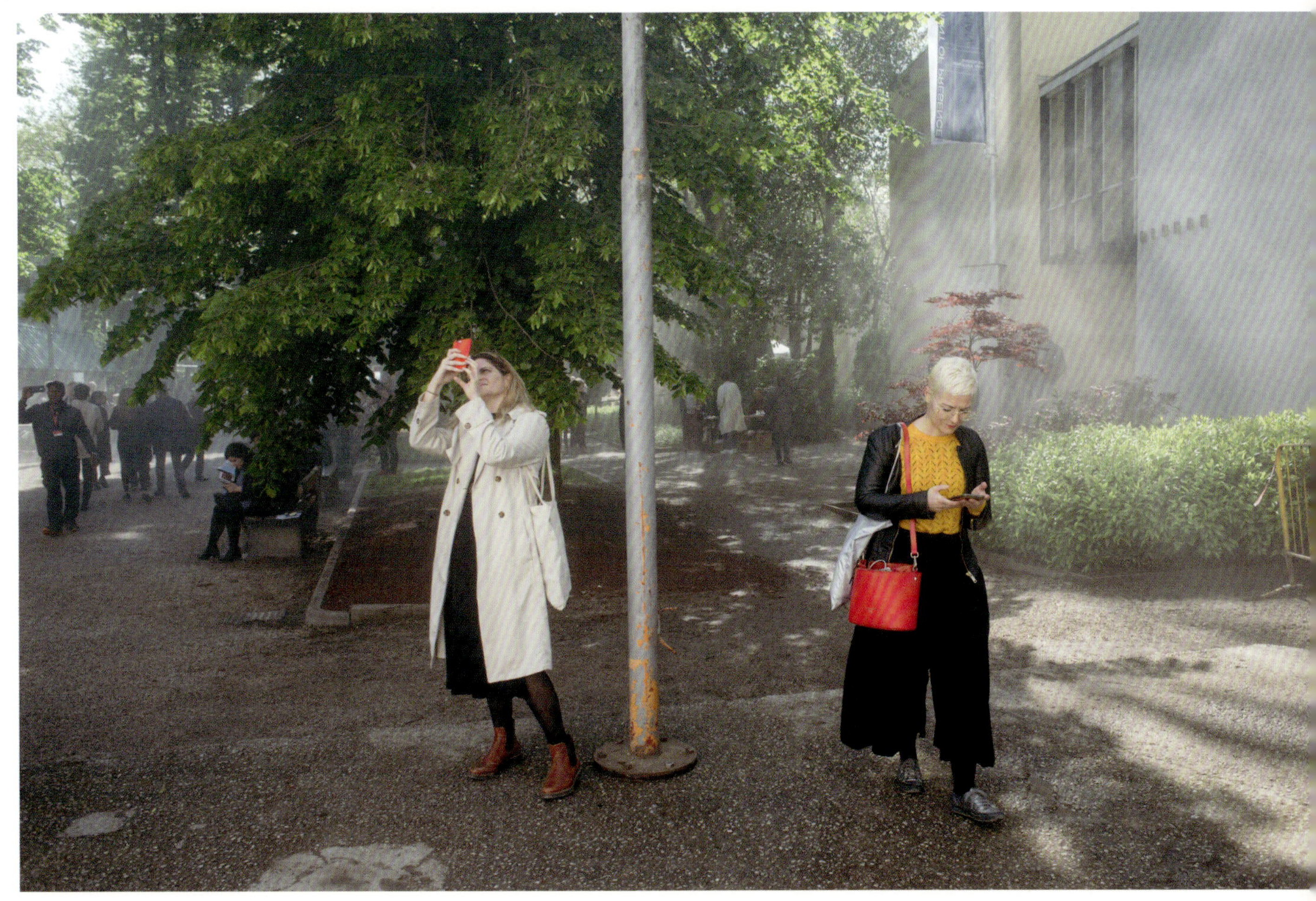

Giardini, Venice 2019

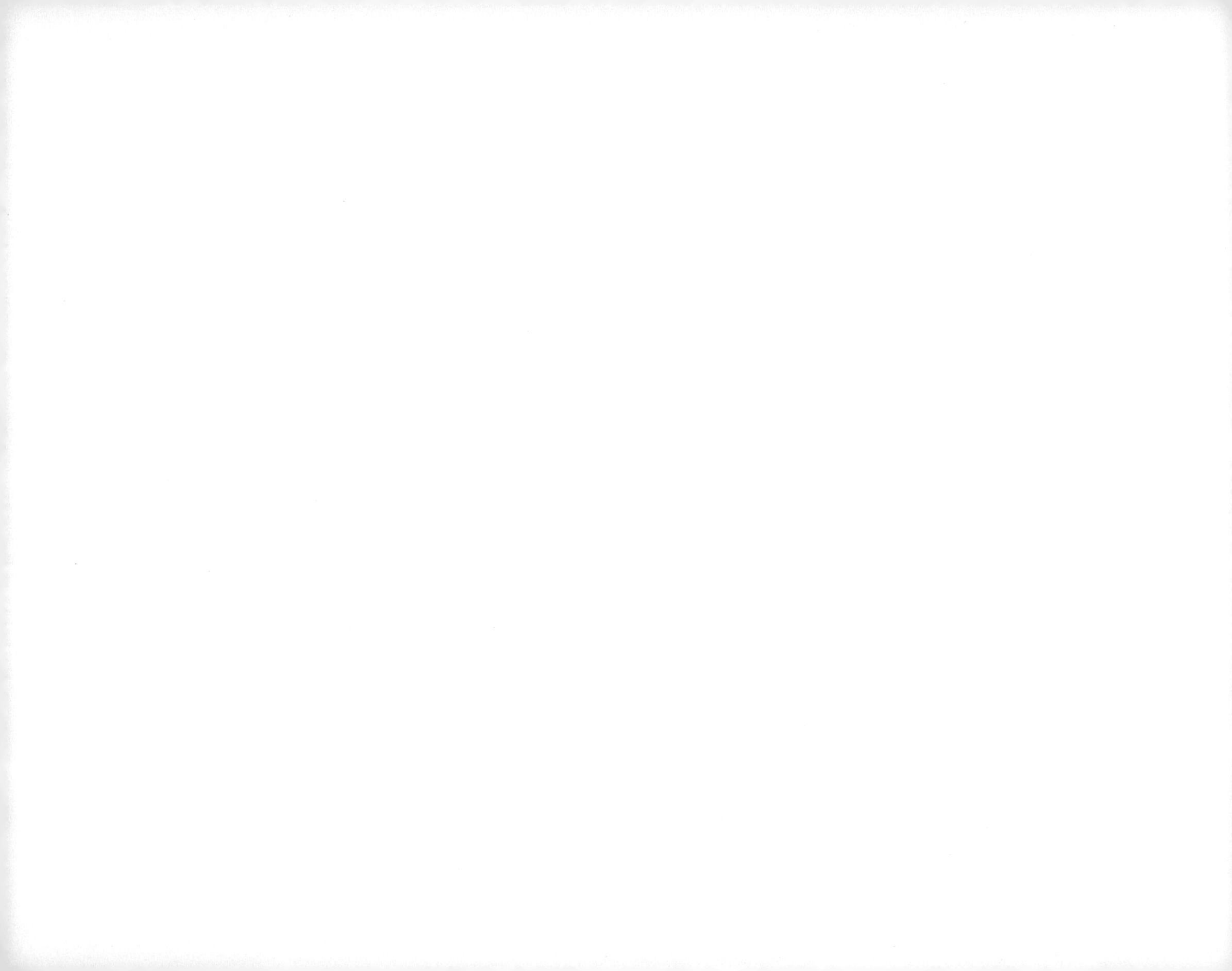

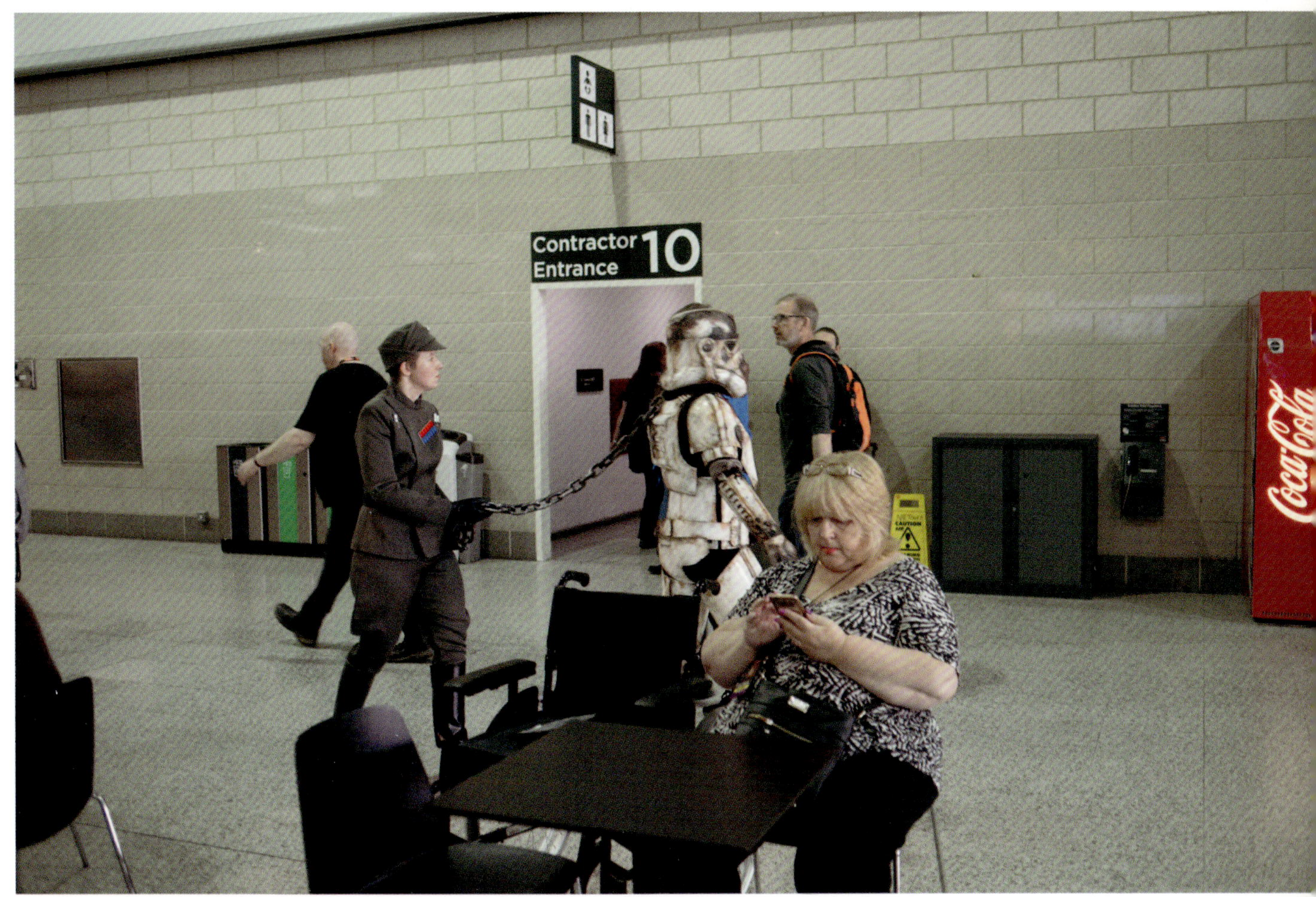

ExCel London 2019

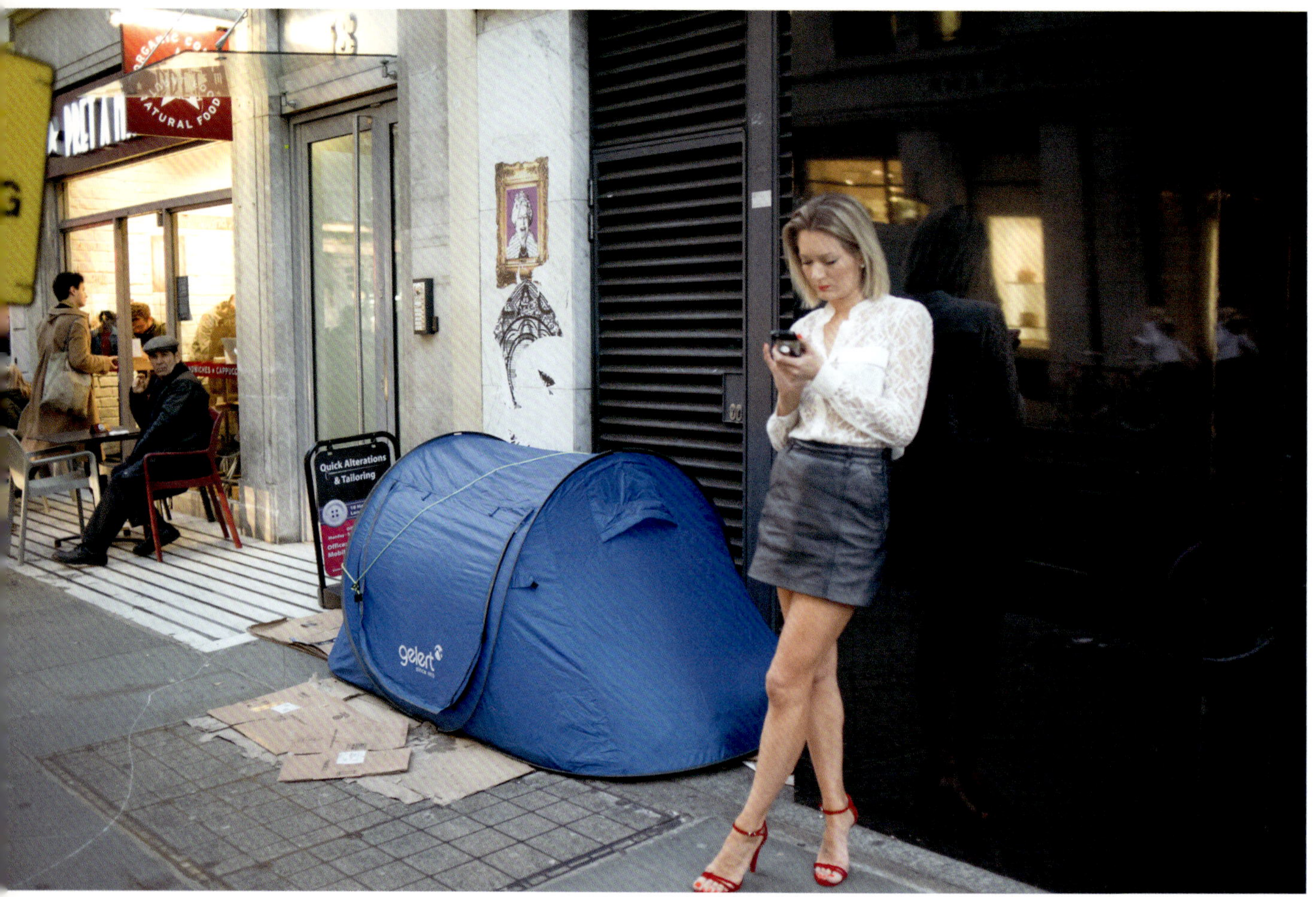

Mayfair, London 2018

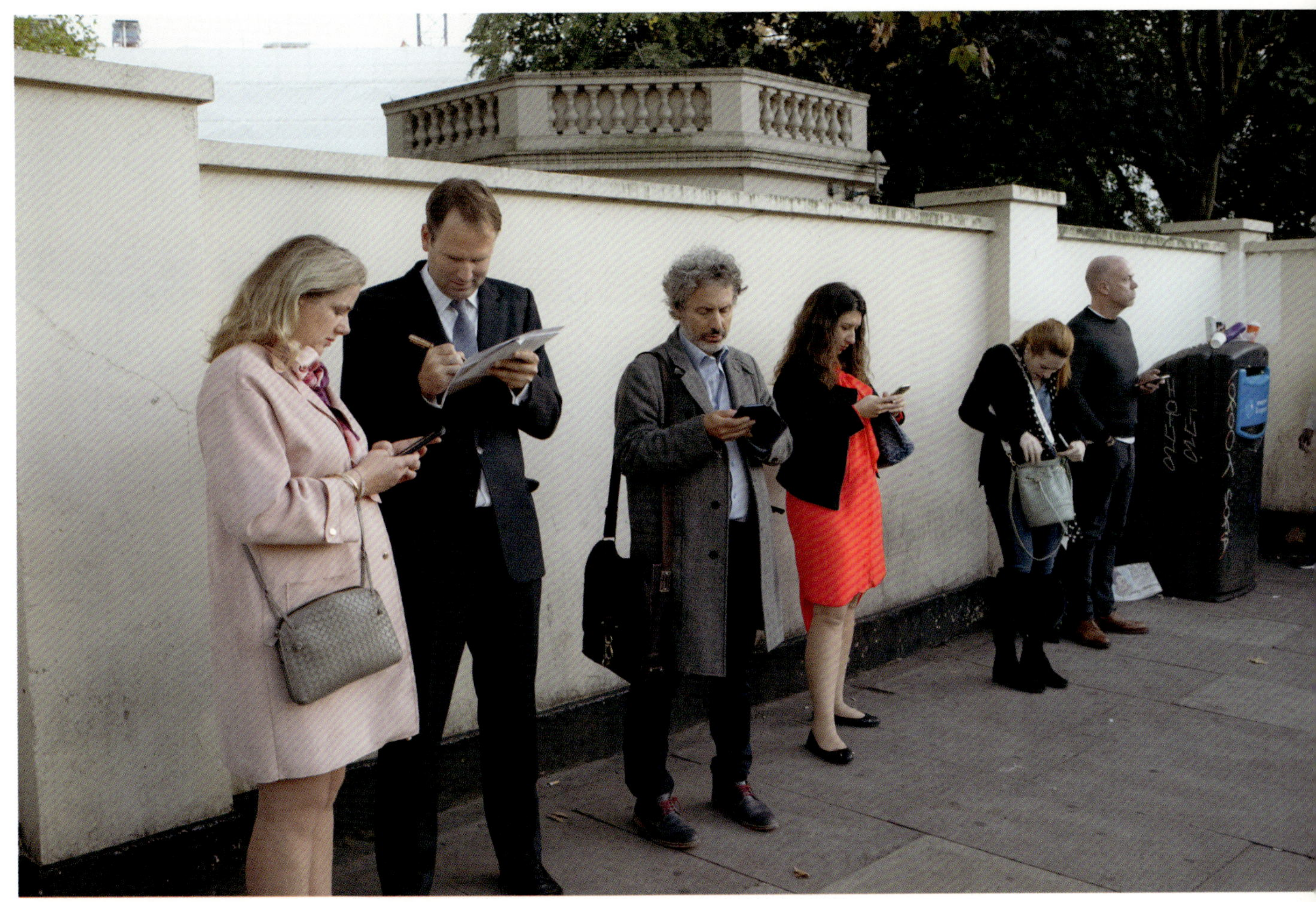

Regent's Park, London 2018

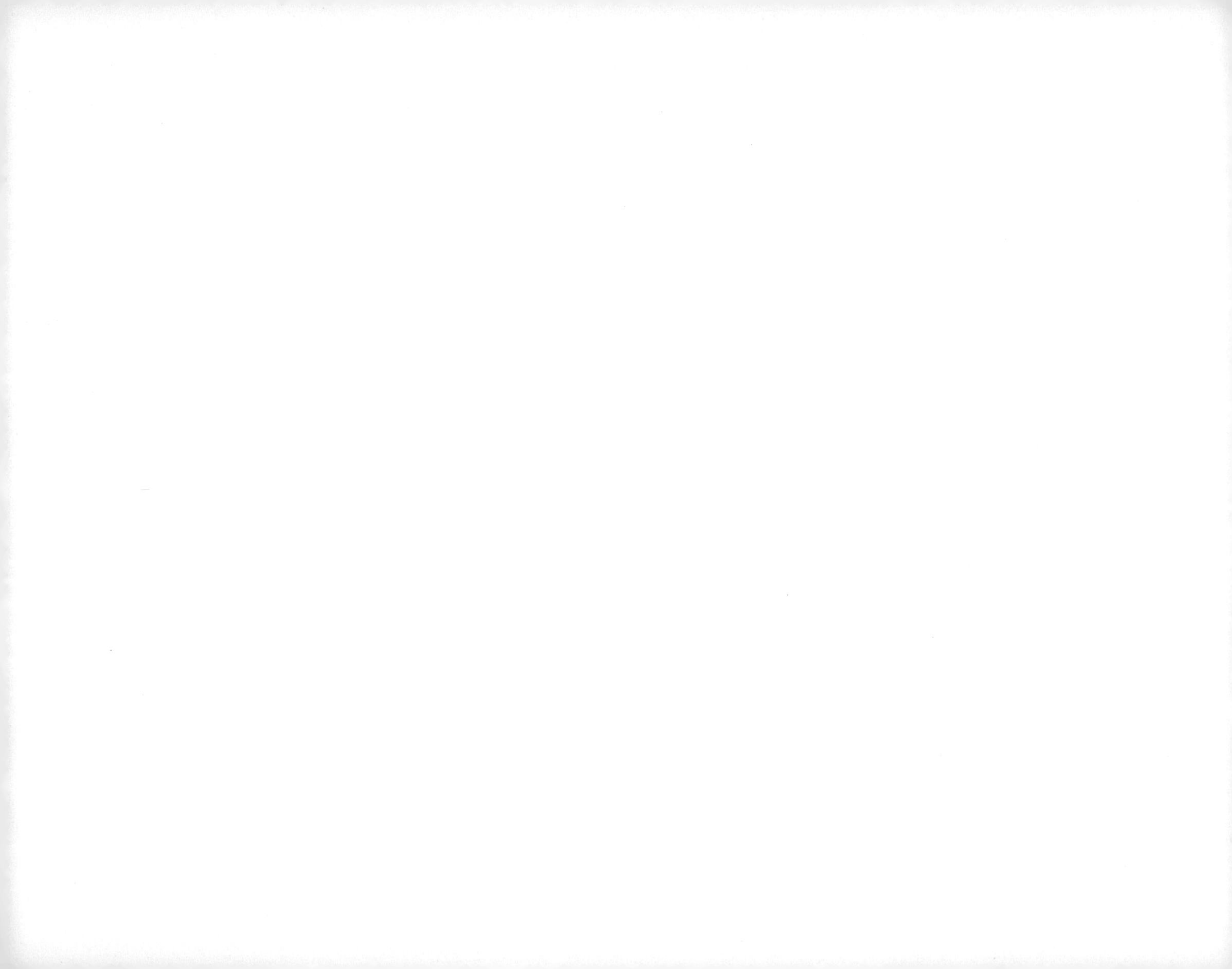

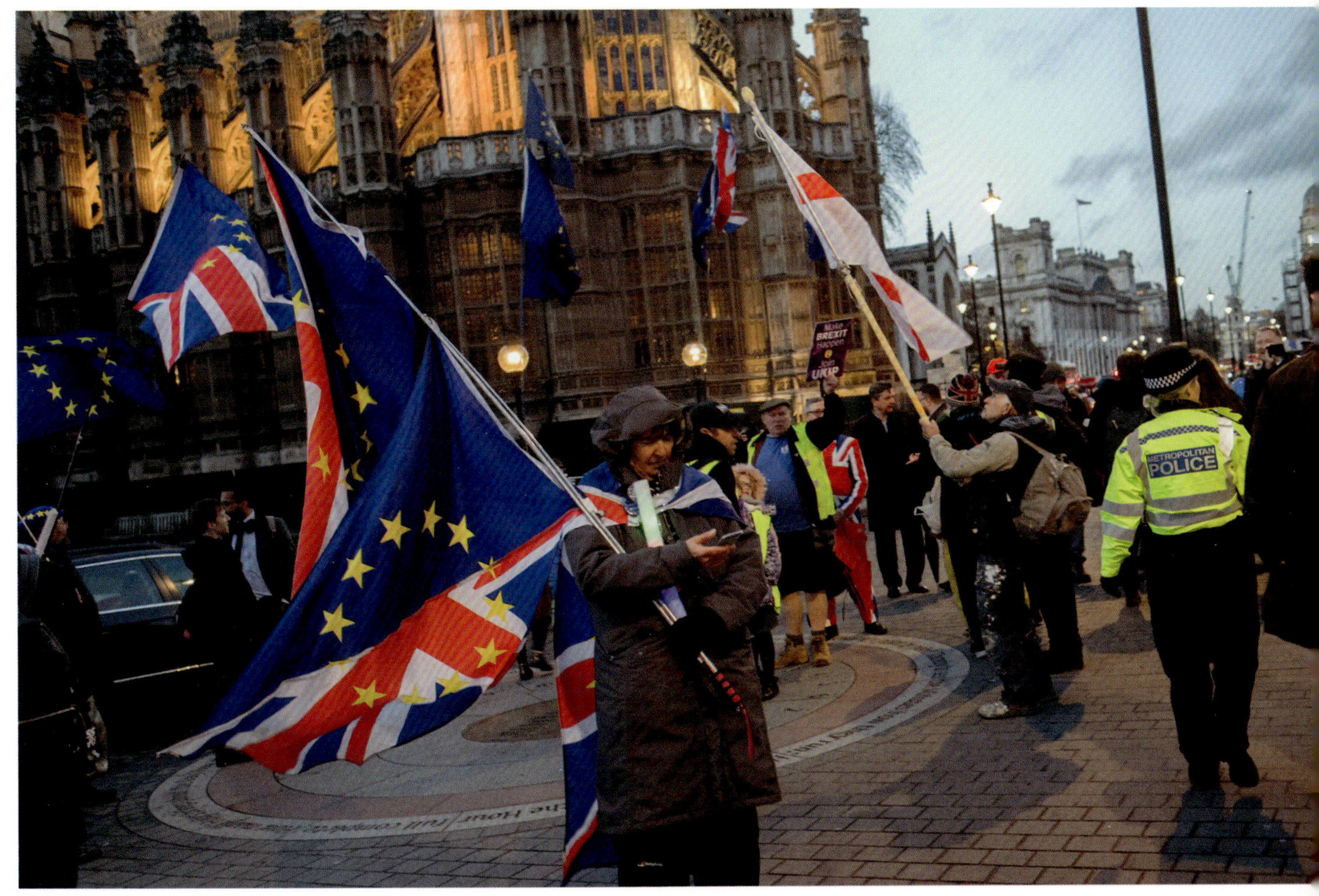

Westminster, London 2019

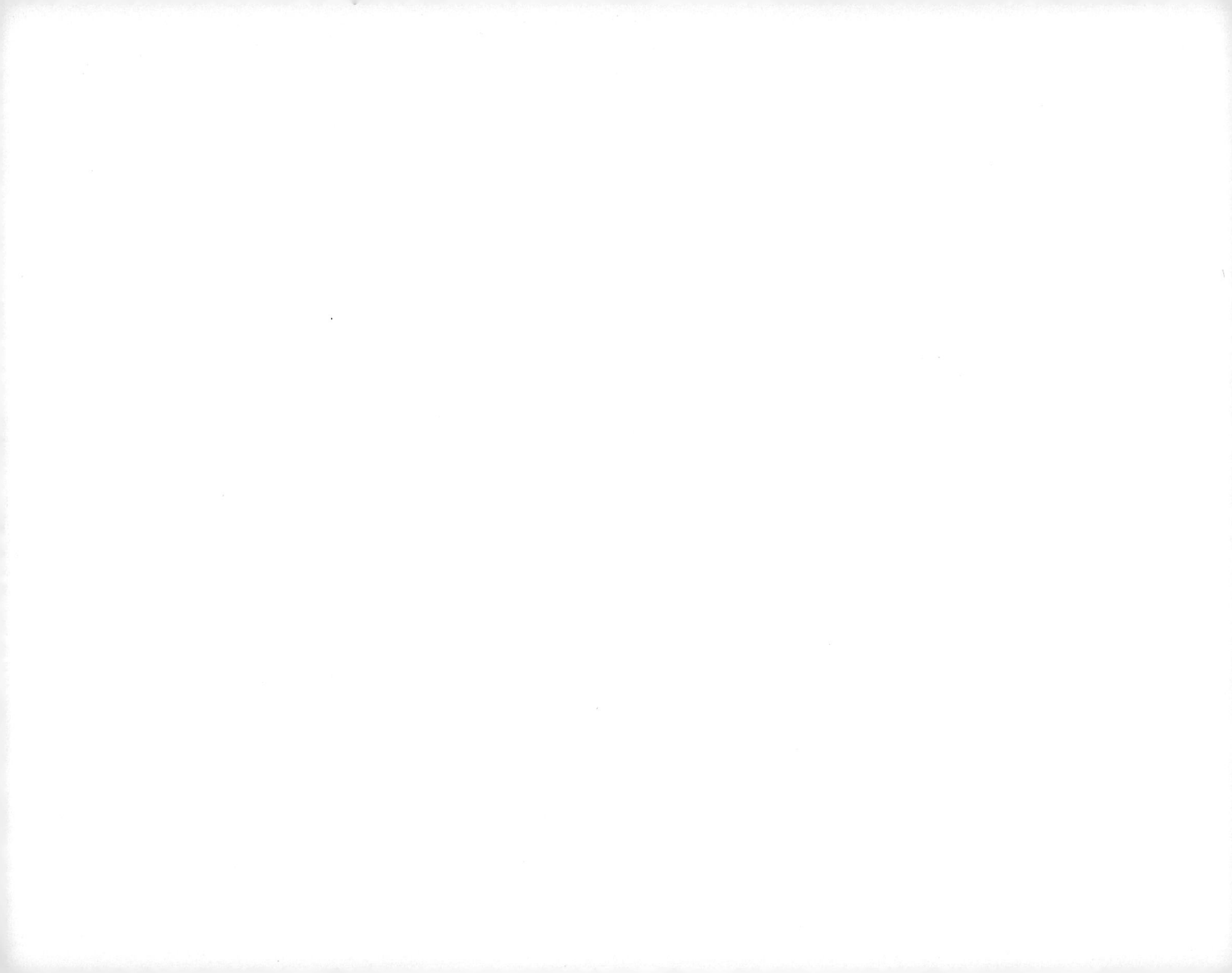

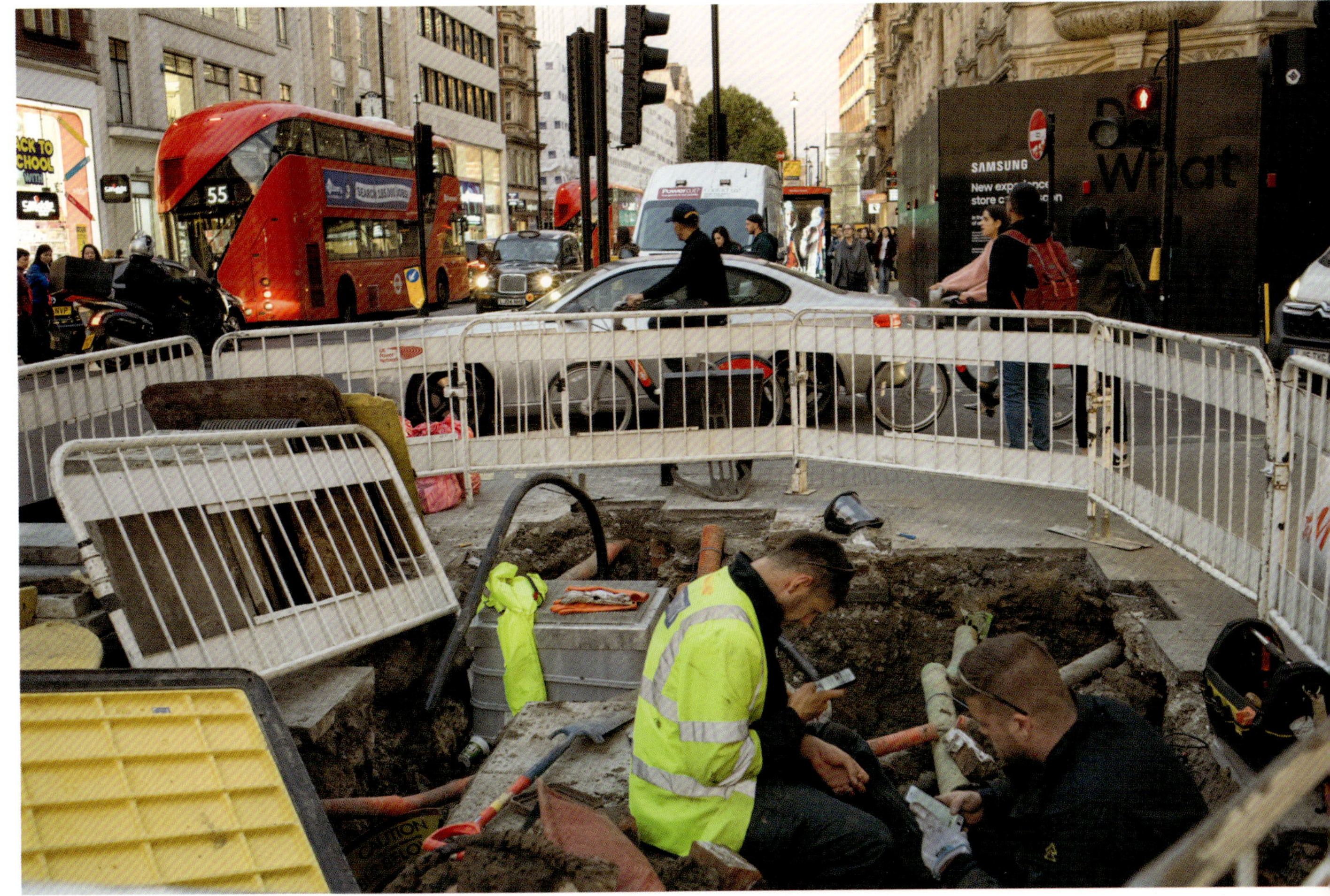

Oxford Street, London 2018

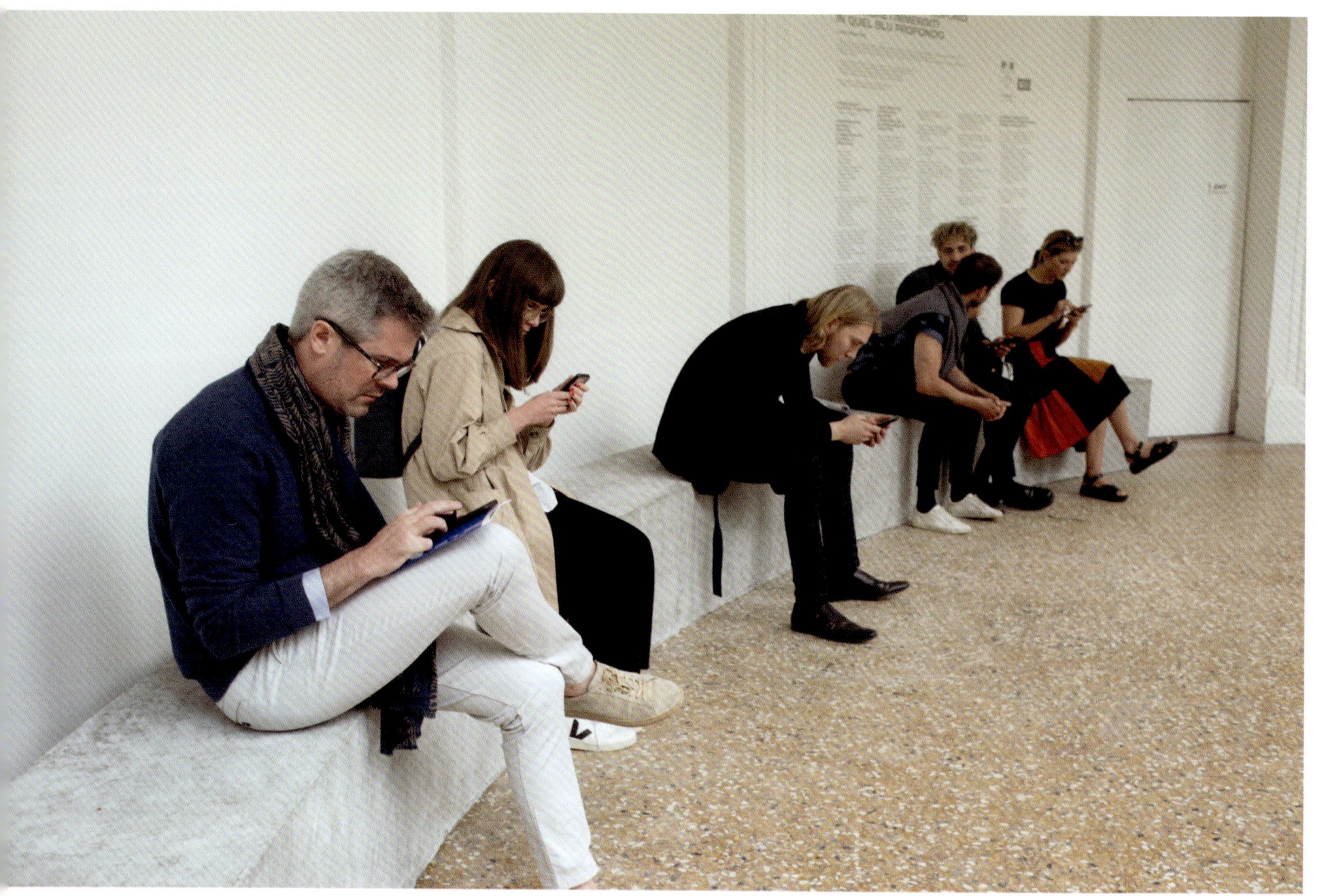

Venice 2019

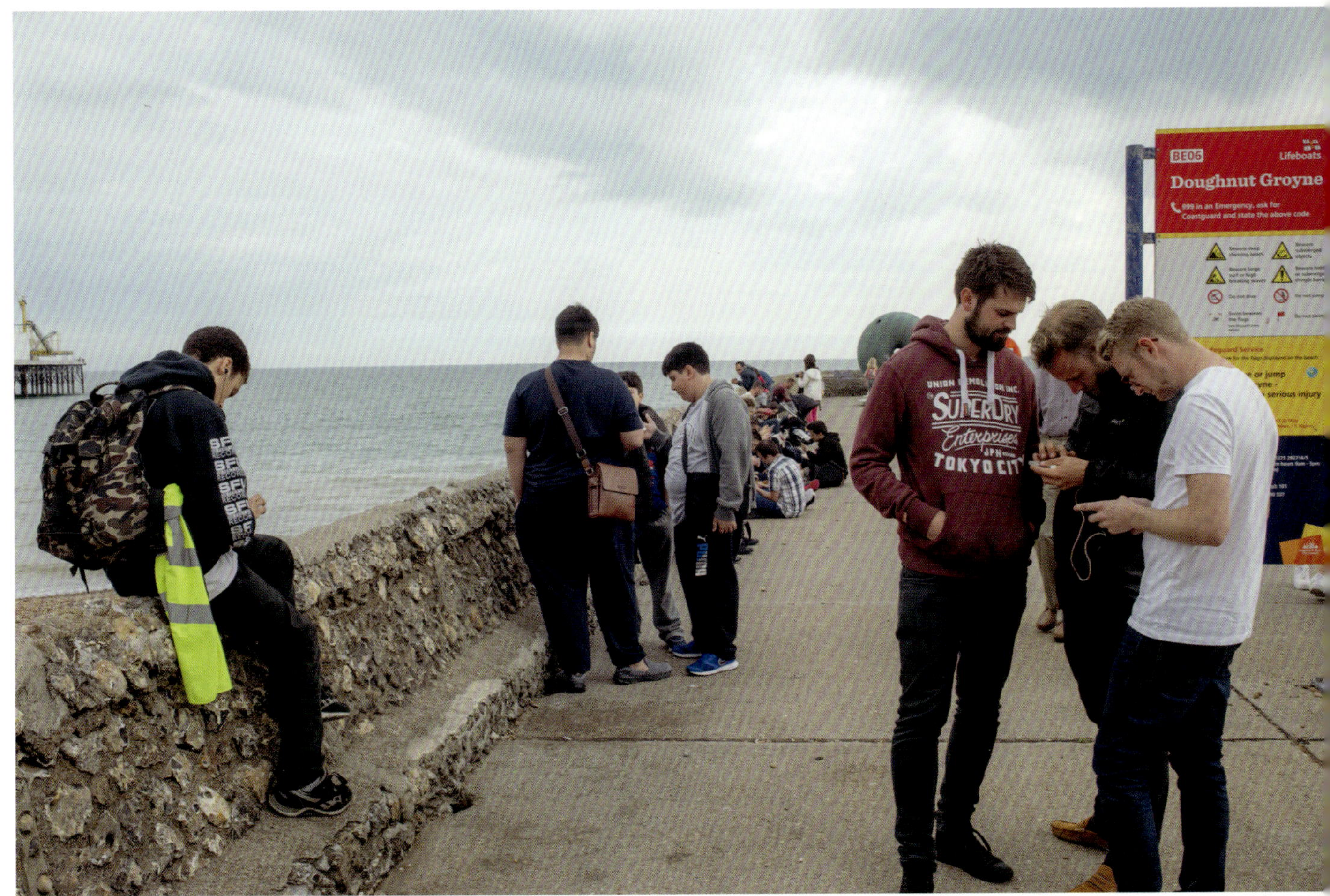

Brighton 2016

Brighton 2016

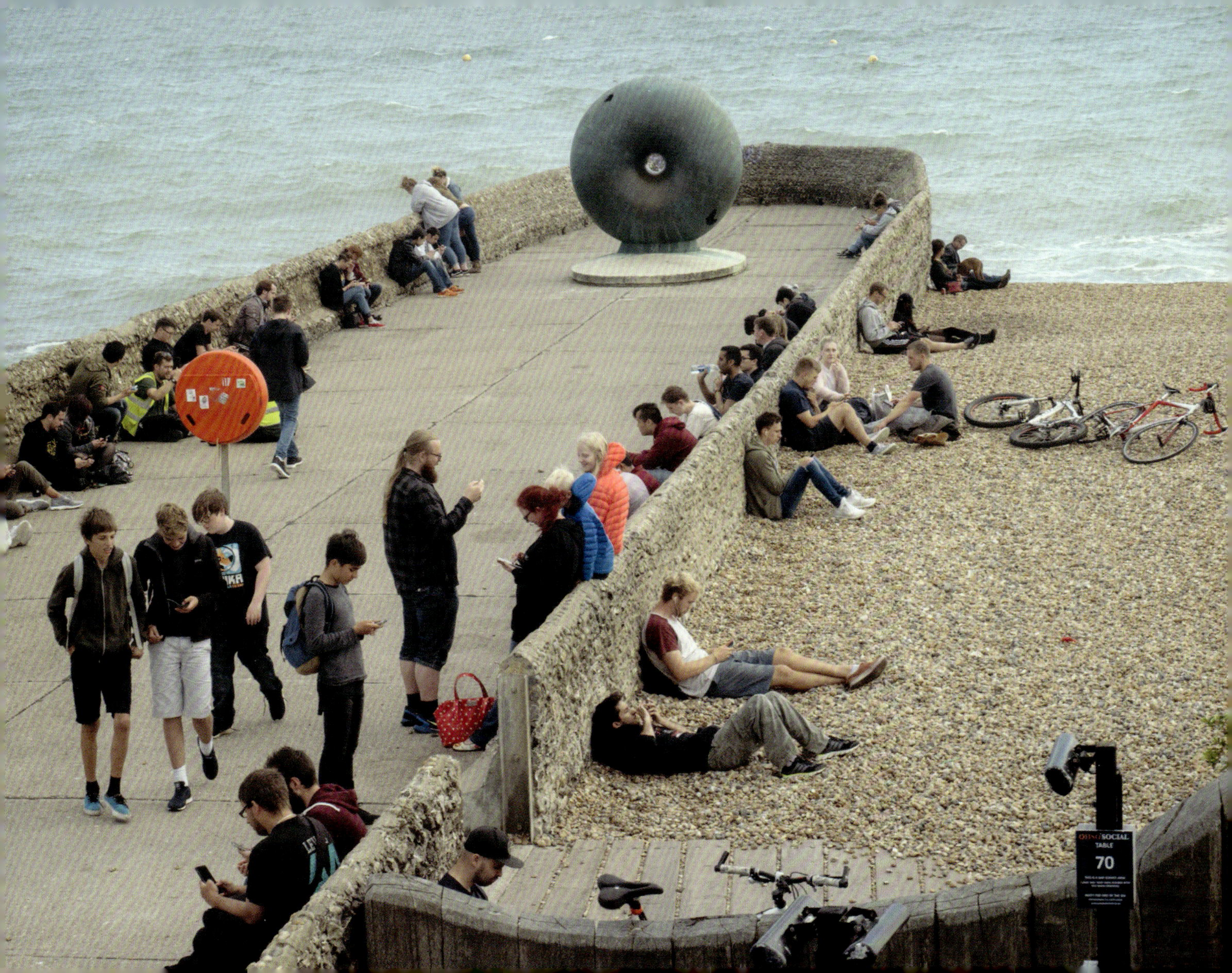
SOCIAL
TABLE
70

First published in 2019 by Circa Press

Circa Press
50 Great Portland Street
London W1W 7ND
www.circapress.com

ISBN 978-1-911422-28-0

Designer: Jean-Michel Dentand

Printed and bound in China